Found Footage
Horror Films

ALSO BY ALEXANDRA HELLER-NICHOLAS

*Rape-Revenge Films:
A Critical Study* (McFarland, 2011)

Found Footage Horror Films
Fear and the Appearance of Reality

ALEXANDRA HELLER-NICHOLAS

McFarland & Company, Inc., Publishers
Jefferson, North Carolina

Permission has been granted to reprint portions of this book derived from these earlier published essays: Material in the Introduction first appeared in "A Pre-History of 'Reality' Horror Film" in *Ol3Media* 4.9 (January 2011). 26–30. http://host.uniroma3.it/riviste/Ol3Media/Archivio_files/ol3media%2009%20Horror.pdf. Material in Chapter One first appeared in "Strangers with Candy: The Highway Safety Foundation and *The Child Molester* (1964)," *Bright Lights Film Journal*, 72 (2009) http://www.brightlightsfilm.com/72/72strangers_heller.php. Material in Chapter Two first appeared in "Snuff Boxing: Rethinking the *Snuff* (1976) Coda," *Cinephile: The University of British Columbia Film Journal*. 5.2 (2009) http://cinephile.ca/archives/volume-5-no-2-the-scene/snuff-boxing-revisiting-the-snuff-coda/. Material in Chapter Seven first appeared in "'The Power of Christ Compels You': Moral Spectacle and *The Exorcist* Universe" from *Roman Catholicism in Fantastic Film: Essays on Belief, Spectacle, Ritual and Imagery* © 2011 Edited by Regina Hansen by permission of McFarland & Company, Inc., Box 611, Jefferson NC 28640. www.mcfarlandpub.com. Material in Chapter Nine was first published in "Finders Keepers: Australian Found Footage Horror Film," in *Metro* magazine, 176 (Autumn 2013) published by Australian Teachers of Media (ATOM) http://www.metromagazine.com.au/magazine/index.html

LIBRARY OF CONGRESS CATALOGUING-IN-PUBLICATION DATA

Heller-Nicholas, Alexandra, 1974– author.
 Found footage horror films : fear and the appearance of reality / Alexandra Heller-Nicholas.
  p.   cm.
 Includes bibliographical references and index.

 ISBN 978-0-7864-7077-8 (softcover : acid free paper) ∞
 ISBN 978-1-4766-1321-5 (ebook)

 1. Horror films—History and criticism. 2. Safety education. I. Title.
 PN1995.9.H6H455 2014
 791.43'6164—dc23   2014010402

BRITISH LIBRARY CATALOGUING DATA ARE AVAILABLE

© 2014 Alexandra Heller-Nicholas. All rights reserved

No part of this book may be reproduced or transmitted in any form or by any means, electronic or mechanical, including photocopying or recording, or by any information storage and retrieval system, without permission in writing from the publisher.

On the cover: Poster art for the film *Exhibit A* (Dom Rotheroe, 2007), courtesy of Bigger Pictures, Ltd.

Manufactured in the United States of America

McFarland & Company, Inc., Publishers
 Box 611, Jefferson, North Carolina 28640
 www.mcfarlandpub.com

For Christian

Table of Contents

Preface ... 1

Introduction ... 3

Part 1: Expanding the Prehistory: 1938–1998 ... 29
One. Safety Films ... 42
Two. Snuff-Fictions ... 58
Three. Television ... 72

Part 2: A Critical Chronology: 1998–2009 ... 87
Four. Revisiting *The Blair Witch Project* ... 93
Five. The Vanishing of the Real ... 112
Six. Approaching *Paranormal Activity* ... 129

Part 3: Further Discoveries: 2007–2013 ... 149
Seven. Exorcism Films ... 151
Eight. The Family ... 165
Nine. Nation, History and Identity ... 178

Conclusion: The Specter of Commercialism ... 192
Notes ... 203
Bibliography ... 217
Index ... 227

Preface

I first saw *The Blair Witch Project* (Daniel Myrick and Eduardo Sánchez, 1999) on a hot summer day, desperate to hide in the cinema's air-conditioned darkness. Spending a lot of time on Usenet and other forums during the 1990s, I was aware of the buzz surrounding this movie, but had frankly grown increasingly bored by horror as that decade progressed; earlier personal highlights like *Candyman* (Bernard Rose, 1992) and Lars Von Trier's *The Kingdom* (1994) were almost distant memories by 1999. To my surprise, I not only enjoyed *The Blair Witch Project*, but it also genuinely terrified me. I'd seen *Cannibal Holocaust* (Ruggero Deodato, 1980) and *Man Bites Dog* (André Bonzel, Rémy Belvaux, and Benoît Poelvoorde, 1992) and had heard the Orson Welles *War of the Worlds* radio broadcast, so there was no danger of being swept away by its claims of authenticity. From this point, however, I developed a fascination with the intersection of horror and "the real" that in the years since led my research in a variety of directions, including snuff-fictions and highway safety films. But I always came back to found footage horror. Not everyone understood this critical obsession of mine, so with its popular renaissance in films like *Cloverfield* (Matt Reeves, 2008), *[Rec]* (Jaume Balagueró and Paco Plaza, 2007), *Diary of the Dead* (George A. Romero, 2007) and of course *Paranormal Activity* (Oren Peli, 2007), my interest was reinvigorated. The book that follows is the result of this long-term interest as both a film researcher and a horror fan.

Thanks to the following for granting permission to include previously published material: Barbara Maio and Corrado Peperoni (*Ol3media*), Brent Strang and Colleen Montgomery (*Cinephile*), Tim Coronel (*Metro* magazine), and Regina Hansen (Boston University), and especial gratitude to Gary Morris at *Bright Lights Film Journal* for his ongoing assistance. I would also like to voice my appreciation to Professor Anne Marsh (Monash University), Professor Rachel Fensham (University of Melbourne), and Professor Julian Thomas

(Swinburne University of Technology), and a special mention to the unrelenting kindness, enthusiasm and support of Dr. Ramon Lobato (Swinburne University of Technology), one of the finest researchers (and nicest people) I have had the privilege to work with. Particular thanks to the inspirational Professor Angela Ndalianis (University of Melbourne): Aside from the personal support she has given my family and myself, she has also written some of the most insightful and exciting work on horror film in recent years.

My thanks to Hannah Fierman, Michael Goi, Rich Lawden, Anthony Spadaccini, Enzo Tedeschi, Stephen Volk, Troy Wagner and Richard J. Wood. Bret Wood has been an inspiration since I first saw his incredible documentary *Hell's Highway: The True Story of Highway Safety Films* (2003). Despite going on to make increasingly brave and intelligent films (*Psychopathia Sexualis* [2006], *The Little Death* [2010] and his upcoming movie *The Unwanted*), Bret has always taken time out to assist my research into the Highway Safety Foundation, for which I am hugely grateful. Mansfield librarian Boyd Addlesperger provided additional assistance in my Highway Safety Foundation research, and I thank him also. A number of other people helped me in a variety of ways, including William Lustig and Greg Chick (Blue Underground), Georgie Nevile (Mungo Productions), Christine Purse (Ignite Strategic Communications), Buzz Remde (R Squared Films) and Clint Weiler (MVD Entertainment Group).

I would like to acknowledge the kindness of my many dear friends and colleagues who were roped into helping with various aspects of this book's creation, particularly Anna Gardner, Craig Martin, Mark Freeman, Tim O'Farrell, Ian Gouldstone, Martin Kingsley, and David Surman. Fiona Drury deserves a special mention, as the book simply would not have made it without her. Thanks also to Dean Brandum, Johnboy Davidson, Jade Henshaw, Kaz Horsely, Alex Hammond, Bernie Guerin and Frankie, Clan Mazarigle, Esther Milne, Neil Mitchell, Rose Moore, Jan Napiorkowski, Matthew O'Callaghan, Catticut Palich, and Martyn Pedler. Most of all, thanks to my family—Richard, Lorraine, Max, and of course my incredible husband Christian and our beautiful son. Everything I am and everything I do is for you guys. (Except the horror movie thing. That's mostly just for me.)

Alexandra Heller-Nicholas
Spring 2014

Introduction

So pervasive is found footage horror that it can be readily identified as the current subgenre *du jour*. Its particular brand of amateur filmmaking aesthetics have opened it up to a range of production budgets, effectively flooding the market and making it close to impossible to remain up-to-date with every new found footage horror movie released. These aesthetics may be considered part of broader cinema traditions that seek to position themselves outside dominant Classical Hollywood filmmaking, but the specific brand of amateur aesthetics in found footage horror is crucial to its construction of verisimilitude. These aesthetics are most immediately identified via its signature rawness, either in the form of diegetically produced shaky hand-held camera footage or surveillance feed. Importantly, this means that movies that *look* like amateur films may not necessarily *be* amateur productions, and *The Blair Witch Project*'s (1999) co-directors Daniel Myrick and Eduardo Sánchez learned this the hard way. Revisiting the film five years after its surprise blockbuster success, *Newsweek*'s Sean Smith noted that for Myrick and Sánchez, "the biggest problem ... was that no one who made the film got the credit for its triumph. Because it was shot by the actors on hand-held video, and the dialogue was improvised from a plot-only screenplay, studio execs doubted that Myrick and Eduardo Sánchez could direct a normal film."[1]

While there are plenty of examples of genuinely amateur found footage horror productions, films like the monster movie *Cloverfield* (Matt Reeves, 2008) have shown the particular rendering of amateur aesthetics that dominates found footage horror could be convincingly replicated by professional Hollywood production teams. *Cloverfield* is emblematic of this paradox: It is a blockbuster movie about amateur filmmakers that cost $25 million to make. *Megan Is Missing* (2011) shows how constructed found footage horror has become and how it draws on this specific aesthetic of amateurism. It was directed by Michael Goi, Emmy-winning cinematographer and president of the American Society of Cinematographers from 2010 to 2012; it would be difficult to challenge his professional credentials. Goi strategically opted for this style to most effectively convey the message he wanted his film to have. Goi's industry recognition adds weight to the claim that found footage horror films like *Megan Is Missing* demand our attention because of their construction of amateurism, rather than their actual status as necessarily amateur productions.

Found footage horror seeks (not always successfully) to create a space where spectators can enjoy having their boundaries pushed, where our confidence that we know where the lines between fact and fiction lie are directly challenged. "The found-footage genre reaches its apex of success," said John Kenneth Muir, "when it transports you so successfully into another life or world that you start to get a little panicky yourself. Like you are actually there ... and unsafe."[2] Since the release of *The Blair Witch Project*, the threat that a found footage horror film may present actual events that occurred in the real world has eroded through the increasing ubiquity and subsequent familiarity of its codes and conventions. Nevertheless, this does not mean the possibility of knowingly indulging in the horror fantasies on offer has vanished altogether.

The contemporary found footage horror subgenre[3] famously began with the phenomenal success of *The Blair Witch Project*. However, the ascendancy of so-called "torture porn"—typified by *Saw* (James Wan, 2004) and *Hostel* (Eli Roth, 2005)—saw found footage horror recede from mainstream attention. The founding of YouTube in 2005 and its spectacular rise during 2006 sparked a growing taste for amateur media, which in turn saw a spike in the production of found footage horror in 2007 with the appearance of *[Rec]* (Jaume Balagueró and Paco Plaza) and *Diary of the Dead* (George A. Romero), and *Cloverfield* in early 2008. Along with YouTube itself, these movies paved the way for the phenomenally successful release of *Paranormal Activity* (Oren Peli, 2007).

Yet found footage horror films were still being produced between the found footage watersheds *The Blair Witch Project* and *Paranormal Activity*, despite the lack of mainstream attention. It was across this period that the codes and conventions of found footage horror were in many ways consolidated, particularly in relation to their specific amateur filmmaking aesthetics and the development of their playful invitation to engage in a fantasy defined through a formal authentic style. Before *Blair Witch*, there were also a number of texts that indicate the contemporary found footage horror category had significant historical precedent. Post–*Paranormal Activity*, the subgenre has flourished and is now understood less as an indicator of authenticity and more as a specific film style.

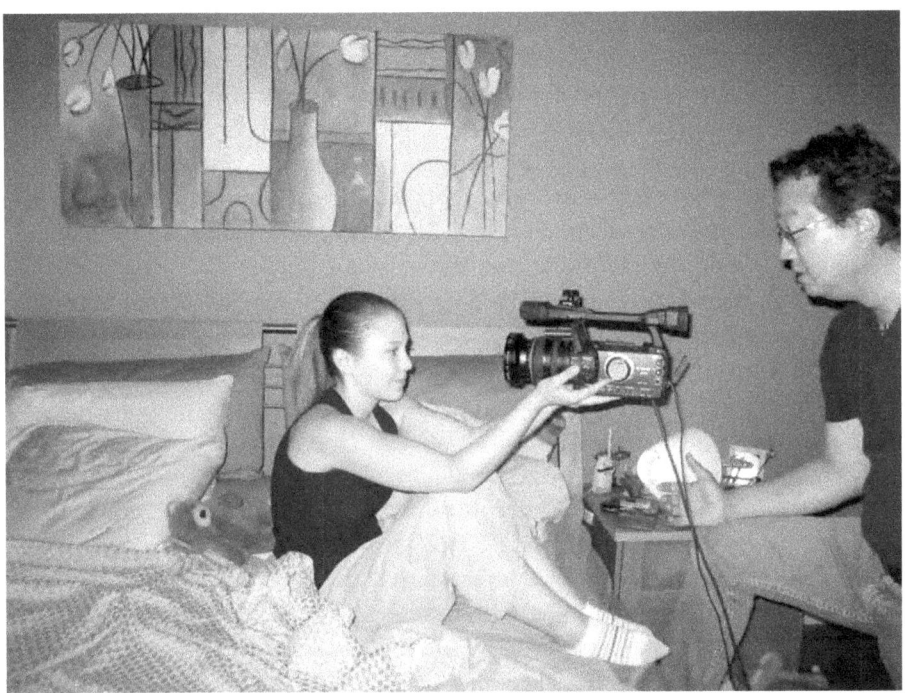

Director Michael Goi and Amy (Amber Perkins) on the set of *Megan Is Missing* (2011) (courtesy Michael Goi, www.meganismissing.com).

It is across this landscape that this book explores the often-complex critical domain of contemporary found footage horror. It addresses a number of features of the subgenre, and while it situates *The Blair Witch Project* as its first fully recognizable instance, it spends some time investigating its genealogy. It examines the significant releases of *Blair Witch* and the *Paranormal Activity* franchise, and considers a range of films produced between them with an eye toward the development of the subgenre across these years. It then explores the diversity of more recent found footage horror movies, examining how it has been deployed in the service of the exorcism trope in films like *The Devil Inside* (William Brent Bell, 2012) and *The Last Exorcism* (Daniel Stamm, 2011), and family-oriented horror films such as *Exhibit A* (Dom Rotheroe, 2007), *Home Movie* (Christopher Denham, 2008), *Apartment 143* (Carles Torrens, 2011) and *Lake Mungo* (Joel Anderson, 2008). With attention to movies including *Cloverfield*, *[Rec]*, *Shirome* (Kôji Shiraishi, 2010), *Trollhunter* (André Øvredal, 2010), and *The Tunnel* (Carlo Ledesma, 2011), it considers the socio-political aspects of found footage horror when produced in different national and cultural contexts. Finally, it explores the relationship between independent and corporate film production, distribution and exhibition in specific relation to *V/H/S* (Adam Wingard, David Bruckner, Ti West, Glenn McQuaid, Joe Swanberg, Radio Silence, 2012) and the highly successful YouTube series *Marble Hornets* (Troy Wagner, 2009–). Permeating many of these analyses is a broader critical interest in gender in particular; because as many of the most rigorous and important critical studies of horror have demonstrated previously, the relationship between the genre and its gender politics is enduring and often complex.[4]

The Blair Witch Project marked the beginnings of found footage horror's recent popularity, but the subgenre's origins stretch back much further. Few would debate the importance of previously identified ancestors such as Orson Welles' notorious *War of the Worlds* radio broadcast from 1938, *Cannibal Holocaust* (Ruggero Deodato, 1980), and *Man Bites Dog* (Benoît Poelvoorde, Rémy Belvaux, André Bonzel, 1992). Less commonly discussed are the safety films of the 1950s and 1960s, typified by the drivers education movies produced by the Ohio-based Highway Safety Foundation, which incorporated graphic footage of actual accident scenes into their didactic re-enactment scenarios. In terms of horror, the relationship between real and represented bodily trauma has been explored in film at least as far back as Michael Powell's *Peeping Tom* (1960). With its story of a man who finds pleasure in filming the killing of women with his gruesome camera-tripod-cum-knife, *Peeping Tom* inextricably links "filming" with "killing." Similar connections have been expanded to varying degrees of success and sophistication in a subgenre of films I identify as snuff-fictions, whose spectacular and affective qualities stem from their association between film and its ability to capture real world horrors such as torture, violence, and death in the moment of their execution. Many films manifest at the intersection between death, film and the real in this context, including *Cannibal Holocaust, Snuff* (Michael and Roberta Findlay, 1976), the Japanese *Guinea Pig* series (1985–1990), *Emanuelle in America* (Joe D'Amato, 1977), *Last House on Dead End Street* (Roger Watkins, 1977), *Hardcore* (Paul Schrader, 1979), *Videodrome* (David Cronenberg, 1983), *Mute Witness* (Anthony Waller, 1994), *Strange Days* (Kathryn Bigelow, 1995), *Tesis* (Alejandro Amenábar, 1996), *8mm* (Joel Schumacher, 1999), and *Demonlover* (Olivier Assayas, 2002).[5] While beyond the specific scope of this book, similar concerns also appear in the broader "reality" horror category, especially in movies that critique popular phenomenon such as "reality" game show television from a horror perspective such as *Battle Royale* (Kinji Fukasaku, 2000), *Series 7: The Contenders* (Daniel Minahan, 2001) and *Slashers* (Maurice Devereaux, 2001).[6] These often-controversial ancestors established many of the boundaries of found footage horror to some degree, setting the ethical and formal parameters of the contemporary subgenre. From this perspective, television also warrants recognition in the prehistory of found footage horror, particularly Lesley Manning's notorious 1992 BBC program *Ghostwatch* and the French series *Les Documents Interdits* (1989–1991).[7]

Contemporary found footage horror has harnessed the conceptual energy of this lineage and redirected it towards the mainstream. This shift from what were often the badlands of cult film fandom to the multiplex blockbuster adds a degree of security to the experience of watching horror films that are explicitly framed around their claims of authenticity. These films are exciting to watch not because their events may or may not have happened, but from the formal innuendo that if they *did* occur, this is how they might look, seemingly filmed as they are on the same ubiquitous consumer-grade technology that many of us have ourselves (home video cameras, mobile phones, webcams, etc.). The paradox—and power—of found footage horror is that its particular type of realism hinges explicitly upon exposing itself as a media artifact. From this perspective, it demonstrates Jay David Bolter and Richard Grusin's notion of hypermediacy, a tendency which implies a beefing-up the presence of the medium itself so that the viewer is forced to "acknowledge the medium as a medium, and to delight in this acknowledgement."[8] Hypermediacy has an often-complex relation with immediacy, which relies on the medium's transparency to obscure our awareness that we are engaging with a medium at all.

The pleasure of this particular type of realism is in its adaption of a set of signifying tropes of the real in a fictional context, but it also speaks in much broader ways about our relationship to new media technologies themselves. In his analysis of Welles' *War of the Worlds* radio broadcast, Jeffrey Sconce stated:

> More than a cautionary tale about irresponsible broadcasting or gullible audiences, *War of the Worlds* continues to fascinate by reminding us of the repressed potential for panic and disorder that lies just behind the normalizing functions of media technology, a terror that is at once terrifying and yet suggestively enticing.[9]

This analysis of found footage horror also does not hinge on considerations of audiences as impressionable dupes. In fact, the knowing suspension of fictionality often allows us indulge in the imaginary "what-ifs" on offer, fantastic possibilities that contain at their very core the titillating potential that the media itself cannot be controlled or contained.

Just as prime-time television series like *CSI* (2000–) and *NCIS* (2003–) have arguably brought a mainstreaming of forensic images to a broad audience, granting them a degree of gore literacy that was previously specific only to trash horror audiences, so too the aesthetics of found footage horror are now commonly understood by audiences not as markers of factuality but as a recognizable cinematic style. These aesthetics let us in turn play with the film frame, deploying a specific stylistic system familiarized through camera phone and webcam use that encourage us to play a subgeneric game of "make-believe reality." Shaky hand-held camera movements and spikes in sound and vision quality are not so much markers of authenticity today as much as they denote an authentic style. In large part, this is because audiences themselves are familiar with the way that amateur footage is produced through the rise of consumer-grade hand-held digital video technology: Craig Hight insightfully observed that "this naturalization of non-professional footage is itself a natural consequence of increased access by audiences to technologies which effectively allow them to play the role of producers."[10] Consequently, as contemporary audiences simultaneously become increasingly saturated in a glut of violent images through mainstream news outlets and television series like *CSI*, *NCIS* and the horror television series *True Blood* (2008–) and *The Walking Dead* (2010–), that these films "look" real no longer has the stamp of authenticity that it once had. This means the modes of reception that dominate contemporary found footage horror is thus significantly different from those surrounding movies like *Snuff* and *Cannibal Holocaust*.

Beginning at least as far back as Welles' radio broadcast, fictional horror (or horror hybrids) products with a patina of "truth" have steadily developed a formal system that signifies "the real." The found footage horror subgenre's veneer of authenticity is the result of a formal code that has developed over time. As will be explored at length in Chapter Five, it is between the two blockbuster releases of *The Blair Witch Project* and *Paranormal Activity* that this system developed so significantly that any threat that these films were "really real" became significantly reduced. Less the result of cynicism than of generic saturation, audiences now no longer assume the signs that once denoted authenticity refer to anything but a specific (and fictional) horror style. This does not necessarily deny found footage horror its pleasures. Rather, the formal encouragement that these films *may* be "real" is often consciously understood by media-savvy audiences as an invitation to indulge in an active horror fantasy, one where we can knowingly accept and embrace the real-seeming film frame while never fully suspending disbelief.

A very particular brand of amateur filmmaking aesthetics define contemporary found footage horror, and is one of its most immediately recognizable features materializing through hand-held shaky cinematography, poor sound and image quality, and almost always through the diegetic inclusion of the camera itself. Marjorie Garber has argued that a definition of the amateur is intrinsically tied up in its relationship to the professional: "[T]hey produce each other and they define each other by mutual affinities and exclusions."[11] Definitions of amateur and professional rely on each other often in disparaging ways, where celebrating one requires a necessary denigration of the other. Working against this tendency and foreshadowing a less binary view that would mark Paul Miller and Charles Leadbeater's concept of the "pro-am,"[12] Garber identifies a gray area of both amateur professionals ("someone who is learning, or poaching, or practicing without a license ... a person trained in one field who writes, thinks, practices and publishes in another"[13]) and professional amateurs ("someone who glories in amateur status"[14]). David Buckingham, Maria Pini and Rebekah Willett have also rejected an either/or view of the relationship between the amateur and the professional in filmmaking, identifying new categories such as enthusiasts (who "invests in technology and creates artistic finished products") and everyday users (who own "relatively inexpensive technology (with no accessories) and do ... not plan or edit his or her films"[15]).

All of these types of producers can be found on YouTube, whose dedication to the creation and inclusion of user-generated content (UGC) is explicit in its slogan, "Broadcast yourself." The rise of YouTube cannot be underplayed in the development of contemporary found footage horror. Founded by Chad Hurley, Steve Chen and Jawed Karim, the video-streaming website was officially launched in November 2005. During 2006, it was one of the fastest growing websites online, with one account claiming that by July that year users were watching over 100 million videos a day.[16] It was purchased by Google for $1.65 billion dollars that same year, and *Time Magazine*'s annual "Person of the Year" issue famously featured a mirror on its cover inside the familiar YouTube interface, celebrating 2006 as "a story about community and collaboration on a scale never seen before ... about the cosmic compendium of knowledge Wikipedia and the million-channel people's network YouTube and the online metropolis MySpace."[17] YouTube appeared at the right place at the right time: Henry Jenkins has suggested that "our society was ready for YouTube when it appeared, which is why it was flooded so quickly with all forms of amateur and noncommercial media production, many of which had been looking for a site for circulation and exhibition."[18] Two thousand six was the year the stories we filmed, often clumsily on our phones, webcams or digital cameras, took over. Found footage horror responded with a dramatic spike that reflected this growth in the acceptance of amateur filmmaking. Thanks to YouTube, by 2007 audiences were ready for found footage horror—movies that looked like they were made for YouTube that we could upload ourselves—to return to the mainstream.

As Dan Hunter, Ramon Lobato, Megan Richardson, and Julian Thomas noted in the introduction to their exhaustive collection *Amateur Media: Social, Cultural and Legal Perspectives*, despite their differences some of the biggest websites on the Internet today—YouTube, Wikipedia, Blogspot, Facebook and Twitter—can hold amateur user-generated content in large part responsible for their huge volumes of traffic.[19] Through YouTube in particular, UGC has become increasingly visible in mainstream media (especially in television news). Buckingham, Pini and Willett note that this can be understood as a "radical evolution" not only regarding sources, but also how news is constructed and how it addresses the viewer.[20] It is in this sense that amateur filmmaking can offer alternatives to mainstream media. Patricia Zimmerman has championed the subversive potential of amateur filmmaking, stating that it "is not an event, but a conceptual formation created by social practices and discourses, a category embroiled in power relations between a dominant, more pervasive culture and marginal cultural resistances and technological formations." Crucially, however, she argued this potential has been neutralized in the past through the relegation of amateur filmmaking to the domain of the home movie, domesticated and tamed into "a privatized hobby for families rather than as a means of communication in the public sphere."[21] This sense of a dilution of the political potency of amateur media when appropriated by the mainstream is not uncommon. As will be examined in Chapter Four, this was a position taken in many critiques of *The Blair Witch Project*.

The commercial success of *America's Funniest Home Videos* and its international variants since the early 1990s[22] brought amateur filmmaking aesthetics into the everyday realm of a large mainstream public long before YouTube. Participation in shows like these simply required access to a camera. Cult, horror and other film fans, however, have arguably been aware of the medium-specific materiality of horror since the onset of the home entertainment revolution itself. According to Lucas Hilderbrand, "bootlegs have been central to fan and film collector culture since the introduction of home video…. [A]lthough it would be impossible to prove definitively, I

The videotape as cult object (author's photograph).

suspect that videotape changed the very nature of media fandom and collecting." Partially this is due to the rarity of these artifacts themselves, as "many of the most intensely interesting, perverted, or loved texts exist only outside legitimate distribution." He added, "The true collector collects those objects that have to be found (and copied) rather than simply purchased at Best Buy."[23] As recalled in *Ringu* (Hideo Nakata, 1998), films deemed "dangerous" were often distributed informally across friendship networks via dubbed videotapes. With quality verging on the indecipherable due to innumerable losses in quality as copies-of-copies-of-copies circulated amongst these fan and friendship networks, video dubs of elusive films such as *Cannibal Holocaust* and late-era *mondo*-style films such as *Faces of Death* (John Alan Schwartz, 1978) and *Executions* (David Herman, 1995) gained in mystique and cultural capital what they lost in quality. The added covertness simply added to the taboo nature of the films themselves.

The generational deterioration that marked the replication processes required for copying videotapes has become a material marker of both their danger and added to the impression of authenticity. Analog or digital tapes and technologies themselves are therefore privileged in many contemporary found footage horror films, as can be seen in just the titles of a number of movies including the *Video X* series (James D. Mortellaro, 2003–2007), *The Mitchell Tapes* (Thomas S. Nicol, 2010), *The Tapes* (Lee Alliston, 2011), *The Poughkeepsie Tapes* (John Erick Dowdle, 2007), *V/H/S* and its sequel *V/H/S/2* (Jason Eisener, Gareth Evans, Timo Tjahjanto, Eduardo Sánchez and Gregg Hale, Simon Barrett, and Adam Wingard, 2013), *Bigfoot: The Lost Coast Tapes* (Corey Grant, 2012), *The Lost Tape* (Rakshit Dahiya, 2012), *The Levenger Tapes* (Mark Edwin Robinson, 2011), *Anneliese: The Exorcist Tapes* (Jude Gerard Prest, 2011), *Tape 407* (Dale Fabrigar and Everette Wallin, 2012), and Sean Stone's 2012 film *The Asylum Tapes* (alternately released as *Greystone Park*). Recording technologies and filmmaking terms even form the basis of some titles, such as *[Rec]*, *Camera Phone* (Eddie Brown Jr., 2012), *Reel Evil* (Danny Draven, 2012) and *Cut/Print* (Nathaniel Nose, 2012).

VCR technology and the home entertainment revolution radically transformed how people engaged with screen media. Joan Hawkins observed that the remote control altered how viewers interacted with culture, because "the viewer can replay selected bits of a film, fast-forward through unsettling sequences, watch the film in installments, watch parts of it frame by frame, or stop it altogether." Hawkins continued

> She can also create composite cinematic texts by alternately viewing two films or by crosscutting between a movie on the VCR and the six o'clock news. That is, she can become a truly active viewer, one who creates her own texts, one who feels free to disrupt the narrative flow.[24]

Laura Mulvey argued a similar point, suggesting that this technology—both video and DVD—has meant that we can control time itself, and the supremacy of narrative has consequently given way to this ability to privilege isolated moments. This results in the potential for pleasure beyond that contained within the linear flow of a film text, played out in a specific and inflexible timeframe. Video and DVD technology has rendered the moving image malleable, and allows viewers to become what Mulvey has identified as "possessive spectators" with "the power of the Medusa's gaze at his or her fingertips, turning the moving figure as it were into stone."[25]

This potential for temporal manipulation is often rendered diegetically in found footage horror movies. In *[Rec]*, reporter Angela (Manuela Velasco) asks her cameraman Pablo (Pablo Rosso) to rewind footage he has just recorded of an elderly woman being killed so she can see it again to verify the shocking event. Also from Spain, the climax of *Atrocious* (Fernando Barreda Luna, 2010) is temporally disrupted by police crime scene photographs and a news report of the aftermath of events we have yet to see. Unlike *[Rec]* or Michael Haneke's *Funny Games* (1997/2007) whose protagonist "rewinds" the film to allow himself to take the narrative in a different direction, in *Atrocious* this act is not committed by a diegetic character from within the story, but by an unknown external force that is never identified. This aligns the act with the spectator themselves, mimicking precisely the active modes of viewing that Hawkins and Mulvey discussed.

The most direct legacy of analog video aesthetics on found footage horror is the low quality of the images themselves. In her work on video art and haptics, Laura U. Marks provides a useful technical overview of video's distinctive look. Video images emerge from communication between the source that plays the video and the screen upon which the image appears, and there is a whole range of possible aberrations from the assumed intended image that affect color, tone, and image quality. This renders the context of exhibition and broadcast as significant as the context of reception. If the haptic quality of video is enhanced over other dominant senses because it is "insufficiently visual," other feature that add to this sense of tactility include contrast ratios and the density of pixels: For example, 35mm film has twenty times more pixels per frame than VHS. Video's visual tactility is also reliant largely upon its ability to be manipulated electronically, and for Marks, the haptic nature of video is most vivid in work where artists experiment with manipulating the image via digital effects and analog synthesis. For instance, now-ubiquitous video effects such as pixilation can make an identifiable object unfamiliar, and at the same time emphasizes the way the viewer experiences textures.[26]

Marks privileges video art over more mainstream manifestations of low-quality video such as "the digitized blobs that replace the faces of crime suspects on reality TV"[27] because they do not actively encourage the tactile sensations upon which her work focuses. Unlike television programs like *COPS* (1989–), however, in found footage horror, sensory experience comes closer to the type of non-visual affective experiences that Marks celebrates. Applying Marks' notion of haptic visuality to horror specifically, Angela Ndalianis argued that "this bodily relationship is all the more marked in that the cinematic body— the audio-visual fictional world presented to us—reflects and amplifies the experience of the horrified, suffering and volatile bodies within the narrative space."[28] In found footage horror, this is coded through the materiality of the medium itself, particularly through the ubiquitous distortion of both analog and digital video. *Evil Things* (Dominic Perez, 2009) offers a useful point of reference as it deliberately displays what can be considered as excessive and severe visual distortion even when compared to other found footage horror movies. With its introductory intertitle confirming the status of its protagonist teens as "Missing Persons," the indefatigable decay of its images are imbued with a haunted quality (even during scenes before any threat has befallen them). The chronic pixilation that dominates the film constructs these characters as ghostly long before the malevolent force enters the story. While the plot itself adheres to the familiar generic terrain of teens under threat by the murderous, unidentified stalker typical of the slasher subgenre, its textural construction is the site of *Evil Things'* affect. The film appears to offer an example of Marks' "haptic image" beyond video art in that it "indicates figures and then backs away from representing them fully.... Rather than making the object fully available to view, haptic cinema puts the object into question, calling on the viewer to engage in its imaginative construction."[29] The *Evil Things* protagonists are sometimes monstrous and frequently vague; that we are so rarely permitted to properly fully see them means that our experience of the film stems from the loss of visual information, rather than the privileging of it. Pixelated digital files now have a far greater function in found footage horror than simply verifying the materiality of the format.

Defining Found Footage Horror

The term "found footage horror" is used loosely in popular discourse. In some cases, it pertains only to horror films that feature material that is literally found or discovered such as *The Blair Witch Project*, *Cloverfield*, *V/H/S*, and *Grave Encounters* (The Vicious Brothers, 2011). It can also accommodate horror movies filmed with diegetic hand-held cameras, surveillance cameras, or both, such as *Diary of the Dead, Apartment 143,* and the *Paranormal Activity* films. This definition begins to get hazy when considering the inclusion of this material in films loosely described as "horror mockumentaries" alongside interviews, voice-overs, and visual documentation (newspaper clippings, photographs), as evident in movies like *The Devil Inside, The Last Exorcism, Lake Mungo, The Ghosts of Crowley Hall* (Daren Marc, 2008), and *The Last Broadcast* (Stefan Avalos and Lance Weiler, 1998).

These definitional issues become more complex when considering "found footage" is a name lifted from an already-established filmmaking practice, typified by Bruce Conner's *A MOVIE* (1958) and Joseph Cornell's *Rose Hobart* (1936). As William C. Wees defined it, found footage films employ material shot by someone else for another reason,[30] and in this sense the link becomes apparent: Found footage horror films rely on the *fictional* premise that the footage from which they are constructed existed previously, and has been re-utilized into a new, separate work. Roger Luckhurst has argued that in the case of science fiction found footage films, the label paradoxically unites *avant-garde* and experimental traditions with an overtly mainstream pop cultural genre.[31] In the case of horror, Nick Rombes has linked the surveillance technologies at the heart of the *Paranormal Activity* franchise with these *avant-garde* traditions, as both share a tendency towards "intense, narcissistic self-reflection" and thus exhibit "a relentless survey of its own practices" which is the very feature that has historically distinguished the *avant-garde* from mainstream cinema.[32] Certainly film works by artists like Michael Snow and Andy Warhol indicate surveillance has historical precedence in the American postwar *avant-garde*.

Although not common, there are cases where found footage horror has employed found material in a way more loyal to its original meaning. *Marble Hornets* uses sound and vision from Gene Kearney's short film *Silent Snow, Secret Snow* (1966)[33] and historical stock footage is incorporated into *Haunted Changi* (Andrew Lau, 2010) and *Shadow People* (Mathew Arnold, 2013). The clearest example of this is Peter Delpeut's *The Forbidden Quest* (1993), a Gothic adventure mockumentary influenced by Edgar Allan Poe. As Deputy Director of the Nederlands Filmmuseum, Delpeut accessed their historical film archives to create his film about the disappearance of the Norwegian ship the *Hollandia* during a fictional Antarctic expedition in 1905. Examples such as these are exceptions rather than norms; beyond these cursory links, it would be erroneous to locate the roots of the contemporary subgenre in found footage filmmaking practices as they are understood in cases such as these.

As David Bordwell has recently suggested, the "found" of the contemporary found footage subgenre pertains to plot (footage is discovered) rather

Poster for *Paranormal Activity* (2007) (Blumhouse Productions/The Kobal Collection).

than to the experimental and avant-garde traditions the name implies.[34] Despite Bordwell's preference for the term "discovered footage," the definitional horse has long bolted from the stable and "found footage horror" is now the most widely recognizable label for the subgenre. A brief look at horror magazines like *Rue Morgue* and *Fangoria* and popular websites—not only horror fan sites such as Bloody Disgusting and Dread Central but more mainstream ones like Wikipedia and IMDb—illustrates just how completely the label "found footage horror" has stuck, regardless of its technical accuracy. *The Atlantic*'s Scott Meslow defines it as follows:

> The found-footage genre is built on the conceit that the movie was filmed not by a traditional, omniscient director, but by a character that exists within the film's world—and whose footage was discovered sometime after the events of the film.[35]

This book will be working with a similar definition, although it takes a consciously more elastic approach to the notion of "discovery." For example, while *Ringu* is a film about the discovery of a mysterious videotape containing strange footage that curses its viewers, the inclusion of this material—while flagging the movie's broader self-reflexivity—is not deployed in the attempt to present the entire film as any kind of factuality-based reality in the documentary film sense. It is clearly a fictional film, and its pleasures do not stem from the assumption we believe otherwise. Those borders may be challenged when Sadako (Rie Inō) climbs out of the television in *Ringu*, but on the whole the fourth wall remains relatively intact. The problem with the translation of "found footage horror" to simply apply to genre films where "footage is discovered" does not do justice to how crucial the subgenre's playful appropriation of documentary codes and conventions are to the pleasure it offers.

The relationship between mockumentary and found footage horror is important. However, from the outset I should make clear that this is not a book about mockumentary or documentary as such. The found footage horror subgenre has advanced in its development far enough to have its own distinct set of codes and conventions. It is not a hybrid form that straddles horror and mockumentary, but rather a distinct horror category with its own readily identifiable features, some of which stem from documentary traditions and associated evolving trends in the field of mockumentary. In their 2001 book *Faking It: Mock-Documentary and the Subversion of Factuality*, Jane Roscoe and Craig Hight offered a useful framework to consider this relationship, emphasizing the fluidity of mockumentary and arguing against its definition as a genre because of its very diversity. They convincingly suggested it instead be approached as a discourse, "informed and shaped through the particular relationships it constructs with documentary proper, with the discourses of factuality, and especially through the complexity of its engagement with viewers."[36] From this perspective, this is a book about a type of horror movie that is in dialogue with mockumentary, amongst a range of other aspects.

Like "found footage horror," the term "mockumentary" is also hazy. Critical treatments often indicate an awareness of this instability, often tiptoeing around it or avoiding the term altogether. For Alexandra Juhasz it is "fake documentary,"[37] Christopher Robbins opted instead for "mock documentary,"[38] and David Bordwell called *The Last Exorcism* a "pseudo-doc."[39] Others, however, have embraced the term: Craig Hight said mockumentary "identifies a deliberate blurring of an assumed fact-fiction dichotomy,"[40] while Alison Lebow addressed it precisely by this name for its ability "to signal a skepticism toward documentary realism."[41] Juhasz contended this category applies to comedy or films with comic elements,[42] and in emphasizing the fundamental role of parody in "mock-documentary," Roscoe and Hight noted that "through a foregrounding of humour, parody allows viewers to enjoy the pleasures of being 'in on the joke'; to appreciate and engage with the 'mocking' of the subject of the parody." They continued, "Mock-documentary assumes a sophisticated viewer able to recognize and participate in the form's largely parodic agenda; in other words, a viewer both familiar with the codes and conventions of documentary and ready to accept their comedic treatment."[43] Regardless of these scholarly considerations, like "found footage" itself, common usage has granted mockumentary a far looser definition. Audiences certainly understand "horror mockumentary" as its own distinct category that does not necessarily entail comic elements.

Bill Nichols' identification of documentary modes offers a basic framework to consider how contemporary found footage horror relates to mockumentary. The poetic mode is concerned less with narrative logic or linearity and is more closely aligned with experimental and *avant-garde* filmmaking traditions with a focus on description and rhythm. The expository mode is often referred to as "voice of god" documentary filmmaking, where a voiceover dictates a singular view and places emphasis on a singular verbal perspective. The participatory mode relies heavily on the interview format and seeks to highlight the way a subject and the filmmaker interact. The performative mode acknowledges the subjectivity of the filmmakers themselves and encourages the provocation of an affective response in the viewer. Finally, the reflexive mode deliberately emphasizes the contrived and constructed nature of the reality a film represents.[44] In this context, mockumentary can be immediately understood as reflexive because it is reliant on an appropriation of documentary's codes and conventions to provoke conscious reflection on the documentary project as a whole.

Finally, the observational mode is crucial to found footage horror. Often described as "fly-on-the-wall" filmmaking, it hinges on the assumption that the movie camera can capture events as they really are. For Nichols, the presence of the camera "'on the scene' testifies to its presence in the historical world. This affirms a sense of commitment or engagement with the immediate, intimate, and personal as it occurs. This also affirms a sense of fidelity to what occurs that can pass on to us as if they simply happened when they have, in fact, been constructed to have that very appearance."[45]

Roscoe and Hight agree that the observational mode relates to documentary's claims of being a truthful record of reality. The two earliest and most well-known observational documentary traditions were the French *cinema verité* movement and the predominantly US–based direct cinema, which while containing notable points of difference, shared a shift towards private spaces and everyday activity as a site of documentary investigation (propelled in large part by technological developments that saw cameras themselves become more portable).[46] The immersive filmmaking techniques that defined both *cinema verité* and direct cinema became recognizable shorthand for a type of realism that the success of found footage horror suggests is only on the rise in the mainstream (although it has historically permeated anti–Hollywood filmmaking).

Observational documentaries imply unrestricted contact with the world as it actually is, supposedly allowing the spectator direct (voyeuristic) insight into reality itself. As Roscoe and Hight have noted, there are significant issues with such an assumption. At the heart of it lies an unquestioning belief that the sign and its signifier have an uncomplicated relationship, where the image's indexical relationship to reality is unquestioned and uncomplicated. This consequently implies that documentary filmmakers themselves exist as purely objective onlookers, "capable of standing outside the socio-historical world."[47] In found footage horror, these assumptions avail themselves to many narrative lessons in hubris; as demonstrated in films including (but certainly not limited to) *The Blair Witch Project*, *The Last Exorcism* and *The Devil Inside*, diegetic "documentary" filmmakers can have their assumed objectivity not only challenged but destroyed. Similar cases can perhaps be identified in documentaries based on found footage that contain horrific revelations, unforgettably illustrated in examples like *Capturing the Friedmans* (Andrew Jarecki, 2003) and Werner Herzog's *Grizzly Man* (2005).

Because of this relationship to the observational mode with its heavy reliance on diegetically filmed hand-held and surveillance material, found footage horror films can be considered part of the broader mockumentary tradition according to Roscoe and Hight's definition as they are movies "which make a partial or concerted effort to appropriate documentary codes and conventions to represent a fictional subject."[48] Like Roscoe and Hight's mockdocumentaries, despite the centrality of the observational mode, found footage horror films also often appropriate participatory and interactive modes especially. Typically, like documentary itself found footage horror frequently presents a range of modal hybrids, appropriating codes and conventions of a number of different documentary modes to create a variety of effects.[49] In this light, "mockumentary horror" and "found footage horror" are not separate, distinct categories as much as they offer a palate of formal and structural possibilities constructed from an appropriation of documentary's codes and conventions. They do this through an emphasis upon the camera's diegetic presence, predominantly through hand-held material or surveillance footage.[50] Despite these qualifications, in practice what is popularly called "mockumentary horror" tends to incorporate observational material with voice-overs, interviews, and other visual evidence such as photographs or maps. At the same time, "found footage horror" is broadly understood as privileging the "fly-on-the-wall" conceit of the observational mode. In practice, the lines between these categories blurs substantially. While the appropriation of observational documentary codes and conventions is a dominant marker of contemporary found footage horror, films recognized by this label frequently include aspects of other documentary modes.

The Blair Witch Project is a useful example of how these aspects blur. It consists of video and film that was literally found (discovered) but it was "mockumentary-ized" in two distinct ways. *The Blair Witch Project* can be understood as both a film about the making of a (fake) documentary and simultaneously a (fake) documentary itself in the framing premise that Artisan Films cobbled together from the various reels and tapes of Heather, Joshua and Mike's recovered footage into a coherent, singular whole, resulting in the film that was released in cinemas. The related promotional television movie *Curse of the Blair Witch* (Daniel Myrick and Eduardo Sánchez, 1999) is a more overt modal hybrid, and includes interviews and visual documentation that acts as "evidence" (photographs, television reports, illustrations, old manuscripts, etc.). As demonstrated by *Curse of the Blair Witch* (a film significantly closer to what the directors originally conceived as their final product[51]), Myrick and Sánchez were fully capable of creating a comparatively slick and polished final product, despite their infamously low budget.

The variety of possible ways that documentary's codes and conventions can be appropriated in found footage horror can also be seen in the lesser known *Video X* series. It begins with *Murder in the Heartland: The Search for Video X* (James D. Mortellaro, 2003), which tells its story through fly-on-the-wall footage alongside other documentary-like materials, while *Video X: Evidence* (James D. Mortellaro, 2003) and *Video X: The Dwayne and Darla-Jean Story* (James D. Mortellaro, 2007) consist primarily of discovered, observational-style footage itself. Again, neither should necessarily be considered more or less a "mockumentary," but rather are best understood as responding to and appropriating different codes and conventions from the palate of documentary modes.

This range of potential combinations is apparent in many other found footage horror films. *[Rec]*, for instance, consists solely of diegetically shot footage that relies heavily on an appropriation of observational documentary's codes and conventions, but part of the footage includes cameraman Pablo's (Pablo Rosso) recorded interviews between journalist Angela (Manuela Velasco) and the residents trapped in the building with them during the mysterious outbreak of a zombie-like virus. *Diary of the Dead* begins with behind-the-scenes news footage of re-animating zombies, and then shifts to first-person hand-held footage of a zombie outbreak filmed by a diegetic camera. This film was edited together by Debra (Michelle Morgan), who tells us via a voice-over at the film's beginning that she has also "added music occasionally for effect." Although the immersive qualities of the film stem primarily from the immediacy of its hand-held, diegetically filmed footage, *Diary of the Dead* is simultaneously explicit in its admission that this footage has been manipulated: It is not raw "found" footage as such, and there is rarely a sense of ambiguity about this fact. While commonly described as a "found footage horror film" and thus emphasizing its reliance on observational documentary codes and conventions, its voice-over in particular also denotes a strong relationship with expository documentary traditions.

J.T. Petty's *S&Man* (1996) shows just how far these boundaries can be stretched as it blurs mockumentary and documentary self-reflexively in relation to horror's own codes and conventions. The film is Petty's interrogation of the relationship between horror and voyeurism, and it includes interviews with notorious horror directors Fred Vogel and Bill Zebub alongside noted horror academic Carol J. Clover. He also interviews "filmmaker" Eric Rost, a fictional character played by actor Erik Marcisak. As the movie develops, Petty becomes increasingly convinced that Rost is making snuff movies, a suspicion that remains ambiguous at the film's conclusion. *S&Man* illustrates just how elastic the horror mockumentary spectrum may be as it delves into the very lines that separate horror fantasy from horrific reality, and mockumentary from documentary.

What underlies the bulk of these films in regard to their relationship with documentary is the fundamental notion of "proof." This manifests in the regular appearance of official-looking intertitles that frame their footage as "official" evidence, and in many cases this is implied by their titles: *Exhibit A*, *Exhibit X* (Brian Shotwell, 2012), *Case No. 666/2013* (Venkat Siddareddy and Purnesh Konathala, 2013), *Case #342* (Allyson Diana, 2012), *Tape 407* (Dale Fabrigar and Everette Wallin, 2012), and two separate found footage horror films called *Evidence*—Howie Askin's 2011 film and the upcoming Olatunde Osunsanmi movie of the same name. Even *Cloverfield*'s title refers to a military case name assigned to the events depicted in Lower Manhattan by the U.S. Department of Defense.

While some of these films use titles like this to validate their status as "real" authorized audiovisual documents of recorded fact, the relationship is often far more complex. If, as Craig Hight has suggested, mockumentary seeks to playfully challenge documentary's underlying truth claims rather than subvert them as such,[52] then found footage horror's frequent mission to capture the elusive and ethereal paranormal grant it a useful position to interrogate the often hazy lines between reality and its representation. The supernatural possibilities upon which so many of these films stories are based highlight their broader relationship to how we culturally engage with new technologies more generally. In his book *Haunted Media: Electronic Presence from Telegraphy to Television*, Jeffrey Sconce noted that "tales of paranormal media are important ... not as timeless expressions of some underlying electronic superstition, but as a permeable language in which to express a culture's changing social relationship to a historical sequence of technologies."[53] Found footage horror movies and the technologies that formally mark them are part of what Sconce has identified as social anxieties around new media technologies that are teased out through considerations of the supernatural.

Not all found footage horror films concern the supernatural, of course. But even in those about real-world horrors like serial killers (as seen in *The Poughkeepsie Tapes*, *Head Case*, and *Megan Is Missing*), villains are still granted more than what would be considered normal in terms of strength, visibility and movement.[54] It is the intangibility of the supernatural and the fact that it is so difficult to capture that makes found footage horror so adept at challenging the truth claims of documentary more broadly. As Roscoe and Hight have argued, documentary has traditionally been valued for its truthful relationship to and accurate representation of the world as it actually is. This is reliant upon an assumed indexical bond between photography as a scientific record and the real-life phenomena it seeks to document. The representation of these events or moments is therefore assumed to be identical.[55] The very thing that these films seek to mock is "the belief in science (and scientific experts) and the essential integrity of the referential image."[56] In the case of the first *Para-*

normal Activity film, Sébastien Lefait has observed that director Oren Peli "chose to exploit the intrinsic supernatural aspect of the camera rather than the spectacular quality of what comes into its field. He drew from the entrenched belief that the camera is endowed with a revelatory power to stage a paranormal appearance that never comes." Put simply, in *Paranormal Activity* "the nature of the footage as surveillance draws on the revelatory power of the camera to make this nothing exist."[57] The pleasure of found footage horror in part stems from spectatorial knowledge that something we rationally know not to be true (the supernatural) can momentarily be reimagined (consciously or otherwise) as "real" because the vehicle in which that information is delivered is one we otherwise trust to provide reliable information.

Approaching Found Footage Horror

The relationship between the movie camera and the psychology of the individual has been of interest to film scholars since the 1970s, particularly with the publication of Laura Mulvey's foundational essay in feminist film studies, "Visual Pleasure and Narrative Cinema." Mulvey responds to Christian Metz's "The Imaginary Signifier"[58] which linked the experience of watching film to Jacques Lacan's notion of the "mirror stage," the period where as a young child we learn to recognize the image in a mirror as our own. Because the child's physical abilities are still developing, they privilege the reflected image with the skills in which they are deficient. The results in terms of identification are complex, because while the child recognizes itself in the mirror, it also *mis*recognize the image as being superior. This process is replicated in the cinema, where we as spectators idealize star images in the construction of our own egos. Mulvey deviated from Metz on the universality of the spectatorial experience, and argued that gender played a significant differentiating role in processes of identification. She also claimed that there is an inherently gendered aggression in the spectatorial gaze in Classical Hollywood cinema that is voyeuristic and channeled through the look of the camera itself. These looks are underscored by a fundamental scopophilic motivation specifically oriented around the sexualization of women's bodies and their "to-be-looked-at-ness,"[59] and as such the dominant gaze of the cinema can be considered not just masculine but also sadistic.

The formal construction of found footage horror is so directly linked to the gaze of the camera and how we identify with characters and their experiences that it can be considered one its major concerns. The assumed masculinity of the cinematic gaze is rendered literal in the *V/H/S* segment "Amateur

Night" (David Bruckner, 2012), where protagonist Clint (Drew Walker) has a video camera built into his eyeglasses: The camera records whatever he looks at. Brigid Cherry's observation that *The Blair Witch Project* is a film "about the way in which technology gets in the way of seeing"[60] could perhaps therefore apply just as easily to the subgenre as a whole. Implied in the camera's presence here is a frustrating of visual control. Rather than acting as a surrogate eye that does our seeing for us, the camera obscures our vision, and stands between our eye and the things we wish to see. Additionally, we often want to look in places that the camera refuses to go. There is a mechanical slowing down that suggests a lack of agency working in direct opposition to the supposed sense of autonomy that a free-moving hand-held camera implies. This hand-held footage is one of the subgenre's most defining traits, and as Roscoe and Hight have indicated, "camcorder footage is very popular within current documentary programming and works to promote the idea of immediacy and the experience of being a 'fly-on-the-wall.'"[61] If we surrender completely to the formal contrivances of found footage horror and find ourselves feeling immersed in the film's action, then technology clearly "gets in the way of seeing."

The camera has traditionally been deployed as a surrogate eye for the spectator in horror and cinema more generally; in found footage horror, this artificial organ is deliberately and consistently exposed as faulty. By exposing the surrogate camera eye of filmmaking technology as incapable of being fully on our side—it "gets in the way of seeing"—these films also formally expose the representational mechanics that lie at the heart of how as spectators we feel a sense of voyeuristic intimacy with onscreen phenomena. At their best, found footage films hold the capacity to undermine the dominant and often sadistic supremacy of the gaze by exposing this inadequacy to fully *see*.

Director and writer of the found footage horror film *In Memorium* (2005), Amanda Gusack has identified precisely what this boils down to in regard to the experience of watching these types of movies. According to Gusack, "[T]he thing that makes it compelling ... is that conventional 'rules' of film are suspended—at least until that convention eventually becomes oversaturated. As a result, our expectations don't work at they normally do. So, since we're looking through a POV that's essentially estranged to us—instead of being able to use convention's rules to determine the outcome of a moment, we fill in the blanks of the story with our own primal terror."[62] Identification is therefore a fundamental part of how found footage horror films seek to scare us, and found footage horror audiences understand these overt formal features as being part of the diegetic world of the film: The camera is part of the story. This is not communicated merely through their formal construction, but also via what is frequently unambiguous dialogue around the act of filming, typified in well-known examples like *The Blair Witch Project* and *Diary of the Dead*.

This sort of self-reflexivity is a significant feature of found footage horror. As Michele Aaron noted, films like *Peeping Tom* and Irvin Kershner's 1978 *The Eyes of Laura Mars* "draw attention to themselves as texts, as artificial, mediated (re)presentations" and thus make it extremely difficult for spectators to forget that we are watching a movie.[63] Found footage horror relies on a similar paradox: On one hand, the formal construction of these films encourages a sense of verisimilitude and suggests that what is being shown is raw, unprocessed "reality." At the same time, however, it does this by making it impossible to forget that we are watching a film: If the shaky camera and the regular glitches in sound and vision fail to remind us of this, then the appearance of and references to filmmaking technologies in many of these films makes it inescapable.

"Realism" and "reality" are a conceptual can of worms that contemporary found footage horror in large part seeks to formally and thematically interrogate, albeit with varying degrees of success. Joel Black has suggested that cinema is itself responsible for our increasing desire to make every facet of our daily lives conceivable as a visible spectacle. For him, one of the most obvious issues about criticizing the relationship between reality and its representation is that by placing an emphasis of "the media's distortion of reality," we are necessarily implying "that there is some independent state of affairs 'out there' that can be objectively verified."[64] As Christopher Williams noted in the introduction to his collection *Cinema and Realism*:

> The problem of realism arises once we have accepted, even as a hypothesis, that the world exists, either as an objective fact for people to look at, or a set of possibilities which they construct through their intelligence and their labor, or as the product of their imagination, or, most plausibly, as a combination of all three.[65]

In Classical Hollywood, the codes and conventions that governed the construction of realism were dominated by its so-called "invisible" style, reliant in large part upon continuity editing which seeks to make the transition from shot to shot as seamless and unnoticeable as possible. However, as outlined above, in found footage horror it is the very *visibility* of the filmmaking apparatus—quite often the self-referential diegetic inclusion of the camera itself— that creates its sense of verisimilitude.

Cynthia Freeland identified "realist horror" as a challenge to definitions of the genre that rely on supernatural monsters such as zombies, vampires or werewolves, typified by Noel Carroll's 1990 book *The Philosophy of Horror: Paradoxes of the Heart*. For Freeland, in realist horror "the monster is a true-to-life rather than supernatural being."⁶⁶ and as such, seeks to blur the lines between fact and fiction. Ndalianis suggested that this realist impulse is critical even in fantastic horror if considered in relation to sensory rather than intellectual knowledge, and she noted that "one of the most powerful effects that horror has is to be able to affect the sensorium in such a way that it perceptually collapses the boundaries between reality and fiction."⁶⁷ Gary Rhodes noted that horror has sought verisimilitude through the construction of the gaze itself, be it the direct address of Bela Lugosi or the deployment of first-person perspective of the slasher killer typified by *Halloween* (John Carpenter, 1978). Rhodes also identified a rise of documentary aesthetics across a range of films including *Psycho* (Alfred Hitchcock, 1960), Georges Franju's *Les Yeux Sans Visage* (Eyes Without a Face, 1959), George A. Romero's *Night of the Living Dead* (1968), and *The Texas Chain Saw Massacre* (Tobe Hooper, 1974), describing these movies as "documentaryesque."⁶⁸

Rhodes traced mockumentary horror back to Welles' 1938 *War of the Worlds* radio broadcast, and also acknowledged the place of *Cannibal Holocaust*. He noted its documentary aesthetics and the deployment of authentic torture footage in places (most notably the scenes of animal torture), and linked it to the Italian *mondo* film that also merged authentic and fake footage in films that "combine the real and the unreal into a collective narrative menagerie that proves difficult for audiences to know where the authentic ends and the fiction begins."⁶⁹ *Henry: Portrait of a Serial Killer* (John McNaughton, 1986) is a key movie that employs documentary elements, playing a role in propelling the shift to more overt horror mockumentaries in the future. Importantly, Rhodes observed that documentary realism manifests in horror through "technical imperfections [that] are understood to be part of the form, and part of what reality on film looks like."⁷⁰ Additionally, the use of black-and-white in these two examples reinforces associations with low-budget documentary film production. To this list he added the importance of hand-held cinematography (a style central in *verité* documentaries, particularly during World War II, the Korean War and the Vietnam War), a rejection to some degree of continuity editing and its goals of invisibility, and a rougher soundtrack and absence of non-diegetic music.

David Ray Carter has presented an equally rigorous analysis in his essay "It's Only a Movie? Reality as Transgression in Exploitation Cinema." For Carter, reality itself is constructed as transgressive in a number of ways in many exploitation films, the most immediate of which is familiar to found footage horror audiences: the simple claim from the outset that a film is a true story (sometimes these claims are more accurate than others: for example, Renny Harlin's 2013 film *Devils Pass* is based on the real Dyatlov Pass incident of

1959). Regardless of the validity of such assertions, these statements attempt to shift a film's action into the same world as its audience. Carter has noted that "fictional films that assert that they are depicting reality blur the line between the actual and the false and thus become hyperreal rather than purely fictional or authentic."[71] Hyperreality thus becomes inherently transgressive as it seeks to undermine the expectations we bring to the film-viewing experience: We expect to indulge in a fictional fantasy, but these films make concrete attempts to usurp this belief, hoping the stories will therefore necessarily become closer to our own realities. Filmmakers seek to unsettle and discomfort spectators through this sudden, unexpected proximity shift, milking our suspicions that what we are watching may in fact have actually happened.

Since *The Blair Witch Project* onwards, however, the recycling of tropes and other found footage horror codes and conventions do not signify ambiguity as much as they once did. These features now allow easy taxonomical identification much more than they support claims of authenticity, and rendering what were once transgressive markers of possible factuality serve instead as simply a tamer, obedient recognition of firmly established subgeneric codes. The tradition of found footage horror has evolved and matured, and in turn audiences can engage with them in a more knowing way. Its pleasures are not reliant on our gullibility, but rather on our willingness to succumb to the *myth* of the real that these films offer through a now heavily codified formal system.

This book will explore how this system evolved, while emphasizing the ways that films in this category both merge and deviate. Part 1 will examine the prehistory of contemporary found footage horror, identifying its oft-cited antecedents before turning its attention to less discussed forbearers such as the safety films of the 1950s and 1960s, snuff-fictions, and television series and programs like the notorious *Ghostwatch* broadcast in the United Kingdom and the French series *Les Documents Interdits*. Part 2 presents a detailed analysis of the two key watershed moments of the contemporary found footage horror subgenre, the 1999 release of *The Blair Witch Project* and the mainstream cinema release of *Paranormal Activity* in 2009. It also provides a brief survey of films produced in the category in the decade between them, suggesting that it was during these years that the subgenre's codes and conventions solidified, allowing the potential to *play* with the threat of the real these films formally offer, rather than accepting them wholesale as authentic. Crucial to this shift was the rise of YouTube in 2006 that saw a spike in found footage horror films that both looked like UGC and also appropriated the codes and conventions of observational documentary. A series of essays then explores some thematic trends that have appeared in the post–*Paranormal Activity* period of found footage horror, including the recurrent exorcism trope, the role and representation of the family and its relationship to technology, and the way this subgenre has interrogated national history and identity. Finally, it explores the indie success of *V/H/S* and the *Marble Hornets* series, reflecting on the specter of commercialism that has hovered over the subgenre since the *Blair Witch* phenomenon in 1999.

As we make our way through this material, we will discover that found footage horror has an often-volatile history. Demonstrating an ability to survive by adapting to technological and cultural shifts and popular trends, the contemporary found footage horror category is a powerful and perhaps surprisingly complex subgeneric experiment in blurring the lines between our quotidian reality and horror's dark and tantalizing fantasies.

Part 1

Expanding the Prehistory: 1938–1998

The search for authentic artistic depictions of death, torture and bodily trauma has a long history, spanning far beyond the cinematic image. Drawings of cadavers were once the primary method for studying the human body for would-be medical practitioners, and the body has been just as central a subject in the arts. As Deanna Petherbridge noted, the body "has been central to Western Art for most of its history, and to represent bodies in all their expressivity artists have needed to study anatomy: dissecting the dead to depict the living."[1] Both Michelangelo and Leonardo Da Vinci produced anatomical sketches based on dissections, and Caravaggio was rumored to have used the bloated body of a drowned prostitute as a model for his painting "Death and the Virgin" (1606). The 18th century French painter and engraver Jacques Gautier d'Agoty is renowned for his vivid and highly detailed anatomical drawings of opened bodies, and Théodore Géricault painted highly detailed studies of severed heads and limbs in the early 20th century, keeping body parts from a local hospital in his studio and studying them as they decayed.[2] These examples demonstrate a historical fascination with verisimilitude in regard to the human form and its representation.

The search for authenticity in horror also evokes Paris's *Le Théâtre du Grand-Guignol*. Running from 1897 to 1962, the *Grand Guignol* specialized in the creation of realistic horror performances, and Adam Rockoff has located it as the origin of the modern slasher film. With many plays reenacting contemporary *faits divers* (sensational and often lurid news stories),[3] *Grand Guignol* performances were renowned for their emphasis on gore. According to Rockoff, because of this the *Grand Guignol* can be considered as nothing less than "the most violent, gruesome and depraved artistic spectacle in the history of civilization."[4] Additionally, the use of documentation and other "found" evidence is also not new to horror, and diaries, letters, and journals form the structural basis of a range of classic literary horror stories from H.P. Lovecraft and Ambrose Bierce and the famous epistolary novels *Frankenstein* (Mary Shelley, 1818)[5] and *Dracula* (Bram Stoker, 1897). More recent examples include Stephen King's *Carrie* (1974) and Max Brooks' *World War Z: An Oral History of the Zombie War* (2006). These texts rely on creating a sense of authenticity by replicating the familiar documentation of everyday life, and thus creating a sense of realism unavailable to the omniscient third-person narrator that has traditionally dominated literary fiction. David Bordwell has also linked films like *The Blair Witch Project* and *Cloverfield* to "the topos of the discovered manuscript" that was a popular feature of Renaissance-era romances in particular, where a manuscript is presented with the understanding that someone other than its author has prepared it for publication, again to grant it a degree of authenticity.[6]

One of the most famous ancestors of the contemporary found footage horror subgenre is Orson Welles' 1938 radio adaptation of H.G. Wells' novel *The War of the Worlds*. It replicated the formal structures and stylistic devices of the newscast format that would have been familiar to its contemporary audience; the panic, confusion and hysteria that followed this broadcast has been widely documented. Some listeners were concerned that an alien invasion was actually occurring, and that what they were hearing was a real news broadcast. Prior to this, advances during the 19th century in print technology and a subsequent rise in access to newspapers corresponded with an increased demand for local content. In this climate, hoaxes became common. Many leading literary figures were involved in the creation of such scandals in their journalistic careers, viewing them as creative writing exercises: Mark Twain (writing as Samuel Clemens) reported in Nevada's *Territorial Enterprise* in 1862 of petrified human remains being found in the side of a mountain, and Edgar Allan Poe was behind the supposed first-person account of space travel published in the *Southern Literary Messenger* in 1835, "The Unparalleled Adventures of One Hans Pfaall." The 19th century also saw much larger scale science fiction–themed media hoaxes such as "The Great Moon Hoax" (1835) about life being discovered on the moon, and horror-inflected ones including "The Winstead Wild Man" (1895) about a wild beast loose in Connecticut.[7]

In the case of cinema, Joel Black cited Thomas Edison's *Execution of Czolgosz with Panorama of Auburn Prison* (1901) as an example of how real death acted as an early cinematic spectacle[8]: While the execution scenes were reenactments, the shots outside the actual prison itself were filmed on the day of the execution. However, when it comes to cinema, there are cases where it has not been necessary to feign sensational material. One need only recall Edison's execution of Topsy in *Electrocuting an Elephant* to find evidence of real death in early cinema. It is therefore not only within the generic domain of horror that the visceral shock of death and bodily trauma has been employed to impact its viewers, and the shock value of body horror is crucial to the notorious road safety films of the 1950s and 1960s. As explored in Chapter Two, the rise in road accident fatalities during this period led to the formation of safety film groups like Ohio's Highway Safety Foundation who incorporated actual car accident footage into their educational movies. Despite their name, the Highway Safety Foundation did not deal exclusively with road safety films, and today one of their most shocking movies remains the 1964 educational film *The Child Molester*. The film contains actual crime scene images of the bodies of two young girls murdered by a sexual predator. To the contemporary imagination, the impact of deploying material such as this is clearly ethically challenging.

Driver education and other safety films from this era certainly cannot be considered "snuff" as such, but along with films like Michael Powell's *Peeping Tom* (1960) they highlight the complex conceptual and ethical terrain that surrounds the relationship between death and its on-screen representation. The term "snuff" is often used so loosely that it has no unified concrete meaning, but it is this nebulousness that grants it its power. This lack of clarity has allowed the formation of a category of films I refer to as snuff-fictions: fictional films about the production and distribution of often sexually charged movies depicting graphic murder. This category includes *Hardcore* (Paul Schrader, 1979), *Vacancy* (Nimród Antall, 2007), *Mute Witness* (Anthony Waller, 1994), *Tesis* (Alejandro Amenábar, 1996), *8mm* (Joel Schumacher, 1999), *Snuff-Movie* (Bernard Rose, 2005) and a vast number of other examples.

It was the controversy surrounding *Snuff* (1976) that brought the relationship between horror and the real to the fore. Like many issues surrounding this notorious text, ascribing authorship to a single figure is difficult. The bulk of the film consists of an unreleased exploitation film called *The Slaughter* made by Michael and Roberta Findlay in South America in 1971, loosely based on a Charles Manson–like figure called Satan (Enrique Larratelli) and the escapades of his female followers in the lead-up to the eponymous bloodbath (climaxing in the killing of a pregnant woman in a clear reference to the murder of Sharon Tate in 1969). Unable to release the technically substandard film as it was, distributor Allan Shackleton hired adult movie director Simon Nuchtern to create a short five-minute coda showing the supposed evisceration of a female "crew member" by its "director." "Re-titled *Snuff* and playing up suggestions that this added sequence was an actual murder in its promotional material, the film was greeted with hostility in New York City especially, where it became a primary text in the burgeoning anti-pornography feminist movement. Although *Snuff* was promptly exposed as a hoax, that it was so difficult to tell "real" snuff from "fake" snuff became precisely the point that many anti-pornography feminists championed. That those final five minutes of *Snuff* are so rich in technical flaws merely emphasized its difference from slick, polished horror films such as Richard Donner's *The Omen* that came out in the same year. These final moments have no non-diegetic sound and no end credits, underscoring Shackleton's deliberate and conscious efforts to make the *Snuff* coda appear as real as possible. Regardless of a number of treatments reducing *Snuff* to a passing curio, however, it is a significant film in the prehistory of found footage horror for a number of reasons that will be addressed further in Chapter Three.

The Usual Suspects

Often cited as a crucial origin point for contemporary found footage horror, Ruggero Deodato's *Cannibal Holocaust* (1980) deliberately blurred the lines between the real and the fictional in a horror context, and in doing so faced great controversy. The movie follows New York University Professor Harold Monroe (Robert Kerman) and his team to the Amazon where they search for a documentary crew that vanished while making a film about cannibalism. Monroe discovers the remains of the crew as well as their surviving cans of film. In New York, the television network that sent Monroe on this trip urge him to host a broadcast of this discovered footage, but Monroe insists on viewing it first. While watching the shocking material, he is horrified to discover the original crew not only set up fake scenarios and presented them as real, but also engaged in a range of horrific acts including rape. The final moments of this discovered footage show the original crew being graphically tortured and eaten, leaving television executives no choice but to agree with Monroe that the film should not only go unaired, but that it should also be destroyed.

Like other films in the Italian cannibal subgenre such as *Cannibal Ferox* (Umberto Lenzi, 1981) and *The Mountain of the Cannibal God* (Sergio Martino, 1978), *Cannibal Holocaust* can be considered what Harvey Fenton has called the "bastard son" of the *mondo* films of the 1960s.[9] *Mondo* films traditionally explored taboo subject matter often in the context of non–Western cultures, typically with more attention paid to sensationalism than fact. Its exploitative peak was probably the *Faces of Death* series (1978–1996). It was promoted as authentic but its validity has been challenged. Mark Goodall has celebrated *mondo*'s influence on a range of contemporary media from *National Geographic* and Benetton's *Colors* magazine through to the novels of J.G. Ballard and surveillance trends in "Reality" TV. Beginning with *Mondo Cane* (Paolo Cavara, Franco Prosperi and Gualtiero Jacopetti, 1962), Goodall argued that at its best, *mondo* has a significant place in documentary history and that it is at least as closely related to *avant-garde* filmmaking traditions as it is to horror, trash and exploitation. In attempting to distinguish the "supreme Mondo"[10] of Jacopetti with its more exploitative and sensational entries, Goodall drew a line between the type of racist exploitation films that *Cannibal Holocaust* is responding to and those he suggested illustrate an important aspect of experimental and documentary filmmaking, a heritage he convincingly argued has thus far been excluded from film history.

With its depictions of so-called "savage natives," even the serious accusations of racism lobbied against *Cannibal Holocaust* paled in comparison next to the storm of legal problems it faced both in Italy and around Europe for its graphic violence. The French magazine *Photo*'s 1981 article "*Grand Guignol Cannibale*" claimed that people were actually murdered in the making of the film, and much of the movie's notoriety stemmed from similar beliefs. The Italian authorities employed a disused law outlawing the torture of animals to ban *Cannibal Holocaust* only a month after it opened in 1980. (After a long court battle, it was eventually released uncut in 1983.) In the United Kingdom, it became a key text in the "Video Nasties" scandal[11] and despite being banned, it was again surrounded with accusations of being a genuine snuff film when a video copy was confiscated in Birmingham in 1993.[12] As David Kerekes and David Slater observed in their foundational book *Killing for Culture: A History of Death Films from Mondo to Snuff*, the sense of verisimilitude that dominated the controversy surrounding *Cannibal Holocaust* stemmed from the convincing effects of bodily violence and from their proximity to the very real violence committed against animals in the film. The scenes of real animal torture "increases the potency of all subsequent acts of violence ten-fold. *Cannibal Holocaust* manages to anaesthetize rational thought with the shock of real live things being killed: *if this is real, what else might be real?*"[13] This was a trick that later filmmakers would also adopt, such as in Michael Haneke's *Benny's Video* (1992) whose introduction shows a video of a pig being killed, footage that is played and then replayed in slow motion to establish the negative influence of video violence on its eponymous teenage protagonist.

Although some of the special effects in Deodato's film may be less shocking today than they were at the time of its release, its graphic scenes of real violence against animals are as powerful and as disturbing as ever. Declaring in 1999 that he believed the film to be a "masterpiece,"[14] Deodato's claims that "all the animals which were killed were then eaten by natives"[15] do little to assuage the fact that these images of cruelty and torture remain inescapably problematic. Significantly, however, these are issues that the movie itself—with its film-within-a-film structure—attempts to address in its own diegesis. When the television station that initially wished to broadcast the discovered footage deemed it unshowable and demanded it be destroyed, *Cannibal Holocaust* paradoxically confirms that the very horrors it has just shown should not be seen. As Fenton noted, "[T]he most pertinent argument pitched against *Cannibal Holocaust* is that it is guilty of the transgressions which it seeks to condemn."[16] Deodato's movie resists the critical instinct to reduce it to a single progressive or reactionary position, making for an ultimately uncomfortable viewing experience because, as Fenton again encapsulated so perfectly:

> It is difficult to watch it without "taking sides" in a battle in which it demands that the viewer must become engaged.... Personally I am left in an impossibly ambivalent state when considering the moral questions which it raises: I no more want to "defend" it than I wish to "attack" it for the embarrassed ethical corner into which it paints itself.[17]

Aside from its primary narrative premise of "discovered footage" providing an obvious link with the contemporary found footage horror subgenre, *Cannibal Holocaust* also taught later filmmakers who experimented with the relationship between film, horror, and the real a valuable lesson: There *are* limits to what audiences (and the law) will accept. Contemporary found footage horror movies like *Crowsnest* (Brenton Spencer, 2012), *Welcome to the Jungle* (Jonathan Hensleigh, 2007), *Home Movie* (Christopher Denham, 2008) and *Long Pigs* (Chris Power and Nathan Hynes, 2007) all share a fascination with cannibalism, suggesting conscious (if not safe) nods to Deodato's notorious work. The television series *The River* (2012)—created by *Paranormal Activity*'s mastermind Oren Peli—also appears to be directly influenced by *Cannibal Holocaust* in its basic premise of a film crew in the Amazon searching for another film crew who has gone missing.

This collision between the real and the fictional is by no means specific to Europe or the United States, and the *Guinea Pig*[18]—or *Ginī Piggu*—films (1985–1990) from Japan offer yet another scandalous instance where fake violence was claimed as real to create its gruesome impact. Although followed by *Flowers of Flesh and Blood* (*Za ginipiggu 2: Chiniku no hana*, Hideshi Hino, 1985) and five other titles, Satoru Ogura's original *Devil's Experiment* (1985) arguably remains one of the most shocking examples of Japanese cinematic ultraviolence. With no plot to speak of and lacking the polish of mainstream horror films from this period in the West, *Devil's Experiment* shows the torture and mutilation of a young woman in close-up for almost an hour. As Jack Hunter indicated, despite the fact that *Devil's Experiment* was marketed as an authentic underground snuff film (the video package contained no credit information, for example), the production values belie this. Like many contemporary found footage horror films, it contains a brief introduction that states the film was received from an anonymous source in an attempt to add weight to its claims of authenticity, but what remains when this is rejected is for Hunter "an effective and surprisingly low-key meditation on the culminative dehumanization that violence causes in both aggressor and victim alike."[19] Later installments of the franchise like *Flowers of Flesh and Blood* for Hunter devolve into more familiar gore territory and therefore lack the thematic clout of the original.[20]

The *Guinea Pig* films gained international notoriety with the rumor that actor Charlie Sheen contacted the FBI about them in the belief that they were genuine snuff films. As David Ray Carter has observed, beyond Japan they were distributed informally as bootlegged videotapes which granted them an added aura of authenticity,[21] and no doubt this was one of the factors that prompted Sheen's action. It was not only authorities in the United States who had concerns about these films, however, and criminal investigations were launched in both Sweden and the United Kingdom. In Japan, the franchise attained notoriety when serial killer Muyazaki Tsutomo—the so-called *Otaku* Murderer—was rumored to have re-enacted specific scenes from *Flowers of Flesh and Blood* when he murdered four children in the late 1980s.[22] Despite these controversies, Jay McRoy has celebrated the *Guinea Pig* films in his lengthy analysis as "a collection of texts that mobilize images of corporeal disintegration, and the (on-screen) forces responsible for their methodical yet gory disassembly, as metaphors for shifting conceptions of corporeal, social, and national cohesion."[23] He noted that *Devil's Experiment* actively undermined its own claims of authenticity with overt evidence of its constructed nature in terms of editing and cinematography.[24] Although not as well known in the West, the legacy of the *Guinea Pig* films and a fascination with snuff-fictions more generally can be seen in a range of other Japanese horror, gore and adult films, including *Evil Dead Trap* (Toshiharu Ikeda, 1988), *Suicide Dolls* (Tamakichi Anaru, 1999), *Tumbling Doll of Flesh* (Tamakichi Anaru, 1998), and *Celluloid Nightmares* (Daisuke Yamanouchi, 1999).

While all of these films collectively played a key part in the development of the contemporary found footage horror subgenre, the Belgian film *Man Bites Dog* (1992) provides the most direct link in this prehistory so far to *The Blair Witch Project*. As Charles Masters has observed, both films rely on a mockumentary format and the makers of each used their extremely low budgets to their advantage.²⁵ *Man Bites Dog* was not unique in combining documentary-styled graphic violence with the serial killer film—John McNaughton's *Henry: Portrait of a Serial Killer* (1986) is a notable previous entry—but as Martin Rubin has indicated, it was preceded by *The Honeymoon Killers* (Leonard Kastle, 1970) and *Badlands* (Terrence Malick, 1973).²⁶ However, the mockumentary format so crucial to *Man Bites Dog* renders it particularly significant to contemporary found footage horror.

Man Bites Dog blends dark comedy with graphic violence as it follows a "documentary" film crew tracing the exploits of serial killer Ben (Benoît Poelvoorde). As Ben commits horrendous crimes in between normal activities like drinking in bars or visiting his family, the crew are increasingly implicated until they become accomplices, raping, killing and disposing of bodies with Ben and accepting stolen money from him to help complete their film. Ben's apparent indestructibility unravels as a mysterious source seeks revenge not only against the killer, but his family, his girlfriend Valerie (Valérie Parent) and the film crew themselves. Like *The Blair Witch Project* seven years later, the final shot of *Man Bites Dog* is suggestive of the death of the entire film crew as a camera lies on the floor, filming from its discarded position.

Ernest Mathjis has noted that *Man Bites Dog* is a densely reflexive text, not only because of its excessive and overt formal construction via the articulation of the nuts-and-bolts of filmmaking itself, but also because it knowingly refers to the broader mediasphere through references to French film figures such as Jean Gabin, Michèle Morgan and Philip Noiret.²⁷ As the film's original title *C'est arrivé près de chez vous* or *It Happened in Your Neighborhood* suggests, the film's punch is aimed squarely at the audience ourselves, emphasizing our complacency as media consumers in how violent imagery is produced and consumed. Alongside the graphic murders, sexual assaults and the other crimes that the film chronicles, the most chilling legacy of *Man Bites Dog* is just how casually Ben and the film crew go about their business. It is unquestionably a gruesome and disturbing film, but taking lessons from *Cannibal Holocaust*, *Man Bites Dog* knew how to most effectively merge ambiguity and authenticity.

It is clear why *Cannibal Holocaust* and *Man Bites Dog* regularly appear in historical overviews of the contemporary found footage horror film.²⁸ Without undermining their importance, the following chapters will now expand on other areas that have not received such detailed attention, demonstrating that its origins are more diverse than often assumed. This does not intend to diminish the importance of films like *Man Bites Dog* or *Cannibal Holocaust*, but rather suggests that alongside the body of critical work afforded to these films lie a number of other texts that are comparatively under-acknowledged.

In terms of marketing strategies alone, the contemporary found footage horror film has harnessed the conceptual energy of these more controversial ancestors—films like *Snuff*, the *Guinea Pig* films, *Cannibal Holocaust* and *Man Bites Dog*—but has directed it away from grindhouses, arthouses and underground fan cultures and towards a more accessible mainstream. This section presents an overview of the prehistory of the found footage horror film and focuses on some key instances that, while perhaps not directly spawning the current phenomenon, are certainly responsible for culturally developing a fascination with the intersection of horror and the real. The chapters that follow are by no means intended as the final word on the prehistory of contemporary found footage horror. Rather, this section will ideally provoke further investigations into this area.

But first, a brief overview of Orson Welles' *War of the Worlds* radio broadcast. While this text has hardly suffered from a lack of critical interest, its inclusion is necessary to fully contextualize the contemporary found footage horror phenomenon that would rise to prominence over sixty years later.

The Birth of Found Footage Horror: War of the Worlds *(1938)*

The essential elements of contemporary found footage horror were to some degree established in this notorious radio broadcast, both in terms of the mechanics that create confusion about the ontological status of a text (is it real? is it fake?), and—perhaps even more crucially—that create fear in its audiences. It was described by Chuck Berg and Tom Erskine as nothing less than "the most sensational program in the history of radio"[29]: Orson Welles and the Mercury Theatre broadcast their adaptation of H.G. Wells' science fiction classic about a Martian invasion the night before Halloween in 1938. Its notoriety stems from the fact that many members of the listening audience believed what they heard to be true primarily because it so convincingly mimicked the familiar news radio format, leading Craig Hight to define it as an "aural mockumentary."[30] Listening to a recording of the broadcast today, it is noteworthy that the fictional status of the Welles' story is flagged throughout, with Wells himself even stating at its conclusion that their adaptation was their "own radio version of dressing up in a sheet and jumping out of a bush and saying 'Boo!'"[31] As has been observed in a number of critical evaluations, however, timing was everything. For a number of reasons, it was highly likely that a significant portion of the original listening audience simply missed these admissions of fictionality.

War of the Worlds was not Welles' first attempt at evoking verisimilitude: He had earlier that same year developed a series called *First Person Singular* where he would directly address his audience to create a sense of intimacy and authenticity. More directly linked to the radio news conceit of *War of the Worlds*, however, was his earlier involvement in the 1937 broadcast *The Fall of the City*, an allegorical treatment on the rise of fascism which also formally replicated a radio news program. *War of the Worlds* was one of a series of literary adaptations undertaken by Welles' Mercury Theatre on the Air group, and they had presented their own versions of *Jane Eyre*, *Julius Caesar* and *Oliver Twist*. Berg and Erskine noted that there was from the outset some tension between CBS (who broadcast the series) and the Mercury Theatre, as while the broadcaster wanted the attempts at verisimilitude toned down in the *War of the Worlds* script, Welles felt that the story would be considered too ridiculous.[32]

The broadcast began with a prologue typical of radio plays at the time, but cut directly to a weather update and a seemingly live cross to an orchestra playing in the Park Plaza in New York City. It is here that the newsflash-style interruptions began, with experts discussing unusual weather on Mars that soon lead to a full-fledged Martian invasion of Earth. Protagonist Professor Pierson ended the play with a description of what it was like to walk around a near-deserted New York City before realizing the invaders had been destroyed by bacterial infections. While only around an hour in length, the impact of the broadcast is infamous even today. By one account, a minimum of six million people heard the *War of the Worlds* broadcast, and around a million reacted with fear.[33] In a foundational study into the phenomenon written in 1940, Princeton-based psychologist Hadley Cantril offered a number of case studies to illustrate the hysteria. In one case, a young gas station attendant offered the following personal account:

> My girl friend and I stayed in the car for a while, just driving around. Then we followed the lead of a friend. All of us ran into a grocery store and asked the man if we could go into his cellar. He said, "What's the matter? Are you trying to ruin my business?" so he chased us out. A crowd collected.... Then people started to rush out of the apartment house all undressed. We got into the car and listened some more. Suddenly, the announcer was gassed, the station went dead so we tried another station but nothing would come on. Then we went to a gas station and filled up our tank in preparation for riding just as far as we could.... Then one friend, male, decided he would call up the *Newark Evening News*. He found out it was a play. We listened to the rest of the play and then went dancing.[34]

Cantril offered a number of other examples, and noted that even before the broadcast had ended, people across America were "praying, crying, fleeing frantically to escape death." He continues, "Some ran to rescue loved ones. Others telephoned farewells or warnings, hurried to inform neighbors, sought information from newspapers or radio stations, summoned ambulances and police cars."[35]

Context and timing were crucial in a number of significant ways. Most immediately was the way that people flicked from station to station, and tuning in late to a particular program was a common radio listening practice.[36] A survey by CBS found that 42 percent of listeners who believed that the broadcast was real tuned in late, while only 12 percent of people who listened to the entire program believed the same thing.[37] The Mercury Theatre's primary competition at this time was the popular Charlie McCarthy program, with Cantril's research suggesting that many listeners came to the Welles broadcast after tuning out of its more popular competitor, thus rendering their experience of the *War of the Worlds* broadcast bereft of its key disclaimers: 18 percent of their survey's respondents claimed that they had listened to Charlie McCarthy, and 62 percent of this number said that they tuned in after the first act of Charlie McCarthy and kept listening to CBS because of their interest in the alien invasion.[38]

Orson Welles records *War of the Worlds* (CBS/The Kobal Collection).

The dominance of radio during this period has been compared to the contemporary role of television, and Cantril estimated in 1940 that of the 32,000,000 families in North America at that period, 27,500,000 had radios—more than had telephones, newspapers, magazines or even cars, plumbing and electricity.[39] Jeffrey Sconce emphasized that the hysteria around the broadcast "was as much a panic over the new and rather suffocating presence of mass communication as it was a panic over extraterrestrial invasion."[40] He stated:

> By simulating the simultaneous collapse of the social body and the radio institution, *War of the Worlds* exposed and then exploited the media's usually faceless gaze as it fell under siege. In the process, the institution of network radio came dangerously close to betraying itself; that is, the *War of the Worlds* broadcast

almost provoked the radio audience into a "crisis of faith" and a potentially unsettling examination of its own investment in the medium.[41]

From this perspective, Sconce suggested that the broadcast itself functioned "as a form of media 'death wish,' expressing a desire for chaos as a return of the repressed for the mechanisms of order imposed by broadcasting that had so recently transformed radio's 'presence.'"[42] I would suggest that a similar "death wish" permeates some of the most fascinating (although admittedly not necessarily successful) contemporary found footage horror films that will be discussed later in this book, explicit in the very titles of films such as *The Last Horror Movie* (Julian Richards, 2003), *The Last Broadcast* and *The Last Exorcism*.

In the United States, 1938 was a period of great cultural unrest. It was marked by social and financial fallout following the Depression, a growing awareness of the war in Europe, and the impending reality that there would be American involvement. As one respondent said, even an allegorical interpretation of the broadcast was still too close to home: "I knew it was some Germans trying to gas all of us. When the announcer kept calling them people from Mars I just thought he was ignorant and didn't know yet that Hitler had sent them all."[43] The broadcast occurred at a time when people were simply used to having their regular programs interrupted by dramatic news updates. In that particular climate, listeners had no reason to consider it unusual that Welles' program would be interrupted with urgent news updates.[44] The inclusion of familiar places and interviews with "experts" added to its sense of authenticity, a strategy still commonly deployed in contemporary found footage horror.

As Marguerite H. Rippy noted, Welles' *War of the Worlds* broadcast effectively initiated a specific set of performance conventions that established a belief that what they were hearing was true. She suggested that there were a number of ways that Welles managed to do this: the employment of voices that sounded like authentic political subjects, mimicry of radio news flash techniques, the diegetic reference to technology like microphones, the inclusion of familiar actual locations, and a splintered narrative that jumps and leaps between different contexts as if unplanned and spontaneous.[45] Notable here is the importance of interruptions: If there is a formal feature that can be pinpointed to generate a sense of authenticity in contemporary found footage horror, it is the inclusion of supposed technical interruptions such as tape hiss, static, and other types of distortion. These interruptions often denote malign supernatural presence, implying a direct physical effect on recording technologies.

Welles' fascination with the often-blurry lines that distinguish fact from fiction continued through later works such as *F Is for Fake* (1973) and the famous "News on the March" newsreel sequences in *Citizen Kane* (1941). In terms of government policy, the Federal Communications Commission—who were, according to Berg and Erskine, attempting to shut down the program during the broadcast—immediately banned the use of fake news bulletins in radio plays.[46] However as Rippy argued, Welles was ahead of his time, and it is only now that mainstream media appear to be "catching up" with his innovative treatment of truth and fictionality. "The primary legacy of the Wellesian brand is to create models for constructing alternative truths," she said. "With his *War of the Worlds* broadcast, Welles opened up the possibility for listeners to construct their own meanings and to pose hypothetical 'what ifs' that were both disturbing and revolutionary."[47]

One

Safety Films

Orson Welles' *War of the Worlds* radio broadcast was not the only popular media artifact that would play a role in the development of contemporary found footage horror. The Highway Safety Foundation's notorious road safety movies have earned cult status through their inclusion of actual footage of real death, and their name is familiar to cult film fans with a taste for gore and kitsch, as well as to those interested in the history of ephemeral film cultures. As their name suggests, the bulk of the Highway Safety Foundation films concerned road safety, like *Signal 30* (1959) and *Wheels of Tragedy* (1963) that combined pantomime-like re-enactments of small town Americana with grisly footage of actual car accidents and their mangled, bloody victims. The juxtaposition of these re-enactments with real-life gore is shocking, even to viewers today. While there is debate regarding the educational effectiveness of films such as these—did they really reduce car accidents, or were they simply exploitation?—there is no escaping the powerful impact of the Highway Safety Foundation films.

Their relationship to horror is unmistakable. For Ken Smith, the status of at least one Highway Safety Foundation movie as horror was obvious as he noted, "[R]eal-life dead people were the stars of *Signal 30,* the first highway safety gore film."[1] For later generations, these films were not seen in classrooms or community centers like they were for their predecessors, but rather lay in the domain of cult and exploitation fandom. They were predominantly packaged in compilations; Mikita Brottman noted that for this later audience, road safety films were promoted with slogans like "real-life traffic splatter" and "two hours of blood and bone crunching horror."[2] The authenticity of their real-life carnage provides their primary lure for its cult horror audience today.

Like many contemporary found footage horror films, the low quality of movies like *Signal 30* "is offered as an index of truth," said Brottman. They pride themselves on their supposed amateur status, but as she explained, this was often the result of a conscious formal strategy:

"This is not a Hollywood production, as can readily be seen," the narrator intones, proudly. "The quality is well below their standards. However, most of these scenes were taken immediately after the accident occurred." This ingenuous disclaimer detracts attention from the fact that the film is, in effect, carefully shot and edited to create a deliberate and specific effect. Camera movements are sometimes loose and jerky, in the best traditions of *cinema verité*, and sometimes they are much smoother, particularly when the camera glides easily over piles of twisted metal, panning for mangled body parts.[3]

Like the contemporary found footage horror subgenre, poor production values are deployed in safety education films like these as a marker of authenticity. This—along with their focus on body horror—grants road safety films a place in the prehistory of contemporary found footage horror films.

This chapter will focus on the Highway Safety Foundation in particular, but its primary case study will not be one of their notorious driver education films. Less well remembered are other safety films they produced, including the gut-wrenching *The Child Molester* (1964). This was an educational film warning against "stranger danger," shockingly ending with graphic crime-scene images of two small girls' murdered bodies. While many of the Highway Safety Foundation's road accident films have today garnered the reputation of bizarre historical novelties, the subject matter of *The Child Molester* is incapable of being so easily dismissed as curious retro kitsch. Evidence that child sex crimes still possess a moral clarity can be seen in popular television series such as *Law & Order: SVU* (1999–present) and the controversial found footage horror movie *Megan Is Missing* (Michael Goi, 2011). Following the abduction, sexual assault and murder of two teenage girls, *Megan Is Missing* is a consciously didactic movie that relies on amateur aesthetics for its impact, creating a sense of authenticity to best convey its safety message to its intended audience. *Megan Is Missing* does not contain actual footage of abused and assaulted children, of course, but the two films still offer remarkable points of comparison. Both *Megan Is Missing* and *The Child Molester* suggest that amateur aesthetics have a persistent capacity to add verisimilitude to screen narratives that are meant for emotional and educational impact.

Educational Films and the Highway Safety Foundation

Rick Prelinger has traced the origins of educational movies back to the early 1900s, when film was used to demonstrate processes difficult to replicate in the classroom. It grew in popularity as a teaching aid for the military during both world wars. Insurance companies commonly sponsored safety films, and Prelinger identified *We Drivers* (1935) as one of the earliest driver education films. At the end of World War II, surplus projectors from the military were transferred to American schools, leading to the 1950s, "the golden age of the drivers ed. film."[4] Ken Smith presented a clear picture of why these movies were successful during this period: Automotive technology had remained relatively undeveloped since the 1920s when there were simply fewer cars on the road, so things like air bags, shoulder belts, roll bars, head rests, and child safety seats were non-existent. It was in this context that drivers were seen as carrying the burden of responsibility for the terrifying increase in car accidents.[5] With the growth of "muscle" car culture, the death toll resulting from car accidents "skyrocketed," and according to Smith, so did sales of Highway Safety Foundation films. By the 1970s, they claimed forty million people had seen their movies.[6]

Road safety films are remembered for their brutality and their no-holds-barred intent to show car accidents in their full bloody reality. As illustrated in earlier road safety films such as the infamous *Last Date* (Lewis D. Collins, 1950), the figure of the out-of-control teenage driver figured largely. The success of this particular title was staggering, with Smith suggesting three million people saw it in its first eight months of release alone; it played not only in

The Highway Safety Foundation's Richard Wayman, center (courtesy Bret Wood).

classrooms, but also in school gymnasiums and movie theaters. Along with films like *Borrowed Power* (1951) and *What Made Sammy Speed?* (1957), these movies ironically had little impact on curbing the growing road death tolls, despite offering the teenage driver as a widely accepted scapegoat. By the late 1950s, Canadian Budge Crawley felt that the increasing death toll meant that more severe tactics were needed and decided to insert actual footage of real-life car accidents. The same idea occurred to Richard Wayman in Ohio at around the same time and, along with Earle Deems, he would go on to form the Highway Safety Foundation.

The Highway Safety Foundation (and its affiliated distribution and production company, Highway Safety Films, Inc.) produced 14 films in total, beginning with *Signal 30* and finishing with *Options to Live* (1979). There are differing accounts surrounding what originally led Wayman to his interest in car accidents. As an amateur photographer in the mid–1950s he and Phyllis Vaughn of Mansfield took color crash scene photographs that assisted police investigators. With public interest in their activities growing, in 1958 they began presenting safety slide shows at the Richland County State Fair in Ohio, and to school and community groups. Enlisting local newspaper photographer John Domer and Vaughn's sister Dottie (who later married Earle Deems), the group turned to moving images. The Highway Safety Foundation became a non-profit organization, and in October 1959 *Signal 30* was screened.[7] The legitimacy of the group has since been questioned, and ex-journalist and private investigator Martin Yant has spoken of controversial rumors about Wayman and the Highway Safety Foundation in the documentary *Hell's Highway: The True Story of Highway Safety Films* (Bret Wood, 2003) and in his books *Rotten to the Core* (1994) and *Rotten to the Core 2* (2004). The most shocking of these include rumors that the Highway Safety Foundation was heavily involved in the production of pornography.[8] The demise of the Highway Safety Foundation was both spectacular and scandalous. Despite receiving $2 million in pledges, the star-studded telethon that screened nationally with Sammy Davis, Jr. as host in August 1973 was financially ruinous.[9]

With their self-confessed shock tactics and use of real-life gore, it remains open to debate whether Highway Safety Foundation films positively influenced road accident statistics. Up to and including the period of *Hell's Highway*'s production, Earle Deems insisted that their films were not exploitation for the simple fact that they had successful results.[10] For Ken Smith, changes in car safety statistics can be attributed more concretely to Ralph Nader's book *Unsafe at Any Speed* (1965) more than any Highway Safety Foundation's films.[11] Rick Prelinger also shared his suspicions, and stated: "Do they work? I'd have to say probably not. We have fewer accidents now per trillion miles driven, but I think that has to do with the fact that we do more freeway driving and cars are safer."[12] *Hell's Highway*'s director Wood was more generous: "I know that they had a strong impact on me, especially in terms of wearing a seat belt," he said. "It has been stated that the films had a strong short-term effect but were ineffectual in influencing long-term driving habits. But I say even if they scared some kids into driving safely for a month or so, during those accident-prone teenage years, I figure it was worth the effort."[13]

"Witch Hunt at Amateur Hour": Highway Safety Off the Road

Combining the clichéd, Baby Boomer suburbia of white picket fences and domestic consumerism with the incorporation of actual motor vehicle accident footage filmed in and around Mansfield, the Highway Safety Foundation movies "offer a picture-perfect view of small-town life in Ohio, then punch a hole in the center of it," according to Wood.[14] Many of their films are available in the public domain on websites such as Archive.org and as DVD extras on *Hell's Highway*; the notoriety of these films straddles cult, ephemera and horror. Wood identified the features that made the Highway Safety Foundation's productions so unique, including elements features crucial to exploitation cinema and to many later found footage horror films like *The Blair Witch Project*, such as their "small town authenticity, the clumsy filmmaking techniques, and the unflinching view of human suffering." For Wood, Highway Safety Foundation films are "grim, gruesome, even morbid, but they are genuine and always earnest in their intentions."[15]

This contradiction is intrinsic to all Highway Safety Foundation's films, but it is most apparent in their non–road safety movies such as the 1964 productions *Camera Surveillance* and *The Child Molester*.[16] While the latter directly engages with the real-life double-homicide in 1962 of two young girls, Jean Burtoch and Connie Hurrell,[17] it is *Camera Surveillance* and the events surrounding its production that have most recently come to public attention through its incorporation into American artist William E. Jones' *Mansfield 1962* (2006) and *Tearoom* (1962/2007) which were shown at the prestigious Whitney Museum of American Art in New York in 2008. Jones' Highway Safety Foundation–based works are powerful pieces in their own right and present eye-opening insight into the historical treatment of homosexuality in small-town America during the 1960s.

The Child Molester and *Camera Surveillance* were closely linked. Only hours after Burtoch and Hurrell's bodies were found on a summer afternoon in Mansfield on Saturday, June 23, 1962,[18] 18-year-old local Jerrel Ray Howell was arrested. When interviewed, he stated: "You guys don't know nothin', you ought to take a look at the men's room in Central Park on the square, that's where I first had oral sex with a man."[19] The Mansfield police were desperate for a way to convince the public that they were responding to the horrific attempted sexual assault and murder of the two young girls; Howell's information led them (with the help of the Highway Safety Foundation) to set up cameras behind a two-way mirror in a public toilet in Central Park, where they recorded anonymous sexual activity that was to become the primary evidence in the conviction of a large number of local Mansfield men with "sex perversion." This material also formed the basis of *Camera Surveillance*.

Jones has succinctly addressed the hysteria that defined this case:

> The Mansfield tearoom busts have an aspect of grotesque disproportion. With the hidden camera, the round-the-clock arrests, and a coda of self-righteous editorials, the whole affair, while strictly defensible in the eyes of the law in that specific time and place, looks more like a witch hunt at amateur hour. A bunch of policemen, given *carte blanche* by a public out for blood in the wake of a brutal murder, peeped on some marginal characters, perfect scapegoats who had no way of justifying themselves, and made a movie about their activities.[20]

Filmed through a two-way mirror over a three-week period, the footage was used to convict anywhere from 38 to 69 men.[21] In an interview with Jones, Wood explained how the film was strategically executed so as to garner the highest number of identifiable participants so as to attain the greatest number of convictions possible.[22]

While the "tearoom" bust footage was filmed in 1962, it was not until 1964 that the Highway Safety Foundation re-edited the footage into the training film *Camera Surveillance*. It was designed to educate police about technology and the way that it assisted them in their investigations. Released the same year as *The Child Molester*, *Camera Surveillance* connected Howell's crimes with the tearoom busts through the following voice-over:

> We were confronted with a terrible crime, the brutal murder of two small girls, aged seven and nine, who were stomped to death by a sex deviate. An 18-year-old boy was arrested by our department within six hours after the discovery of the children's bodies. The quick solution to a crime such as this is possible only when the police department knows their sex deviates.... As police officers we realize that a child molesting is the most revolting crime we can be faced with.... Think of the terror, and as you think of it, the lesson is clear. We must know the sex deviates in our community. Know them and watch them.

This ideologically problematic connection between homosexuality, so-called "sex deviates" and the child murders was the sole assumption that prompted the Central Park stakeout.

The Child Molester is not unique amongst Highway Safety Foundation films for showing graphic images of dead or injured bodies, but in no other context are those scenarios the result of a topic that is so highly charged today as child sexual abuse. Contemporary discourse about this sensitive subject is still riddled with contradictions, confusion, anger and fear, and because of this, *The Child Molester* can be examined as a historical document haunted not only its initial historical context, but by the ghosts that still remain lurking in its shadows almost fifty years later. These will be considered to provide a point of comparison with the found footage horror film *Megan Is Missing*, a 2011 movie about the murder and sexual torture of two teenage girls that was produced with similarly didactic intent, justifying its use of graphic and shocking violence as a way to educate its audience in ways notably similar to *The Child Molester*.

Genre Shock: The Child Molester *(1964) and* Megan Is Missing *(2011)*

For contemporary audiences, *The Child Molester* may not be the most graphically violent Highway Safety Foundation film, but it is the one that remains the most shocking because its subject matter is still so controversial. *The Child Molester* does not allow the luxury of retrospect that accompanies other Highway Safety Foundation films, but rather emphasizes the shocking reality of crimes contemporaneous with any point in history since. Both *The Child Molester* and *Megan Is Missing* achieve their impact through a process of generic shock: In both cases, the films play out initially like an after-school television special, with no indication of the gruesome and graphic turn they will take in their conclusions. Tonally, the impact of their extreme violence is rendered even more shocking because there has been nothing to prepare us for it. At the heart of this genre shock lies their authenticity: Although the footage in *Megan Is Missing* is not real like that in *The Child Molester*, the jolt it causes is regardless very similar.

The Child Molester was directed and written by Herbert J. Leder, known to trash film fans for *It!* and the Nazi science fiction movie *The Frozen Brain* (both made in 1967). Leder was in his early 40s when he made *The Child Molester*, and had by this time garnered some professional repute having worked on successful B-grade movies like *Fiend Without a Face* (1958), *Pretty Boy Floyd* (1960), and *Nine Miles to Noon* (1963). As Bret Wood speculated, it was unlikely that Leder had any association with the Highway Safety Foundation outside of being a directorial "gun for hire." Wood says that Deems told him that "when they were going to make a film, they would often hire a director who was experienced in educational-industrial films, because it was more efficient than one of them trying to stage a dramatic scene."[23]

The Child Molester begins with a young girl named Mary playing hopscotch when a stranger appears and offers some candy. She accepts it and asks if her friend Jeannie may also have some. He also offers some to their friend Cathy, but she refuses as the other girls leave. A man and an elderly woman notice them getting into a car with the stranger. The scene shifts to a woman nervously pacing her kitchen; a male voice-over states, "It's past lunchtime, and Jeannie still isn't home." The woman puts down her cup and rushes to the telephone. A montage sequence of the places she calls in hope of finding her daughter follows, narrated by the same male. As Jeannie and Mary drive away with the unidentified stranger, Cathy walks home. By refusing to accept candy from the stranger, Cathy is contrasted with Jeannie and Mary as an example of good behavior. Interrupting her daydream about her potential new toy, Cathy remembers that she should inform her mother about the incident in the park. Meanwhile, the stranger has taken Mary and Jeannie to a deserted parkland underneath a bridge and the two children are now aware of the seriousness of their predicament and clearly frightened. Jeannie manages to escape, and the stranger forcibly drags Mary behind him as he tries to capture the other girl. Mary escapes also, but her face crumples as she hears Jeannie scream off-screen. When the stranger catches her after a lengthy pursuit through the woods, her terrified face suggests she knows she is to meet the same fate as her friend. Intercut with police procedurals and witness responses, the film ends with the shocking still images, with the voice-over claiming they are the bodies of the two missing girls.

The representation of the child predator in *The Child Molester* is worth considering. In the opening moments, a man's ominous shadow appears over Mary's hopscotch board prompting specific associations with *M* (Fritz Lang, 1931), thus identifying itself as part of the same representational tradition. This stranger is shown as an unidentified, shadowy figure throughout the film, gaining power in his anonymity and thus representing a ubiquitous threat. When he offers Mary sweets, the film employs a first person perspective shot. Showing the point of view of a monstrous character in this manner is typically associated with the horror genre, and in keeping with these traditions *The Child Molester* seeks to uncomfortably align the spectator's gaze with its villain from its opening moments. As Carol J. Clover has observed, in the slasher film this "habit of letting us view the action in the first person long before revealing who or what the first person is" is typical of the subgenre.[24] John Carpenter's 1978 film *Halloween*, she noted, provides a famous example of this, which she declares is "probably the most widely imitated—and widely parodied—cliché of modern horror."[25] In Carpenter's famous slasher film, "we are invited to look not through a murderous camera, but with our own murderous eyes,"[26] proving her claim again that in horror, "we are both Red Riding Hood *and* the Wolf; the force of experience ... comes from 'knowing' both sides of the story."[27] The roots of the slasher film go back at least to *Psycho*, so to privilege *The Child Molester* with establishing this tradition in horror film would of course be incorrect. Nevertheless, the shock factor of this formal strategy cannot be underestimated, even before the graphic imagery at the film's conclusion is shown.

Shock tactics are deployed in other ways. For example, the very title makes clear that it is child *molestation* that is the source of its interest, not child *murder*. Although the subject matter is undeniably serious, nothing about the title suggests that this film will end with its gruesome display of children's corpses. On this count it deviates from other Highway Safety Foundation films. As Prelinger observed, one of the most important features of driver education films was their sense of inevitability:

> If you think about the drama of safety films, they really lead towards one thing: You are waiting for the accident to happen. The great tease is to whom will the accident happen, at what location and when, and it's throughout the whole film you are supposed to be inculcated with the safety message but you're really waiting for the accident to happen.[28]

But *The Child Molester* works very differently. It is unique because it deliberately undermines these expectations from the outset. Wood explains this further: "I think the driver's ed films are deeply disturbing when you first see them ... but after so many of them, you grow used to the formula and become almost immune to them.... *The Child Molester* gets under the viewer's skin because it isn't following a formula that we can predict. And, of course, the fact that the crime is against children is even more disturbing."[29]

Aside from the stranger telling Mary and Jeannie in the woods, "Keep quiet or I'll kill both of you," there is no indication that the film is going to end with images of the girls' dead bodies. The gravity of their situation is only made explicit in the concluding moments. Contrasting dramatically against the bureaucratic and didactic tone of the "dos-and-don'ts" preceding it, the visceral shock of the sudden cut to actual crime scene material is overwhelming, even by today's standards. In these final moments, the narrator states, "The missing girls were found. These are the actual police films of the tragedy. Your children put their trust in you. Do not betray them. Teach them all the safety rules. Give them their chance at life." The film's final moments focus on the dead bodies of the girls, and these images are filmed in a much more amateur style and grainier film stock than the parts that preceded it. This juxtaposition, combined with the voice-over and an association with other Highway Safety Foundation films that employ actual footage of dead bodies, in large part denotes their authenticity.

The Child Molester is marked by its historical context in a number of obvious ways, and aside from its 1960s-styled *mise-en-scène* most notable of these is the kitsch idealism against which this repulsive crime is so dramatically contrasted. Over time, many of the assumptions about child sexual abuse have also changed: It is almost unnecessary to note that today we understand "stranger danger" as only one of many possible scenarios that place children at risk from sexual predators. It is therefore curious when watching this film almost half a century later that the narrator's voice is not wholly dissimilar to that of the "child molester." It is gentle and while not elderly, it still exudes an authoritative adult masculinity. It may be speculated that for a viewer of this film in the early 1960s, an association between the authoritative narrator and the sexual predator would have seemed illogical, but for contemporary viewer with an understanding that strangers are not the primary threat to children's safety, the possibility is both real and chilling.[30] The similarities between the threatening presence (the child molester) and the figure of authority (the narrator) for a contemporary audience debunk the film's intended "stranger danger" lesson, thwarting its original moral message and channeling that meaning into a strikingly different direction.

As demonstrated in *Megan Is Missing*, however, child sexual predators unknown to their victims are still a threat today. At its outset, the film establishes via intertitles that Megan Stewart (Rachel Quinn) went missing on January 14, 2007, with her best friend Amy Herman (Amber Perkins) disappearing three weeks later. Beginning on January 2, the film spends a great deal of time developing character profiles of these 14-year-old girls. Megan is sexually active and acts beyond her years, while Megan's party friends ridicule Amy for her inexperience. Struggling with her insecurities, Amy experiments with makeup and parties, and gently chastises her loving parents for treating her like a little girl. Despite this, there is evidence that she herself does not want to fully let go of her childhood, demonstrated by her child-like affection for numerous Teddy bears. In contrast, Megan is sexually adventurous and uses drugs and alcohol in her hard-partying lifestyle. Her relationship with her mother is hostile, with Megan explaining to Amy that this is because her mother's boyfriend raped her (Megan) when she was nine, and her mother never forgave her daughter for his imprisonment. "Guys like me, they've always liked me," she confesses to Amy. "I'll pretty much do what you want but you have to tell me you love me." Megan and Amy's strong friendship is a positive and healthy outlet for both girls: While Megan appears to be superficially popular with a party crowd, both girls at different points in the film make it clear that the other is the only true friend they have.

Desperate for love and approval, Megan flirts online with Josh, an apparently shy teen skater who maintains visual anonymity by telling her that his dog had broken his webcam. Consequently, he could see Megan during their online contact, but she could not see him. When he fails to reveal himself at a party he invites her to, they make an appointment to meet after Megan introduces Amy to him online. Television news clips inform us of Megan's disappearance, and Amy confronts Josh online and asks if he is responsible. At first Josh is flirtatious, but when he realizes Amy suspects him he becomes cruel, calling her fat and friendless. Amy reports Josh to the police, and he retaliates by threatening her and her mother. Photographs appear on an online fetish forum of Megan being tortured, and three weeks after Megan's disappearance, Amy is also grabbed by a shadowy figure. Amy's video camera is found in a trashcan. It is here that the film takes a dramatic shift as the last 22 minutes claim to be raw and unedited footage taken directly from Amy's camera. This end section of the film shows the brutal torture and rape of Amy before Megan's corpse is revealed to her in a large plastic barrel as she is locked in it alongside her dead friend. The final chilling scene is a single shot of Josh digging a large ditch in an unidentifiable wooded area as Amy pleads desperately with him from within the barrel. He ignores her, and buries the barrel before picking up the camera and his flashlight and walking away.

Megan Is Missing consists predominantly of material we believe is shot by the characters themselves with a range of digital technologies such as mobile phone cameras, camcorders, and webcams, thus creating a sense of authenticity through its deployment of its diegetically filmed amateur aesthetics. While the hi-tech world of *Megan Is Missing* contrasts strikingly with that of *The Child Molester*, it is significant that despite these differences, the two films merge in a number of ways. Most crucial of these is the way that amateur aesthetics are deployed to imply authenticity, but it is notable that their construction of the offender is also similar.

Josh first appears is when Megan's party friend Lexie recommends him as a potential chat partner. Lexie sends Megan a photograph of a handsome blonde teen they both accept as Josh. Although he talks to Megan at length, the first appearance of this figure is in the grainy black-and-white television footage played on the local news about Megan's disappearance. This footage of Megan being approached by an adult male and led away is zoomed in to 200 percent and then to 500 percent, making him increasingly indistinct. He next appears as a black shadowy figure in the background as Amy records her

One. Safety Films   53

Amy (Amber Perkins) on the set of *Megan Is Missing* (2011) (courtesy Michael Goi, www.meganismissing.com).

video diary direct-to-camera underneath a bridge in a park where she and Megan used to share secrets, and where Amy has hidden her most beloved Teddy bear. It is here that he snatches Amy a few weeks later, with his arm appearing suddenly from the left of the screen and paused dramatically over her as he grabs her. In the grueling final third of the film as Amy is raped and tortured, Josh is never shown in full.[31] His clothes also offer no distinctive mode of identification, as he wears basic sneakers, blue jeans and t-shirts.

Like *The Child Molester*, this anonymity is crucial in its construction of terror. If the predators in each of these movies were to be shown in full and to present identifiable features, then their villainy would specifically apply only to those individuals. However, these figures are never identified, their only notable features being that they are anonymous. Therefore, the threat becomes much more omnipresent. As he tells Amy, Josh is not even his real name: There is simply nothing known about this figure. Thus, when the film lingers on the shadowy image of the man (who has just buried Amy alive in a barrel with the corpse of her dead best friend) re-entering the world at the end of the movie, there is an implication that he will continue to abduct, torture, rape and murder teens unhindered. That he filmed this sequence and deliberately left it in a location where he knew the police would not only find it but also immediately link it to Amy's disappearance underscores the extent of his sadism, vanity and confidence. This in turn increases our sense of fear.

Technology and the hand-held amateur aesthetics of its cinematography are obviously crucial to the film's construction of verisimilitude. This is visible in the first section of the film, before Megan's disappearance, when the everyday experiences of its two central characters are considered in detail. By establishing a sense of authenticity in these less dramatic moments, it necessarily implies that the more violent and intense climax is also just as real. This tonal shift is marked by the sudden display of the shocking photographs of a tortured Megan that appeared on an online fetish website. These photos are taken with a bright flash and imply a lack of compositional forethought: They are constructed as amateur snapshots taken in the heat of the moment. Similarly to *The Child Molester*, it is not just the sudden change in tone but also the shift to a much cruder aesthetic that heightens the shocking impact of *Megan Is Missing*'s revelations. While what happens to Amy after these images is even more violent and cruel, part of the horror of her torture and rape stems from the *duration* of the abuse. Added to this is the fact that the camera's gaze which earlier in the film belonged to the girls themselves has been viciously turned against them by this sadistic predator. The impact of *Megan Is Missing*, like *The Child Molester* before it, stems from its particular construction of authenticity through amateur aesthetics, its representation of the child sexual predator as an anonymous figure, and its deployment of these elements in the pursuit of presenting its fundamentally didactic message. Whether this educational intent quarantines these films from accusations of exploitation, however, is another matter entirely.

Exploitation or Education?

Even today there remains some confusion regarding the intended demographic of *The Child Molester*. Bret Wood believes that the Highway Safety Foundation intended it solely to be a training film for adults, and has stated, "Deems insisted that the film was not meant to be shown to children; that it was made for the police, parents and educators." Wood remained skeptical, however, as this does not gel with the fact that the Highway Safety Foundation catalogue stated the film was "cleared for television," implying they were happy with it being viewed by a much broader audience.[32] Either way, there is no doubt that children did see the film: One of the most memorable moments

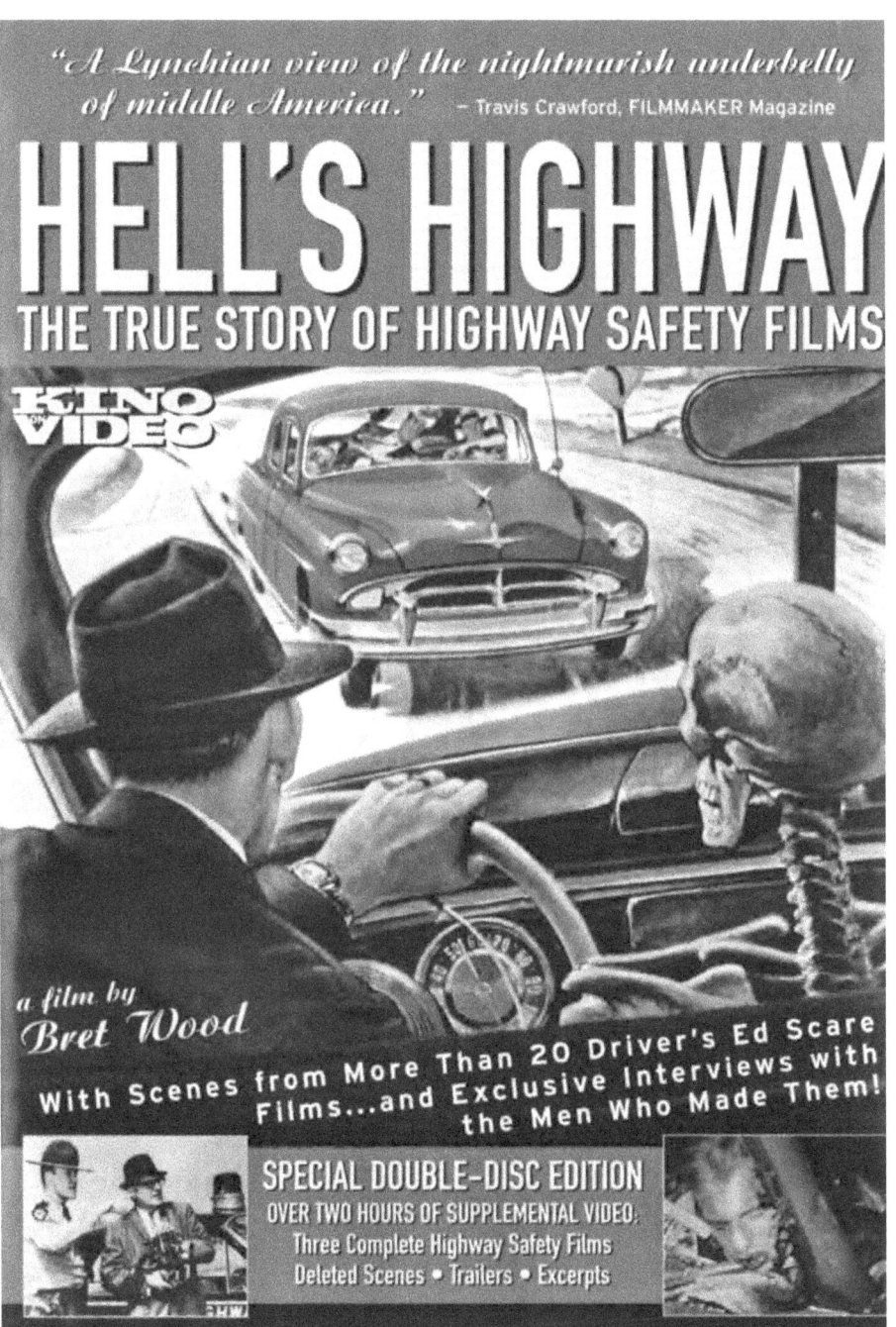

Hell's Highway: The True Story of Highway Safety Films (Bret Wood, 2003). Released by Kino Lorber (courtesy Bret Wood).

of Wood's *Hell's Highway* documentary is when brothers David and Eric Krug recall watching the film as children at school in the 1970s, and the trauma that resulted.

The sincerity of Michael Goi's intent behind *Megan Is Missing* is also unquestionable. His professional credentials are remarkable: He has over fifty credits to his name as cinematographer, earning Primetime Emmy nominations for his work on *My Name Is Earl* in 2005 and *Glee* in 2009. He was president of the American Society of Cinematographers from 2010 to 2012, has served on the National Executive Board of the International Cinematographers Guild, and has been a member of the Academy of Motion Picture Arts and Sciences and the Academy of Television Arts and Sciences. Since *Megan Is Missing*, Goi's cinematography credits include *American Horror Story* and *Web Therapy*. Although known primarily as a cinematographer, Goi took on additional roles in *Megan Is Missing* including writer, producer and director. As he stated on the official *Megan Is Missing* website, he was deeply affected by real-life stories like Megan's and Amy's that appeared on the television news, compelling him to take action. Combining elements of seven different real-life cases—five about the murder and abduction of children, and two about online predators—Goi maintains that the details of the film were based on fact, and claimed "there is not a single incident in the film that I made up entirely out of thin air." Even the dialogue is based on actual online chats by teens around the age of Megan and Amy. Goi wrote the script in ten days, and it was shot in a little over eight. He also insisted on the presence of his young actors' parents on set so that they were fully aware of their children's involvement.[33]

As a subgenre, found footage horror powerfully granted Goi the space to avoid what he has called the "Hollywood treatment" of such stories. "No cutaways to shots of leaves blowing in trees to suggest sexual assault," he has said. "I was going to show what it feels like to go through what the news describes in five seconds." Goi was unequivocal in his determination for *Megan Is Missing* to make a difference: "I'd like the things that happen in the movie to never happen to another child again."[34] *Megan Is Missing* also had the significant support of Marc Klaas, founder of the Klaas Kids Foundation and father of Polly Klaas, who was abducted from her home and murdered by a sexual predator in 1993. In a letter to Goi published on the film's website, Klaas calls *Megan Is Missing* a "difficult, but important, film to watch," and one that addresses the contemporary risks children are exposed to online.[35] Goi has stated that his intention with *Megan Is Missing* was "to shake people up and have them look at their child's world for what it is, as disturbing as it may be,"[36] and it was a similar desire to issue a "wake-up call" about the existence of child sexual predators that fueled the Highway Safety Foundation's *The Child Molester.*

Realistically, the reception contexts of these films are often very different to those their respective filmmakers may have ideally envisaged. Derek Long has noted that films like those produced by the Highway Safety Foundation tend now to be understood more as "objects of cult fascination."[37] And despite Goi's stated objectives, not everyone embraced *Megan Is Missing* as the well-intended warning he intended it to be. In 2011, the New Zealand Office of Film and Literature Classification categorized the DVD release of the film as "objectionable" and banned it in that country:

> Although an attempt has been made to present the material in the context of a cautionary tale ... the feature's material is strongly prurient and exploitative. The film relishes the spectacle of one girl's ordeal including a three-minute real time rape scene. The feature also sexualizes the lives of these young teenage girls to a highly exploitative degree.

As such, this national censorship body felt that *Megan Is Missing* in this instance was "likely to be injurious to the public good."[38] How practical such steps are in an age where films are easily accessed online by savvy consumers is, of course, open to debate.

Whether educational or exploitative, inherent to these movies is their construction and deployment of the real: to present in as convincing a manner as possible the threat of child sex offenders. In *The Child Molester* and the Highway Safety Foundation's broader oeuvre of road accident movies, this impact relies specifically upon their inclusion of genuine footage of dead or dying bodies, shown in grisly detail. That a film like *Megan Is Missing* seeks to create a similar sense of authenticity through found footage horror conventions and its particular brand of amateur filmmaking aesthetics is a clear indicator that these earlier safety films deserve at least some recognition as belonging to this prehistory. As the following chapter will elaborate further, snuff-fictions—fictional films that diegetically concern the existence of "real" death movies—may also be added to this list.

Two

Snuff-Fictions

The specter of so-called "snuff"—films that show real death for the arousal (sexual or otherwise) of their audience—has long haunted found footage horror. Scott Meslow called *The Blair Witch Project* a "snuff film with a safety net,"[1] and the "discovered" footage conceit is crucial to a majority of films that fall under the snuff-fiction umbrella. This "safety net" offers titillating potential, allowing us to speculate what it might be like to watch "real" death with the moral reassurance that no one is actually being hurt. This pleasure has manifested in other ways in the past, illustrated by the public fascination with the on-set deaths of Brandon Lee on *The Crow* (Alex Proyas, 1994) and Tyrone Power on the set of *Solomon and Sheba* (King Vidor, 1959). Snuff-fictions—fictional movies predicated on the assumption that snuff exists—diegetically feature fake snuff films to provoke this fascination with this link between real death and film. Snuff-fictions and found footage horror rely on particular amateur filmmaking aesthetics in their construction of their "real" material, and also often make filmmaking technologies overtly present in their narratives and *mise-en-scène*. Historical associations between pornography and snuff make it impossible to talk about snuff-fictions without engaging with the complex history of gender politics, in the United States especially. Put bluntly, snuff aesthetics are porn aesthetics, where the aesthetics of amateur filmmaking are focused on opened bodies, be they real or fake. Despite its relative shyness in showing exposed flesh and sexual images compared to its raunchier subgeneric cousin the slasher film, the legacy of porn aesthetics on the contemporary found footage horror category should still not be underestimated.

The power inherent in the word "snuff" is dependent upon its vagueness; its enigmatic force stems directly from its elusiveness as a concept. Not only has snuff been defined in different ways across a range of different contexts, it is the haziness with which the term is applied in practice in both critical and non-critical discourse that makes it such a resilient taboo. At its most basic level, a contemporary understanding of snuff is located at the intersection of film, death and "the real." When we think of "snuff" we think of a number of other uses of the word: to snuff out or extinguish a candle, or of snuff boxes used to store powdered tobacco. Mikita Brottman noted that the verb "to snuff out" is a synonym for extinguishing life (like the flame on a candle) that has been active since around the seventeenth century,[2] but its association with drug uses also link it to contemporary associations with supposedly real on-screen murder. Its meaning as a drug simultaneously permits associations with a substantial cache of meanings regarding illicitness and both bodily and social transgression. Drug use denotes danger, but at the same time has during different historical periods contained a degree of cultural capital, be it the LSD experimentation of the 1960s, the heroin-chic of the 1990s or the use of laudanum during the Romantic and Victorian periods by literary luminaries as Percy Bysshe Shelley, Thomas De Quincey, and Lewis Carroll.

It is pivotal to its current usage that many of the cultural associations it conjures—the relationship between danger, subversion, transgression and the body—existed long before the invention of the moving image. The etymological origins of "snuff" suggest that the roots of its contemporary meaning (and the consequent force of that meaning) spread far beyond the scope of cinema. The snuff movie may be intrinsically filmic in form, but its impact—the fear, anger, revulsion and fascination it produces—function at the core of contemporary discourses of gender, power, and the very notion of representation itself.

Problems of Definition

To define the contemporary meaning of snuff is no simple task: The force of the term itself appears to outweigh its specific meaning in myriad debates that address the depiction of real-life death on film. David Kerekes and David Slater pinpointed Ed Sanders' book *The Family: The Story of Charles Manson's Dune Buggy Attack Battalion* (1971) as the first time the phrase was used, in relation to claims that Manson and the Family were making "brutality" films.[3] As Kerekes and Slater defined it, "snuff films depict the killing of a human being; a human sacrifice for the medium of film."[4] Beyond these basic components, opinion is divided. Framed in reference to the anti-pornography debates of the mid–1970s, Eithne Johnson and Eric Schaefer identified the fluid nature of the term, and while they define its context during this period in gendered terms as "a pornographic movie that culminates in the actual murder and mutilation of a woman," they acknowledge this has changed over time, garnering further meanings that apply to "any film that depicts simulated murder."[5]

This definitional volatility means in practice that debates about snuff can morph mid-breath. Many critics have dismissed the existence of snuff as an actual underground subgenre of pornography,[6] but as Julian Petley noted, even if "the commercially made 'snuff' movie is an entirely imaginary creature ... this is definitely not ... to deny the possibility that real murders may have been filmed or otherwise recorded by their perpetrators for purely private purposes."[7] Few would also deny the exploitative nature of death films, including *mondo* films like *Executions* (David Herman and Arun Kumar, 1995), the bizarre public reactions to the amateur Saddam Hussein execution video that was an Internet sensation in 2007 that then went on to become a hit on a number of horror and gore fan sites,[8] and even the exploitation DVD *Maguindano Massacre* that featured the graphic four-hour crime scene cleanup of the notorious 2009 massacre in the Philippines, appearing in pirate markets only weeks after the event.[9] Considering snuff in this broader sense, Joel Black has cited the gruesome videos made by real killers Charles Ng, Leonard Lake and Melvin Henry Ignatow in the 1980s as evidence that "sexually sadistic killers do make visual records of their deeds."[10] More recently (2007), the so-called Dnepropetrovsk Maniacs (Viktor Sayenko, Alexander Hanzha, and Igor Suprunyuck) who went on a killing spree in the Ukraine murdering 21 people kept recordings of their crimes. One of these videos was leaked online and went viral under the title *3 Guys 1 Hammer* (a play on the *2 Girls 1 Cup* viral video that had previously swept the Internet). In 2012, a similar video of real-life torture and murder appeared from Canada, and it was linked to the alleged murder of Lin Jun by Luka Magnotta. Again highlighting the viral-like disposability of such material, it was titled *1 Lunatic 1 Ice Pick*, also referencing *2 Girls 1 Cup*. Muddying the waters even further is the bizarre world of custom snuff fetish video that David Kerekes investigated in 2010, where filmmakers produce made-to-order faux snuff films in scenarios requested by clients.[11]

Paradoxically, if there really *is* a market for snuff, it is the urban legend itself—propelled by snuff-fictions—that has triggered it. For a phenomenon so steeped in its status as a forbidden text, snuff has an ironically visible presence in fictional cinema. Many critics have agreed that it is this presence that has provided the momentum of snuff's longevity as an urban legend. Joel Black has observed, "Not only do fictional horror films in the tradition of *Snuff* incorporate staged snuff sequences to make themselves appear shockingly real, but these fictional films also give reality to snuff films.... [I]n making use of snuff sequences to arouse terror in viewers and to produce the horror effect, horror films and thrillers also play on people's suspicions that an underground subculture exists in which snuff films are made and marketed."[12] Scott Aaron Stine suggested that it is precisely these fictional engagements that grant the concept of snuff its real-world power, because "every time that snuff films are even mentioned in modern fiction and cinema, they are giving credence to the rumors, playing on the reader's or viewer's assumptions that they are real to begin with."[13] For Julian Petley, "[G]ullible and hyped-up press reports about the existence of commercially produced 'snuff' films are major contributory factors to the apparently widespread belief that such a genre actually exists."[14]

Discourse surrounding snuff therefore often finds itself trapped in a rhetorical *mise-en-abime*, so to avoid this conceptual gridlock this chapter considers only snuff-fictions, these purely fictional films about snuff movies and the underground networks that produce them. As will be discussed, however, these fictional films are informed to a large extent by broader associations with pornography and real death, so these aspects cannot be wholly separated from how we evaluate and engage with snuff-fictions themselves.

Snuff-fictions themselves can be broken down into a number of sub-categories. Michael Powell's *Peeping Tom* (1960) follows a man who films and kills women for sexual satisfaction. There are films whose premise assumes an inherent link between snuff and pornography, such as *8mm* (1999), *Mute Witness* (1994), *Strange Days* (Kathryn Bigelow, 1995) and *Hardcore* (Paul Schrader, 1979). Others examine the events surrounding the filming of diegetically coded "actual" murder, such as *The Brave* (Johnny Depp, 1997), *The Last House on Dead End Street* (Roger Watkins, 1977), *Special Effects* (Larry Cohen, 1985), and *Henry: Portrait of a Serial Killer* (1986). Many of these snuff-fictions attempt with varying degrees of success to place the onus on the spectator to accept responsibility for the existence of snuff in the first place, such as *Cannibal Holocaust* and *Snuff Movie* (Bernard Rose, 2005).

What these films share—and what makes them such a notable predecessor to contemporary found fiction horror—is their formal construction of the real. Like found footage horror, they often rely on specific amateur filmmaking aesthetics and diegetic technologies (the inclusion of sound recording devices and cameras within the film itself). In many cases, the discovery of the footage is a major part of the unfolding narrative. In these films, snuff and porn aesthetics often overlap, and some of the key stylistic features they share are later found in the contemporary found footage horror subgenre. As Alan McKee has noted, this commonly includes low-quality sound and image quality.[15] That snuff is so closely associated in the popular imagination with pornography renders a brief historical snapshot of the climate where the terms became

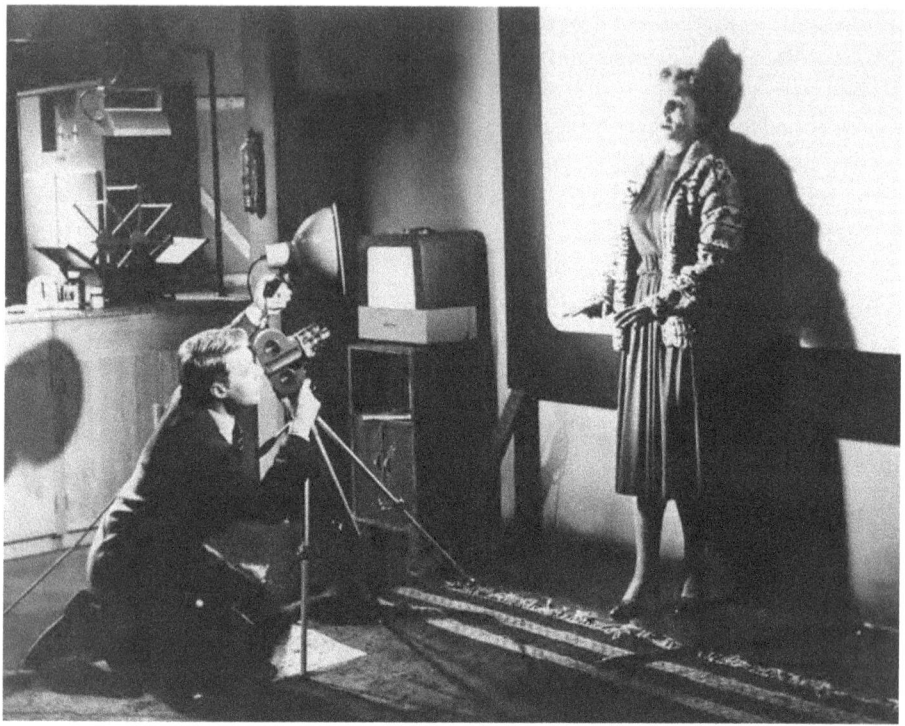

Mark (Karlheinz Böhm) behind the camera in *Peeping Tom* (Michael Powell, 1960) (Anglo Amalgamated/The Kobal Collection).

so intimately linked necessary. By doing so, it will contextualize the development of snuff-fictions and the aesthetics that overlaps so significantly with contemporary found footage horror.

Snuff and Pornography

In the early 1970s, the increasing acceptance of pornography was demonstrated with the commercial success in mainstream cinemas of the hardcore feature *Deep Throat* (Gerard Damiano, 1972). It comes as no surprise that this growing acceptance of pornography was of great concern to many within the feminist movement at this time, so much so that Deborah Cameron has noted that debates about pornography can be considered the central mobilizing issue for American feminism when the radical momentum of the previous decade began to wane.[16] Snuff film became an integral element of the pornographic landscape for anti-pornography feminists, and much of the discourse surrounding the threat of pornography held the reality of snuff as central to their claims. The idea that the real murder and rape of women was being committed to propel a commercial film interest for men's sexual pleasure understandably terrified and gave direction to the movement at this time.[17]

Inextricably linked to the controversy surrounding the 1976 feature film *Snuff*, the rhetoric of many anti-pornography feminists found little need in lieu of the scope and publicness of the controversy to offer additional evidence that snuff actually existed. As Johnson and Schaefer indicate, up until the scandal surrounding this film the women's movement was split over the importance of the rising mainstream acceptance of pornography: "*Snuff* served to galvanize feminists because it seemed to bear out the theory that it was a short leap from film to actual murder."[18] This is typified by leading anti-pornography feminist Catherine MacKinnon's view that

> only for pornography are women killed to make a sex movie, and it is not the idea of a sex killing that kills them. It is unnecessary to do any of these things to express, as ideas, the ideas pornography expresses. It *is* essential to do them to make pornography.[19]

Whether snuff refers to the actual killing of women or fictional-faked accounts is neither here nor there; anti-pornography feminist rhetoric does not usually require a distinction to be made, as what is key here is its pure symbolic force. For Jane Caputi, the confusion between real murder and its simulation was precisely the issue: "[T]here seems to be no sure way to discern on film what is faked and what is ... real, which is a 'symbolic annihilation' and which is an actual one."[20] In terms of reception, this indistinguishability rendered them regressively the same. Snuff film therefore holds a significant position in the history of anti-pornography feminist discourse as it shifts seamlessly between the symbolic and the literal. Actual violence against women in the snuff film is unable to be separated from symbolic violence against women in pornography in general, and it was this—rather than the is-it-real-or-isn't-it debate—that made it one of the primary elements that rallied 1970s feminism in the United States.

Not all feminists shared these same views. Pro-sex feminist Camille Paglia described this vision of snuff as MacKinnon's "puritan hallucinations of hellfire."[21] Avedon Carol suggested that there is a daunting significance to the moral panic surrounding snuff felt by many feminists during this period:

> It's understandable that many women are frightened, hurt and angry enough at some of the things that men do that we are willing to believe the worst of men. Or maybe we suspect men of being so angry at us that they are bound to have "snuff" fantasies.... Yes, the idea of snuff films is a very scary one; but perhaps

more scary is the fact that, even when the evidence is that no snuff film exists, we are still so willing to believe in it.[22]

Snuff is a crucial cinematic artifact as many of these debates manifested specifically from the controversy surrounding it. The following analysis reveals that while the issues concerning its authenticity are now redundant, the questions that once surrounded it as a genuine snuff film have proven to be a successful long-term distraction from the actual content of its infamous coda: The fact that we have ignored the details of what takes place on screen before us is itself ideologically concerning. The *Snuff* coda also demonstrates clearly that the codes and conventions of found footage horror were firmly located in these earlier snuff-fictions, borrowing the aesthetics of low-budget pornography in the creation of their own version of authenticity.

Case Study: Snuff *(Findlay, 1976)*

Snuff might not be the "best" film produced in the Americas in the 1970s, but it may be the decade's most important "worst" film. Rumored to depict the actual murder of a female crew member in its final moments, its notoriety consolidated the urban legend of snuff film.[23] Despite *Snuff*'s status as a unique trash artifact, the suddenness with which the controversy exploded into the public arena allowed it very little time for a "micro" analytical moment. The *Snuff* enigma was so intoxicatingly extra-diegetic that it instantly transcended the nuts-and-bolts details of the film itself. The shocking impact of those final five minutes appeared to render close analysis unnecessary: *Snuff* the movie—like the broader conception of snuff film more generally—was predicated upon a hyperactive theatricality of ambiguity, rumor and moral panic.

Now over thirty-five years since its release, *Snuff* receives very little critical attention outside of historical analyses of film violence and the anti-pornography movement, or paracinematic critiques that more often than not mock the undeveloped gore-literacy of those who fell for the hoax at the time of its release.[24] However, considering that snuff film has remained such a consistent urban legend despite shifts in both camera technologies and modes of distribution, an exhumation of the *Snuff* coda reveals an alternate dimension to this unique moment in film history. While the unnamed "director" figure and his blonde victim remain two of the most notorious onscreen figures in exploitation cinema history, the presence of a third figure, "June" (the only named person in the entire sequence[25]), has gone almost completely unacknowledged.[26]

The production history of *Snuff* is appropriately complex. The 1976 theatrical version was a conglomerate of two sections, filmed four years apart. The first 74 minutes were made in 1971 by husband-and-wife director-cinematographer team Michael and Roberta Findlay, who were renowned for their "roughies" such as *Body of a Female* (1965), *The Ultimate Degenerate* (1969), and the *Her Flesh* trilogy (1967–8). Initially called *The Slaughter*, it was a low-budget exploitation film made in South America based loosely on the Charles Manson "Family" murders. The gory coda, made in 1975, was funded by distributor Allan Shackleton of Monarch Releasing Corporation.[27] Shackleton bought *The Slaughter* years earlier, but had encountered difficulties releasing it on the Findlays' familiar grindhouse circuit due to what were—even by forgiving exploitation standards—severe technical problems with the audio dubbing.[28] Shackleton hastily organized the filming of the notorious coda in New York with director Simon Nuchtern and marketed the final product as an actual snuff film. His promotional campaign included the release of phony newspaper clippings that documented the outrage of non-existent moral conservatives.[29] By the time the hoax was exposed, it was too late: *Snuff* had captured the interest of the public, and an urban legend was born.

With its gimmicky, self-imposed "X" rating for violence, the blurring between "hard-core gore" and "hard-core porn"[30] meant that for many—most notably Beverly LaBelle in her 1976 essay "*Snuff*—The Ultimate in Woman-Hating"—the authenticity of the violence was unquestionable. If sex in X-rated porn is real, it follows that so is murder in X-rated gore films. In large part, this blurring of porn and horror can be understood as manifesting in the amateur, low-budget aesthetics of the contemporary found footage horror subgenre: Many of these films look "real" because they mimic the low-quality, amateur construction of low-quality porn film. The scale and voracity of this type of anti-pornography feminist discourse rendered close analysis of the film itself redundant. As Johnson and Schaefer observe, its broader cultural meaning was always the source of attention: "Among those who denounced *Snuff*, morality assumed greater significance in their arguments than the film itself, which was often inaccurately described, whether for rhetorical effect or for lack of close analysis."[31] So great was the symbolic force of the *Snuff* coda that it overshadowed interest in its actual content. The absence of June in the vast amount of criticism concerning the film suggests this still has yet to be remedied.

Many have observed that formal traits such as continuity editing belie the authenticity of the *Snuff* coda as an actual murder filmed in one continuous take.[32] Of greater concern to contemporary considerations of the film and the surrounding scandal is the omission of this third figure. *The Slaughter* ends with pregnant actress Terry London (a character not wholly dissimilar to

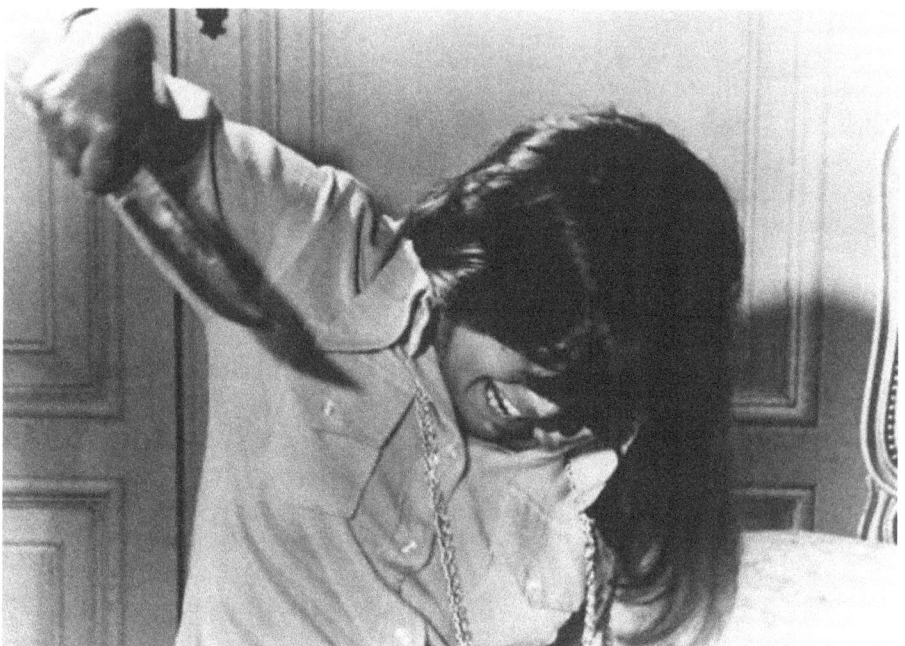

Snuff (1976) recalls the murder of Sharon Tate (Monarch/The Kobal Collection).

Sharon Tate) being stabbed on a bed by a female member of the Family-like cult. This scene fades and then cuts to a long establishing shot of 51 seconds that marks the beginning of the *Snuff* coda. The shot is composed of a group of people surrounding the bed. In the center of the room is a blonde woman dressed in (virtuous) white, and in the foreground on the side, a brunette woman dressed in (villainous) black who carries a clipboard. Once the "cut" command is given, everyone works busily. The camera pans across, and more crew members are shown in the background. In the foreground is a second bed. Its illogical introduction into the scene, combined with its privileged placement in the foreground, foreshadows its significance.

This is the moment where the link between the behind-the-scenes action and the profilmic event blurs, as the former becomes the center of attention. After *Cannibal Holocaust* and *Man Bites Dog* in particular, this blurring will become typical of many found footage horror films in the future, from *The Blair Witch Project* onwards. It is at this stage of the *Snuff* coda that two separate groups now form. On the center left, the "director" speaks to the blonde woman. They touch each other in a sexually familiar way, and he tells her how the murder scene they just shot aroused him. On the center right, three crew members are in discussion, including the brunette woman later identified as

June. This woman walks off camera to the left of the shot momentarily, only to reappear at the head of the unused bed where she adjusts a pillow and takes notes on her clipboard.

The blonde woman expresses discomfort at having sex in front of "all these people," but regardless, she and the director kiss. There is an abrupt shift to hand-held camera movement that, when combined with the shots of cameras and other cameramen in the frame, creates a sense that these events are being filmed "live." Zooming in on the couple shows that the director is holding a knife, while in the background June is focused intently upon her clipboard. As the couple lie kissing on the bed, June puts down her clipboard; this small act significantly alters her involvement from a "crew member" to an active performer in the action that follows. The blonde woman becomes increasingly agitated when she realizes that she and the director are being filmed. June stands at the end of the bed next to a small table with a collection of weapons placed upon it, and a toolbox on the floor. The blonde woman becomes more frantic; the brief point-of-view shot of June from the director's perspective that follows is integral to this re-evaluation of the *Snuff* coda. This shot could be easily mistaken for a point-of-view shot of June from the victim's perspective; it is only logical perhaps to feel that another woman, June, is the blonde woman's most likely ally, and her only means of possible escape from this increasingly dangerous situation. However, the shot is not from the victim's perspective at all, which begs the question: Why would the director stop at this pivotal point and look to see what June's reaction was? Regardless of the answer, there is no denying this look formally includes her in the action unfolding onscreen. The presence of June in the *Snuff* coda therefore rejects the simplistic "men versus women" scenario that it is so often purported to be, and upon which much of its ideological debate is based. Its sexual politics are far more complex. The female victim is not only at the mercy of a man, she is tortured by a man, and restrained by a smiling woman. An off-camera male voice directs June to "hold her down." It may be argued that June is following these orders to avoid being tortured herself. Significantly, however, the coda does not provide any evidence to support such a reading, and her smiling face challenges such claims.

This formal inclusion of June is reiterated just before the first act of violence when the blonde woman's shoulder is cut. During a three-second shot (as the director asks his victim, "You think I'm kidding, do you?"), June is also granted a point-of-view shot as she looks at the director. While it is only a brief shot, it is a crucial one, since it is June's perspective that is formally privileged and it reciprocates the glance just described. This shot not only sets up a formal relationship between June and the director, but acknowledges that a woman is watching these events. This suggests the presence of an active and sadistic *female* gaze, and so once again, the battle lines between men and women may not be as clearly demarcated as has been commonly contended. Moreover on this point, June becomes increasingly excited in her remaining time on screen. On numerous occasions, she is shown in the same shot as the victim and the director, smiling and restraining the woman. After a saw is introduced to the gruesome proceedings, her pleasure becomes even clearer. As the victim's suffering and terror increase, June's reaction—her legs apart, mouth open, smiling—implies a sexual aspect to her involvement. The last shot of June's face (there is a brief shot after this of her hands holding the blonde woman down) is taken from the point of view of the director, whose gaze captures his accomplice's arousal at the victim's trauma. June's involvement in the violence is confirmed once more as she is granted the privileged reaction shot to the most shocking gore shot thus far when the victim's hand is severed.

This is the last time June is shown onscreen. As the violence enters its second, more explicit stage, it is worth asking: Where did she go? The soundtrack becomes increasingly ambiguous as the sound of the victim's final breaths blurs with groans of pleasure presumably coming from the director. In the moments before the blonde woman is eviscerated, a heartbeat is also heard. Whose heartbeat is it? It may be the victim's, because the sound is only heard when her exposed organs are shown. As she is dying, one may deduce that her heartbeat would not be so steady. Alternatively, it may be the director's, but the sound appears to come from a point closer to the camera. Perhaps it is a synthetic estimation of the spectator's own heartbeat from the perspective of their surrogate onlooker, the cameraman. If the latter is the case, the emphasis of the soundtrack is significantly not on the onscreen bodies themselves, but rather upon the spectator's own capacity to enjoy the spectacle of onscreen violence. This also bears particular significance to the later found footage horror genre, as it would appear to consciously acknowledge the spectator's complicity in the onscreen violence by blurring the lines between diegetic and non-diegetic spaces. In doing so, a self-reflexive awareness becomes apparent through the articulation that appears to say "Yes, audience, the bodily violence on display is there solely for *your* benefit." That snuff-fictions and screen violence in general are so often addressed in terms of the visual makes this a unique aural indictment of the spectators and their involvement with onscreen violence.

One can also speculate that there is another possibility: The heartbeat may belong to June. Having been so pleasurably involved in the action, it makes sense that she is still watching. If this is the case, despite her physical absence within the frame, she is (again) granted a privileged position that suggests the victim's torture has in fact been a twisted sexual union between the director and June. That she shifts from assistant to audience at the same point that the violence so drastically increases exposes what has been implied throughout the entire sequence: the possibility that the *Snuff* coda may be a filmic haiku of deviant romance between June and the director on par with longer cinematic love ballads like *The Honeymoon Killers* (Leonard Kastle, 1970) or *Natural Born Killers* (Oliver Stone, 1994).

Taken less symptomatically, this twisted romance between June and the director also reflects one of the key aspects of the first 74 minutes of the film itself. *The Slaughter* and the *Snuff* coda are often viewed as separate entities because of their production history; it is perhaps too easy to miss how directly the coda relates to the film as a whole (the writing of Johnson and Schaefer, and that of Mikita Brottman, are notable exceptions). That *The Slaughter* tells of a group of women on a murderous rampage neatly provides a contrast with the coda, marking it as a desperate, and both physically and formally violent, return to a male-dominated status quo. A simple body count supports this claim: As Brottman states, "[V]irtually all the violence in *Snuff* is perpetrated by women on men, or other women."[33] After the all-girl killing spree that makes up the bulk of *The Slaughter*, it is of note that the first time a man kills anyone in the film is almost an hour in (and in his defense, he shoots one of the female gang members after he himself has been stabbed and the women have killed an elderly woman and a young female child during a robbery). Even more directly, *The Slaughter* concentrates much of its (admittedly loose) plot upon a deviant romance between Angelica (Margarita Amuchástegui) and its Charles Manson figure, Satan (Enrique Larratelli); the gruesome relationship between June and the director provides a neat parallel to this plot element within *The Slaughter*. Like June herself, this brief and degenerate affair has been lost to history, sacrificed in favor of the ideological debates that so famously marked the film's original release.

The last moments of the film indicate another clear legacy to contemporary found footage horror. In these final seconds, the director disembowels his victim, removing viscera and lifting it victoriously above his head with a scream. As the screen fades to white, two male voices whisper and ask, "Did you get it all?" Here *Snuff* recalls *The Blair Witch Project*'s absence of credits that played a role in creating its sense of authenticity: Bereft of these traditional features and lacking other formal indicators of closure, the suddenness of *Snuff*'s conclusion adds weight to claims of its genuine status as a real snuff film. Even to gore-literate viewers today for whom the ketchup-red splatter and cocktail-wiener guts may seem a little kitsch, it is difficult to deny the disorientating effectiveness of this trickery.

Aside from establishing many of the features that would become familiar in later found footage horror films, there are also broader ideological observations that can be made. While few would defend *Snuff* as any great cinematic masterpiece, that previous analyses of the film have generally ignored the role of June is a telling omission. This does not suggest that the presence of June magically transforms *Snuff* into a progressive text—there is a strong argument to be made that the idea of a woman being sexually aroused and complicit in the torture of another woman is evidence of some deeply regressive male fantasies regarding violence against women. To place this in historical context, the film from this perspective functions as an active breaking down of the united force of women, one visible at the time of the film's release in the shape of the very feminist movement that rallied so passionately against it. Nevertheless, the fact that June has been so widely ignored means that these aspects have yet to be properly addressed. It is of no small interest to debates on gender and film that in the name of championing the rights of women, one woman has been eradicated completely from film's historical memory. Any attempts to grasp the broader phenomenon of snuff film—be it as an urban legend, a popular fictional trope or as a real, tangible part of contemporary screen cultures—must reconsider the ease with which historical perspectives regarding *Snuff* have been so dramatically skewed away from any reading that incorporates the presence and function of June.

Snuff DVD artwork (courtesy Blue Underground, Inc., www.blue-underground.com).

Along with *Cannibal Holocaust* a few years later, *Snuff* demonstrated only too forcefully the impact on the popular imagination of fictional films that made claims of authenticity through their promotional strategies, formal construction or explicit diegetic declarations. Twenty-three years after the explosion of negative attention and valuable publicity that *Snuff* received, *The Blair Witch Project* mimicked many aspects of its predecessor, features that would later become regular (though not compulsory) characteristics of contemporary found footage horror. As this exploration of the under-explored prehistory of this subgenre will now examine, the roots of this subgenre continued to flourish throughout the 1980s and 1990s, particularly on television.

Three

Television

This chapter provides a brief overview of found footage horror's television heritage leading up to the release of *The Blair Witch Project* in 1999, examining the ways that a variety of programs responded specifically to their historical contexts, how television as a medium was uniquely suited to such material, and how these texts set the scene for future formal experimentation. Certainly the marketing that drove the phenomenal success of *The Blair Witch Project* played on just how suitable a vehicle television was for this type of supernatural quasi-verity: The *Curse of the Blair Witch* mockumentary that screened on the SciFi channel in the United States just before the feature's release was a hugely successful element of its promotional campaign.

In his excellent book *Television Mockumentary: Reflexivity, Satire and a Call to Play*, Craig Hight argued that mockumentary and television are uniquely suited because the codes and conventions of the latter have become so familiar they are ripe for appropriation. Television viewers are often highly adept at reading these codes and conventions that govern television's particular mode of representation, and are aware of how the medium has changed over time. As Hight noted, unlike cinema, television tends to rely on tight framing and uses a lot of close-ups to create a sense of intimacy which, along with editing techniques designed to give it an on-the-fly quality, adds to television's sense of immediacy. "[T]elevision is preoccupied with 'being there,' with capturing things 'as they happen,' with cameras being present at the unfolding of every intimate aspect of an event."[1] This sense of immediacy is of course also crucial to contemporary found footage horror.

The Rise of Television Mockumentary

Cynthia Miller has located the importance of a short three-minute April Fool's Day hoax shown on the British current affairs series *Panorama* in 1957 as a crucial point in mockumentary history. This story focused on a non-existent Swiss spaghetti harvest, and was presented by the reputable journalist Richard Dimbleby. It included faked footage of the supposed annual harvest of the spaghetti tree—claiming this was where spaghetti came from—and noted that due to the eradication of the spaghetti weevil, 1957 provided an impressive crop. After broadcasting the story, the BBC received many calls from viewers complaining about this serious news program's deviation from fact, while others wanted information on how to grow their own spaghetti trees. Although the story would perhaps be easily dismissed today, in the late 1950s spaghetti was considered exotic in Britain.[2]

While the comedic capacity of mockumentary is visible in this instance, eight years later the potential to unsettle by blurring fact and fiction became only too vivid. Peter Watkins is widely regarded as one of the forefathers of docudrama, and much of his radical and often confrontational work addresses the nature of the media and documentary in particular. His 1965 television special *The War Game* combined aspects of documentary filmmaking with dramatizations to construct his exploration of the nuclear fears that dominated the Cold War. Mimicking the format of the news magazine style typical of the time, *The War Game* combined participatory interviews, expository voice-over narration, and other documentary modes in its "coverage" of the events surrounding and following a fictional nuclear attack on the United Kingdom by the Soviet Union. Familiar British locations become the site of horrors that loomed large in the popular imagination: The only thing more terrifying than the likely death-toll statistics was the misery that awaited the survivors, such as radiation sickness and wider social and cultural collapse.

According to Nick Muntean, Watkins researched his subject "scrupulously" and erred on the side of conservative approximations so as to not be accused of being too over-the-top. The motivation behind the project was to communicate the possible consequences of a nuclear attack on Britain, addressing what Watkins believed to be a gap in public knowledge disproportionate to the substantial budgets dedicated to nuclear weapons themselves.[3] The BBC refused to play it as planned in 1965 (scheduled to mark the 20th anniversary of the nuclear attack on Hiroshima), deeming it too shocking for television audiences. As Keith Beattie explained, the real reason behind the cancellation of *The War Game*'s original broadcast was that it might negatively influence the country's nuclear defense policy.[4] Despite not being shown on television, *The War Game* went on to win the Academy Award for Best Documentary Feature in 1966. The BBC finally aired it in 1985 (the 40th anniversary of Hiroshima), and in Nick Muntean's words, it has become possibly "the most terrifyingly realistic depiction of nuclear war and its aftermath ever committed to film."[5]

Echoing Orson Welles' *War of the Worlds*, *Alternative 3* (1977)—also made for British television—established television mockumentary as the perfect vehicle to execute a successful large-scale hoax on the viewing public. For Hight, "[T]elevision mockumentary hoaxes are fictional texts which both play with audiences' assumptions of commentary modes of representation and involve the direct complicity of a host broadcaster,"[6] and are premised on thwarting the expectations audiences hold about the authoritative nature of television. Produced by Anglia Television and screened on ITV in the United Kingdom, *Alternative 3*—like the Panorama spaghetti tree hoax twenty years earlier—was intended to screen on April Fool's Day, but was not broadcast until June. It was the final episode of the scientific news series *Science Report* but unlike other episodes, it opted instead for a fake documentary format that outlined in detail a mass conspiracy linking missing persons cases with climate change, the Cold War, and exploration on Mars. The program was presented by its regular host Tim Brinton which, along with its traditional investigative documentary format, also afforded it a degree of authenticity.

The project began as a fictional teleplay by writer David Ambrose called *Disappearing People*. These roots are apparent in the opening moments of *Alternative 3* as it focuses on three unsolved missing persons cases, with heartfelt and often melodramatic interviews with their concerned families. Frustrated with the direction of the original work, Ambrose discussed it with director Christopher Miles and together they decided their missing people were going to Mars, inspired by a recent issue of *Paris Match* with images from the unmanned Viking mission on its cover. Miles and Ambrose decided to opt for a "fake documentary" format, and from that point they found the project became extremely easy to write.[7] With *Science Report*'s team of investigative journalists, the conspiracy Brinton seeks to uncover begins from an earlier investigation into Britain's so-called "brain drain," examining the disappearance of a number of highly trained scientists and other experts. The unusual circumstances surrounding the death of Professor William Ballantine in a car accident leads the team to discover that he had given a friend a mysterious videotape that only played static. A suspenseful interview with U.S. Apollo astronaut Bob Grodin (Shane Rimmer) reveals that he had discovered an unpublicized lunar base while on the moon. Through further research, it is revealed that the missing scientists and others were a part of a mass U.S.-USSR conspiracy to move significant figures from Earth to a space station because, as revealed in a key interview with scientist Dr. Carl Gernstein (Richard Marner), the rise in pollution and other environmental hazards meant global climate upheavals were imminent. Gerstein outlines the three options international governments had to choose from in answer to the looming threat of climate change: to reduce the number of people living on Earth, to move populations underground, or to leave the planet altogether. The latter—the eponymous "Alternative 3"—was the one that international governments agreed on. In Gerstein's words, the plan was to "get the hell of this [planet] ... while there's still time." After establishing the possibility that there already exists a lunar colony on the moon as part of "Alternative 3," the *Science Report* team finally attained the hardware to descramble Ballantine's videotape to reveal secret 1962 footage that shows evidence of life on Mars.

Many have noted the remarkably prophetic nature of *Alternative 3* in regard to climate change, with Hight, Ambrose, Miles and Brinton all drawing parallels with Al Gore's *An Inconvenient Truth* (David Guggenheim, 2006).[8] So convincing was the mockumentary that despite its creators' admission that it was a hoax, many remained unconvinced and it has gone on to form the foundations of still-active conspiracy theories.[9] While it is a stretch to refute the claims of the filmmakers themselves that *Alternative 3* was a hoax, the mockumentary skillfully employs a variety of different tactics to create its sense of verisimilitude. Some of these techniques would become familiar conventions in mockumentary horror, such as the presentation of a range of different types of documentary evidence such as newspaper clippings, interviews, re-enactments, photographs, hidden camera stings, infographics, and the inclusion of recognizable stock footage and news items. Like *Cannibal Holocaust* three years later, it also deploys a film-within-a-film structure in places that again becomes a feature in many later found footage horror movies. The intensity of *Alternative 3* stems from its sense of urgency and immediacy: Brinton refers to a telephone call made to their office "48 hours ago," and emphasizes that the revelation of the contents of Ballantine's videotape is being played back in full "as we saw it." This footage—as well as the 8mm hidden camera interview with Bob Grodin—is contrasted by its scratchy, low quality appearance, and typifies the authenticating value of material corruption and distortion with the appearance of tracking lines, snow, and poor audio marking the Ballantine tape in particular. This decomposition and interference is, as discussed elsewhere in this book, also typical of how found footage horror creates its sense of authenticity.

Like *Alternative 3*, a number of other television mockumentary hoaxes mimicked the formal construction of news, current affairs programs and documentaries with political intent. In the United States, the TV movie *Special Bulletin* (Edward Zwickland, 1985) replicated a typical American network television schedule with station idents and advertisements for other programs appearing in between increasingly urgent news updates about terrorists armed with a nuclear bomb in South Carolina. There are a number of other TV movies that followed a similar structure: The Canadian production *Countdown to Looking Glass* (Fred Barzyk, 1984) also concerns a fictional nuclear showdown between the United States and the USSR, while the science fiction films *Without Warning* (Robert Iscove, 1994) and *Special Report: Journey to Mars* (Robert Mandel, 1996) contain apocalyptic themes, albeit in more fantastic fictional narratives.

The dark-tinged science fiction overtones of such material also paved a route to contemporary found footage horror. An early television precursor was *Alien Abduction: Incident in Lake County* (1998), released initially as *UFO Abduction* (Dean Alioto, 1989). Along with Paul Chitlik, Alioto remade it for television the year before the release of *The Blair Witch Project* as a found footage science fiction special with horror overtones. The U.S. broadcast of this remake caused similar confusion to many of these earlier titles regarding its ontological status.[10] The U.S. documentary television series *In Search Of...* (1976–1982) contained strong paranormal and conjectural leanings, and was also cited by *The Blair Witch Project*'s directors as influencing their film.[11] Although these earlier televisual examples clearly prefigure contemporary found footage horror films in a broader way, *Alternative 3* and the nuclear holocaust television movies can also be appreciated for their horrific and terrifying effect, so much so that *The War Game* ranked 74th on British network Channel Four's *The 100 Greatest Scary Moments* program on October 26, 2003. Of even more direct interest to the concerns of this book, however, was #41: the 1992 British television event *Ghostwatch*.

Ghostwatch *(Lesley Manning, 1992)*

When examined in terms of its pure plot mechanics, there is little about *Ghostwatch*'s central narrative that suggests it could have caused the pandemonium it did at the time of its initial broadcast. The nuts-and-bolts storyline of the BBC1 television special was familiar generic material even in the early 1990s: Single mother Pam Early (Brid Brennan) and her two daughters Suzanne and Kimmy (played by real-life sisters Michelle and Cherise Wesson) live in a North London council house that is plagued by supernatural activity such as loud noises, moving objects, and physical attacks on Suzanne. It is revealed during its ninety-minute screen time that the Early house is built on the site where a notorious female child murderer drowned babies in her boiler at some unidentified earlier point in history. In the 1960s, child molester and kidnapper Raymond Tunstall let a room in the house the Early family would later inhabit, where he began wearing dresses because of increasing delusions about an elderly woman (implied to be the aforementioned baby killer). Tunstall hung himself in the space under the stairs but was left alone in the house for 12 days where he was attacked by hungry cats. Naming the ghost "Pipes" after their mother's initial dismissal of what was making the banging noises, Kimmy's drawings match the description given by audience members who had viewed footage of the girls' bedroom: a bald man with bleeding eyes in a dress.

However, these details do not do justice to the elements of *Ghostwatch* that made it so controversial. According to one account, the BBC received approximately half a million calls during its climactic five minutes, although it received only 2215 official complaints afterwards.[12] The current affairs forum program *Bite Back* that screened just after the 1992 broadcast included one outraged viewer who accused the BBC of having unethically "toyed with the emotions of the audience." *Ghostwatch* reached the international news circuit when a British family claimed it caused their son's suicide five days after the broadcast, and Hight noted one British newspaper even reported a claim made in a medical journal that linked *Ghostwatch* to the first recorded instance of post-traumatic stress disorder in children.[13] It is of no small significance that *Ghostwatch* not only narratively concerned a family, but also that families featured heavily in the heated public discourse that followed, and were considered its primary victims. Jeffrey Sconce has recalled the famous scene from Tobe Hooper's *Poltergeist* (1982), where Carol Anne's (Heather O'Rourke) parents look on as she places her hands on the static-filled television screen and utters the famous words, "They're heeere." For Sconce, "this tableau of the innocent family slumbering in front of the hissing presence of the TV set emblematizes the long history of cultural anxiety over the seeming vulnerability of the family before the unwavering eye of television."[14] The widespread and vocal fallout during and after *Ghostwatch* in Britain at the time of its initial airing vividly link it to these same cultural anxieties.

The details of the central ghost story at its core grossly underplay just how convincing *Ghostwatch*'s simulation of a legitimate live investigation broadcast was. As Elizabeth Evans has indicated, even its very title evoked comparisons with the BBC's crime reconstruction program *Crimewatch* (1984–present) that encouraged viewers to call in with new information.[15] This sense of authenticity existed despite a number of what (in retrospect) are seemingly obvious factors flagging its fictionality: Like Orson Welles' *War of the Worlds* radio broadcast in 1938, it contained disclaimers. It included writing credits at the beginning for Stephen Volk that were added at the last minute,[16] and its closing credits included a cast list typical of fictional films and programs (including one for the "ghost" himself, played by Keith Ferrari). The *Radio Times* television and radio guide also printed a cast listing, as is typical of TV movies and fictional series. Most of all, of course, was the over-the-top fantasy upon which it was based. So taking these things into account, how did *Ghostwatch* cause the panic that it did?

Most obvious was its formal construction as a supposedly live investigative broadcast. *Ghostwatch* was broadcast at 9.25 p.m. on October 31, 1992, as a Halloween special. Focusing on the paranormal events in the Early household on Foxhill Drive in Northolt, the program switched between three primary locations, each hosted by a celebrity who would have been instantly familiar to its intended audience: Inside the Early house with personality Sarah Greene, the street outside with actor and comedian Craig Charles, and the BBC studio with TV presenter Mike Smith as the phone-in presenter, and highly regarded British journalist, author and broadcaster Michael Parkinson as the host. Appearing with Parkinson was parapsychologist Dr. Lin Pascoe (Gillian Bevan), with apparently "live" crosses to New York to interview skeptic Dr. Emilio Sylvestri (Colin Stinton). As Hight summarized it, *Ghostwatch* was "constructed as a textbook example of an unfolding real-time narrative, using all the familiar tropes of live television broadcasting (for British television in the 1990s)."[17]

Ghostwatch director Lesley Manning and writer Stephen Volk (© Rich Lawden 2010, www.ghostwatchbtc.com).

The program's opening statement suggests that *Ghostwatch*'s creators—writer Stephen Volk and director Lesley Manning—had at least some idea of the powder keg they were playing with. "The program you're about to watch," says a sharply dressed Michael Parkinson as the program begins, "is a unique live investigation of the supernatural. It contains material that some viewers may find to be disturbing." From the outset, *Ghostwatch* evokes the oral traditions of the ghost story. The privileging of technology in these opening sequences underscores the modernization of the ghost-hunting trope, and much attention is focused on the heat-seeking cameras and other specialized equipment that the *Ghostwatch* team use in their investigation. At one point, a reel-to-reel tape player is even literally placed on a pedestal: Ghosts represent an archaic world, the program implies, that will be victoriously conquered by a new technological one. *Ghostwatch* proudly deploys technology in pursuit of its prime-time ghost-hunting spectacle, but as revealed in the program's final shocking moments, Pipes turns the tables and uses technology to *his* advantage. The very title contains an insightful (and ominous) double meaning: We watch ghosts through television, but they may also be watching us.

Parkinson's presence should not be underappreciated in *Ghostwatch*'s construction of authenticity. As one of the adult interview subjects recalling their childhood experience of the program in the fascinating documentary *Ghostwatch: Behind the Curtains* (Rich Lawden, 2012) put it, "Parky wouldn't lie." Bringing a level of *gravitas* to the proceedings, Parkinson has been described by *The Guardian* as nothing less than "the doyen of British talk show hosts."[18] By his own account he has interviewed over 2000 celebrities[19]—mostly on his well-known chat show *Parkinson* (1971–1982, 1998–2007)—and he is noted for his often-confrontational interviewing style. In *Ghostwatch*, Parkinson is initially open-minded, and during his first "live" cross to the North London house, he describes it as the place where "it might all happen, or it might not." Parkinson's signature adjectival cache is deployed readily throughout the broadcast, with frequent references to events being "extraordinary," "quite remarkable" and "fascinating." When it is revealed that Suzanne herself was making some of the banging noises—typical, claims Dr. Pascoe, of children in these situations who feel pressure for poltergeists to reveal themselves—Parkinson's tone becomes skeptical and dismissive.

Like snuff-fictions and television mockumentary before it (and contemporary found footage horror films after), *Ghostwatch* formally codes its material as authentic through technical interruptions, disruptions and glitches. What is so fascinating about this program when viewing it today, however, is the degree to which it extends this logic. In Dr. Pascoe's own words, the broad-

Teaser poster for the documentary *Ghostwatch: Behind the Curtains* (Rich Lawden, 2012) (© Arfon Jones and Rich Lawden 2012, www.ghostwatchbtc.com).

cast acted as a "massive séance," forming a literal conduit for Pipes to transmit *himself* through television into viewers' homes and, even more spectacularly, into the BBC studio. As Dr. Pascoe realizes that the broadcast has offered a way of condensing and dispersing paranormal energy across the country, a large gust of wind blows through the studio. At the Early house, Kimmy and Pam escape but Sarah and Suzanne are lured and trapped underneath the stairs where Pipes can be briefly seen. Back in the studio, cats yowl, lights blow, sets collapse, cameras move around on their own and finally the power cuts out completely. Struggling to maintain his professionalism, Parkinson narrates the events, even though by his own admission he is unsure if anyone is still watching. Terrifyingly, his commentary morphs into gibberish and the program ends with a shadowy close-up of the bottom half of Parkinson's face as he says in monotone "round around the garden like a Teddy bear," his voice finally shifting to the same one Pipes had earlier used to speak through Suzanne. This final revelation of the nation's beloved "Parky" succumbing to Pipes' supernatural control was simply too much for many of *Ghostwatch*'s viewers, already unnerved by the events that had preceded it.

Hight has identified a certain playfulness to television hoaxes such as this, but ultimately considers them a one-trick pony, arguing that they "are inevitably less interesting when viewed again or by audiences that are already aware of their status as fiction."[20] I would argue that this depends on your perspective: From the point of view of someone interested only in the evolution of television mockumentary this may be true, but the broader significance of *Ghostwatch* is much more than this. In his compelling essay "The Ghosts in the Living Room," British filmmaker Adam Curtis offered an impressive historical overview of the media culture in which *Ghostwatch* first appeared, suggesting the rise of suburban ghost stories in factual British TV from the 1970s led logically to the 1992 broadcast. In Curtis' words, *Ghostwatch* had an inherently ideological message as it "showed clearly where the real ghosts of our society had now gone to live. They are inside television itself—a strange nether world of PR-driven half-truths, synthetic personalities, and waves of apocalyptic fear."[21] Stephen Volk has openly acknowledged that it was his concerns about the mass audiences' often unquestioning susceptibility to television that lay at the project's heart, and has said that *Ghostwatch* was designed specifically to "challenge people's preconception of trust and what they believe in." As he put it, the British viewing public inherently trusted the BBC

> not to dick around with them ... which of course is exactly the reason that I thought it was perfect for the BBC to do it, because the piece—as a piece of drama—was all about who do you trust. Do you trust the information you are being given, is that person really an expert, are they bullshitting you? I was trying

in drama to ask those kind of questions, challenging people to not just gobble up what they're watching.[22]

In a country still reeling from seeing the first Gulf War unfold before it on television, the urgency of this mission has significant symptomatic pertinence. For Volk, the intent behind the program was much more than a mere Halloween prank. With *Ghostwatch*, he sought to turn the audience's attention back on their own increasingly passive viewing habits; the ensuing brouhaha arguably only served to emphasize the urgency of his project. The surface aesthetics of *Ghostwatch* plant it firmly in British television of the early 1990s, but both the relevance of this message and its horror legacy stretch well into the present, where found footage horror films reign as the generic format *de jour*. Any doubt as to its influence can be dismissed by even the most cursory comparative glance at *Paranormal Activity 3* (Henry Joost and Ariel Schulman, 2011): At times shot-for-shot, despite receiving having only a small-scale official release on VHS and DVD in the past, the influence of *Ghostwatch* and its ensuing controversy has been tangibly demonstrated.[23]

Les Documents Interdits

Jean-Teddy Filippe's series *Les Documents Interdits* (1989–1991) presents further evidence of found footage horror's roots on television in the decade leading up to the release of *The Blair Witch Project*. Initially consisting of twelve self-contained shorts ranging from four to fourteen minutes in length,[24] the French television series is so prophetic that it could be reasonably considered a basic road map for the direction the subgenre would take in the 2000s and beyond. *Les Documents Interdits* first screened on French television in the late 1980s,[25] a decade before *The Blair Witch Project* and quite a few years before *Ghostwatch*. While the deployment of many of the defining codes and conventions of contemporary found footage in *Les Documents Interdits* may in retrospect seem unremarkable, considering how early they predated *Blair Witch* it should be considered anything but.

Like *Ghostwatch* in Britain a few years later, *Les Documents Interdits* is a sharp, insightful critique of television culture itself. With a background in advertising, Filippe had ample experience making high-impact short films, but this series saw him turn away from commercially oriented material to something far more conceptual. Filippe has argued that the central power of television is to authenticate the emotional experience of everything it broadcasts: It is a medium whose immediacy and emotional intensity dominates all other aspects, often despite our own capacity for reason and logic. It frequently tells us how we are to consume and respond to its images. *Les Documents Interdits* challenges this by emphasizing his belief that televisual images are not only complex but also fundamentally volatile.[26] These short films force us to become active viewers by urging us to participate in the decoding of their images. Time and time again, *Les Documents Interdits* openly instructs us to be critical: "Watch carefully what is about to happen," we are told in the episodes "The Castaway" and "The Extraterrestrial." "Pay close attention to what is now about to happen," says the narrator of "The Divers," and we are instructed to "watch what is going to happen" during "The Witch." In a remarkable interview on the French website Cinétrange, Filippe states that his goal was to incite the viewer to be attentive and critical, as he claims we should be when we see *any* image.

This undermining of television's assumed empiricism also manifests in the series' frequent use of dual multi-lingual voice-overs: Russian, Hungarian, English, French, German and Spanish. This formal corruption of the authority of the traditional single voice-over of expository documentary emphasizes the constructedness of what we so often accept as untarnished "factuality." These dual voice-overs expose not only the highly constructed nature of television "factuality" itself, but also stresses that there is often a *cultural* bias in these constructions through the slight differences in translation. Filippe's broader intentions are therefore intrinsically linked to his deployment of a faux found footage format. The benefits of focusing on supernatural subject matter— haunted houses, witches, telekinesis, aliens and Lovecraftian tales of the sea— are twofold. Firstly, with narratives that engage with unexplainable phenomena, the frequent (although not absolute) deployment of amateur filmmaking aesthetics adds a sense of authenticity to what may otherwise be deemed fantastic, even absurd scenarios. Additionally, Filippe noted that television as a medium encourages us to swallow its version of reality unchallenged. The surface authenticity implied by its formal construction as amateur found footage contrasted with the fantastic nature of its content work in unison in *Les Documents Interdits* to challenge our assumptions about television's broader relationship to truth.

The eponymous "documents" take a variety of forms and are historically and geographically diverse. "The Castaway," "The Divers" and "The Soldier" are sea mysteries that focus on unexplained oceanic disappearances. All three consist of hand-held, amateur black-and-white footage with no diegetic sound and a narrator (or narrators) providing voice-over(s). "The Castaway" is filmed by the only survivor of a Soviet cargo ship that inexplicably sank during the 1950s, and follows his submission to an unidentified phenomenon he sees in the sky and that somehow assists in keeping him alive. "The Divers" is undated, and records a military exercise concerning an unidentified marine-based assassin, a "human weapon" with abnormal strength and speed. "The Soldier" concerns footage taken by a U.S. soldier just after the 1943 Sicily landings, who calmly and determinedly walks into the ocean until he vanishes completely after meeting a woman and child coming and returning to this strange, undefined realm. Color home movies from the domestic sphere also appear in *Les Documents Interdits*. "The Child" follows the terrifying power of telekinetic Peter in Montreal from his birth in the late 1970s through to the 1990s, while "The Crown Film the Young" reveals the truth behind a small-town American murder mystery from the perspective of kindly amateur Herbert Crown. Supposedly edited and narrated by the elderly Crown himself, it contains footage shot from the first camera he received at 17, right through to just before he donated his archive to the Church Road Library in 1973.

As the "documents" become more modern, they begin to reflect the formal hybridity of contemporary screen media. "The Extraterrestrial" contains a number of intertitles brandishing conflicting quotes from military officials and experts about so-called rumored collaborative research by the U.S. and USSR concerning a confrontation with aliens on the non-existent Takohamo plateau. "The Extraterrestrial" combines these titles with other types of material—surveillance footage from different sources whose contents are often contradictory and hand-held footage taken from the now-abandoned Takohamo research facility—to link the conspiracy to the 1969 Apollo 11 moon landing. Maintaining the science fiction leanings of this short, "Siberia" is a darkly comic investigation into the difficulties faced after the Cold War by the 12,500 half-men, half-machine cyborgs experimented on by the Soviets. Beginning with a credible station ident for the fictional Australian Television Broadcasting Authority, "The Madman at the Crossroads" is a convincing simulation of a North American television news story from the 1990s, again concerning alien activity on Earth and its impact on Hungarian immigrant Tibor Nagy. Contemporary interviews, reenactments, stock footage and Nagy's footage of his own abduction form the basis of this short.

Direct plot parallels can be made between the episode "The Witch" and *The Blair Witch Project*, such as the enigmatic representation of the witch herself, her ability to manipulate the spatial logistics of the environment to confuse and disorient, and the fact that the story is told from the perspective of outsiders, a documentary crew. "The Ferguson Case" convincingly replicates live broadcast television programming as host Henry Matthews speaks directly to camera from the control room of WACN and references *Les Documents Interdits* by name; he is presenting his story for the series itself. Matthews discusses his involvement in the "At Once" program, which took calls from the public three times a week about a story which audience members felt needed to be addressed, and WACN would dispatch a mobile crew to the site to investigate. He underscored the importance of technology to the program, as the show was predicated on the fact that the crew could go anywhere. Matthews replayed a call they received on May 15, 1989, at 8.45 p.m. from a Mrs. Ferguson from 1036 Sun Avenue, who can be barely heard through a static-filled line saying, "They've been moving in the darkness for two weeks."

Matthews cuts to archival material of the initial broadcast, and a "WACN Live" logo appears in the bottom right corner. For the benefit of viewers, times and a summary of events also scroll across the bottom of the screen. A journalist and his crew arrive at the large manor house and enter despite the house appearing uninhabited. As they walk through the building, the journalist provides a running commentary of their visit and marvels at the artwork and collectibles, all the while calling for Mrs. Ferguson. When there are technical problems with the live feed, the studio dispatches a second crew to the property. These disruptions increase in intensity and duration until the journalist is narrating his experiences in near-total darkness, mentioning at one point that he believes he can see a figure on a sofa and—even more strangely—that a room he enters is full of what appears to be snow, leading him to suspect the entire building is decomposing. It is revealed that the second crew has arrived at the same address, but disturbingly found no house at all. Matthews fills in the rest of the story: The first crew was never seen again, and the initial telephone call they received was forensically traced to Adelaide Ferguson, a woman who had lived in the house in the 1930s who was making the call to rat exterminators. An intertitle reveals that after the "At Once" program, the property was declared a forbidden zone and was buried under lead and concrete. Many of the formal and narrative features of "The Ferguson Case" will become recognizable in later years as readily identifiable conventions of the found footage horror subgenre. Most significant is the connection made between supernatural activity and technical distortions: While the paranormal is marked in this way by earlier films such as *Poltergeist* (Tobe Hooper, 1982), it is "The Ferguson Case" that presents it in the specific manner that will be regularly deployed in later found footage horror, from *The Blair Witch Project* onwards. Many films would follow investigative television crews into haunted spaces—typified not only by *Ghostwatch*, but *The Last Broadcast, Grave Encounters, The Burningmoore Incident* (Jonathan Williams, 2010), *The Feed* (Steve Gibson 2010), and *7 Nights of Darkness* (Allen Kellogg, 2011).

This did not mark the end of found footage horror's relationship with television. British station Channel 4's series *Shockers* (1999) employed it in the episode "Parents Day," and there are a number of other horror mockumentaries and found footage horror television series and programs such as *The Lost Tapes* (2008–2010), the science fiction–horror hybrid *Jeopardy* (2002–2005), *Werewolves: The Dark Survivor* (Edward Bazalgette, 2009), the comedy mockumentary series *Garth Marenghi's Darkplace* (Richard Ayoade, 2004) and *The River* (2012). The latter, a *Lost*-meets-*Cannibal Holocaust* series created by *Paranormal Activity* mastermind Oren Peli, was cancelled after only one season. Its inability to capture the television audience in the same way as his *Paranormal Activity* movies did not mark the end of "reality" television horror, as the success of *Ghost Hunters* (2004–present) and *Most Haunted* (2002–2010) attest.

As contemporary found footage horror unfolded from the late 1990s, the lines between film, television and the Internet blurred. With the rise of the Internet especially, television lost its unique status as the primary medium of immediacy and authenticity. The scares horror audiences once experienced with found footage and mockumentary horror on television have become clichés, the ubiquity of ghost-hunter and paranormal investigation–themed reality programs now reducing its one-time recipe for a successful hoax into familiar codes and conventions. These not only survived on film, but they flourished there: It is the cinema where contemporary found footage horror has reigned, and the next section will explore two of the most successful moments the subgenre has yet offered, *The Blair Witch Project* and the *Paranormal Activity* franchise, and the fascinating history of what happened between them.

PART 2

A Critical Chronology: 1998–2009

The millennial cultural phenomenon of *The Blair Witch Project* (Daniel Myrick and Eduardo Sánchez, 1999) brought found footage horror dramatically to the attention of mainstream audiences. There is little argument that the blockbuster success of this low-budget film about amateur filmmakers going missing in the Maryland woods marked the beginnings of contemporary found footage horror. *The Blair Witch Project* and *Paranormal Activity* are arguably the two major watershed moments of the found footage horror subgenre as we currently know it. As will be explored shortly, however, found footage horror did not disappear completely during the decade between these two films. Many of these films may not be instantly recognizable to mainstream audiences, but in horror circles at least, movies like *The Last Broadcast* (1998), *The Last Horror Movie* (Julian Richards, 2003), and *Behind the Mask: The Rise of Leslie Vernon* (2006) were known to many fans. Other titles made during this period may not have been as widely distributed or as well received, but still demonstrate the ongoing evolution of the codes and conventions of contemporary found footage horror.

With the arrival of YouTube in 2005 and its phenomenal rise during 2006, filmmakers responded by taking found footage to the mainstream in the creation of films that encouraged us to believe not only that we could have seen them on YouTube but that we could have made them ourselves, resulting in films such as *Diary of the Dead* (2007), *[Rec]* (2007) and of course the blockbuster monster movie *Cloverfield* (2008). These films spoke to cultural anxieties about the ubiquity of camera and surveillance technologies and amateur videography more generally, and interwove them with horror traditions that were decades old. They also emphasized the more playful aspects of found footage horror spectatorship, paving the way for the extraordinary success of the *Paranormal Activity* franchise when it received wide release in 2009.

Taken independently, *The Blair Witch Project* and *Paranormal Activity* offer significant insight into the mechanics—both formally and ideologically—of found footage horror, and are as fascinating for where they overlap as much as for where they diverge. In the spirit of *Peeping Tom* (Michael Powell, 1960), they construct the diegetic camera as a weapon, and linger on the banality of their isolation in locations feminized in different ways and to different thematic ends. In this manner, they typify what Adam Lowenstein identified as "ambient horror" and both hinge on their rejection of glossy, highly produced spectacle horror.[1]

While the first part of this book has discussed the development of the subgenre's prehistory, it is *The Blair Witch Project* that popularized the concept itself, familiarizing audiences with its affective potency. As Jane Roscoe noted, *The Blair Witch Project* took "mock-documentary out of the arthouse and into the mainstream."[2] Paul Wells identified its significance for horror more broadly, offering it as a near-textbook example of the genre's ability to reinvent itself. He argued that *The Blair Witch Project* actively sought to recover aspects of horror like allusion and suggestion, which were all but lost during the previous decades.[3] As the following chapter argues, many past debates surrounding *The Blair Witch Project*'s politics have underplayed vital evidence regarding gender fluidity within the film, distracted by the whistles and bells of its phenomenal success and wider extratextuality. While the landslide of critical attention that followed soon after seemed to expend its energies upon everything about *The Blair Witch Project* except the film itself, it was the feature movie's construction of authenticity that allowed the *Blair Witch* myth to flourish. Its directors did this through an approach that would become central to the contemporary found footage horror subgenre: "Myrick and Sánchez have achieved a sense of actuality by systematically repudiating virtually every feature of the film industry's formula for realistic drama," said James Keller. "They have achieved realism by rejecting realism."[4]

Two years after the release of *Blair Witch*, the very notion of fear, horror, terror, and threat went through a mass cultural metamorphosis on September 11, 2001. On that day, the America that horror film in the 1990s sought to critique and challenge changed forever. While this will be discussed further in Chapter Nine, a brief outline of the impact of the 9/11 attacks is necessary to contextualize the lull in mainstream attention on the subgenre between *The Blair Witch Project* and *Paranormal Activity*. John Kenneth Muir's 2011 book *Horror Films of the 1990s* presented an exhaustive overview of the genre during that decade, and noted that beyond the success of *Scream* and *The Blair Witch*

Project horror was marked by a significant slump for a number of reasons: the rise and dominance of relatively unimaginative police procedurals in the genre, the wider accessibility of filmmaking technologies allowing aspiring directors to stray from the traditional "training wheels" of horror, and television series such as *The X-Files* and *Buffy the Vampire Slayer* also vying for the attention of horror fans.[5] After 9/11 the already struggling horror genre faced new challenges. Aviva Briefel and Sam J. Miller described this scenario:

> How could American audiences, after tasting real horror, want to consume images of violence on-screen? The omnipresent post-traumatic response of "It was like a movie" seemed to herald the death of a genre that would either remind viewers of catastrophes they wanted to forget or pale in comparison to the terrors of the real thing.[6]

But they also noted that some saw horror as an ideal vehicle for teasing out the colossal challenges that 9/11 and the subsequent so-called "War on Terror" signaled, and claimed that "in a context where we could not openly process the horror we were experiencing, the horror genre emerged as a rare protected space in which to critique the tone and content of public discourse."[7]

It is from this perspective that films like the *Hostel* and *Saw* franchises have been described as "thinly veiled war allegories,"[8] the plot of the first *Hostel* in one case summarized as "a transposition into horror film terms of the animosity that the Bush administration's policies—the attack on Iraq, the extraordinary renditions and torture, the extra-legal prisoner limbo at Guantanamo and the CIA's black prisons—elicited around the world."[9] While it may be tempting to draw a direct allegorical parallel between films such as these and the fallout from September 11, Matt Hills highlighted the importance of seeing the *Saw* films not as outright metaphors, but rather that these movies "circle thematically around contemporary political controversies, without quite being 'about' them."[10] Whether it was the slow fade of its political relevance, the realization that its visceral bark was more powerful than its ideological bite, or simply that the formula had become stale, by the end of the 2000s, the popularity of films like *Hostel* and *Saw* were notably on the decline. Combine this with the rise of YouTube and the subsequent broader acceptance of and familiarity with amateur UGC aesthetics, and the climate was perfect for the mainstream return of found footage horror.

Although not manifesting the same intensity as *Hostel* and *Saw*, the legacy of 9/11 appears in contemporary found footage horror through the inclusion of diegetic surveillance footage, which is in some of the subgenre's most well-known recent entries—the *Paranormal Activity* franchise in particular—just as important (perhaps even more so) as the hand-held material. David Lyon has indicated that while surveillance certainly was not absent beforehand, it was in the aftermath of 9/11 that there was a widespread rise in awareness of just how much we are now being watched.[11] As demonstrated in his example of parents using hidden cameras to spy on their children's nannies, surveillance is far from an "us vs. them" scenario. Via the increase in access to technologies like mobile phones and GPS, we are often both the watchers and the watched.[12] The everyday matter-of-factness of surveillance has permeated many aspects of contemporary life, and as Adam L. Penenberg has noted, far from being frightened, we are on the whole accepting of it. Citing examples such as taking cash from an ATM machine to knowingly buying mobile phones that can be used as tracking devices, he observed that "they're not spy technologies—but they might as well be."[13] Surveillance is not considered a threat; it is even embraced as the foundation of many successful reality television programs such as *Survivor* which offers what Penenberg has described as "round-the-clock surveillance as entertainment."[14] *Paranormal Activity* underscores just how accepting we have become of the ubiquity of surveillance technology. Sébastien Lefait has usefully linked surveillance culture to the way that the first *Paranormal Activity* constructs its frights. "[The film] constantly reminds the spectators that the reality of the presence rests on their willing suspension of disbelief," he said. "In this regard, the film's specificity lies in the way it unilaterally associates the suspension of disbelief to the alleged revelatory power of the surveillance camera."[15]

The blockbuster success of the *Paranormal Activity* franchise effectively eradicated what by 2009 was the already-dwindling box office impact of the *Saw* franchise, which had dominated horror's lucrative Halloween period since 2004.[16] David Edelstein famously decried movies like *Saw* (James Wan, 2004), *Hostel* (Eli Roth, 2005), *Wolf Creek* (Greg McLean, 2005) and *The Devil's Rejects* (Rob Zombie, 2005) as "torture porn," extremely violent movies that had a sudden spike in popularity around the mid–2000s.[17] The name stuck, and is today the subgeneric label that for many immediately categorizes this group of films. But in his blurring of the horror and pornography body genres, Edelstein problematically repeats the merger of what Eithne Johnson and Eric Schaefer described as "hard-core gore" with "hard-core porn"[18] that marked the *Snuff* controversy in the United States in the mid–1970s (as discussed in Chapter Two). Adam Lowenstein has also challenged the term in his essay "Spectacle Horror and *Hostel*: Why 'Torture Porn' Does Not Exist." Opting instead for what he calls "spectacle horror," Lowenstein defines this less provocative term as "the staging of spectacularly explicit horror for purposes of audience admiration, provocation, and sensory adventure as much as shock or terror, but without necessarily breaking ties with narrative development or historical allegory."[19] From his perspective, spectacle horror provides a useful binary to understand the relationship between the *Saw* and *Paranormal Activities* films: It is the "loudness" of spectacle horror that marks it "as a mode of direct, visceral engagement with viewers,"[20] thus distinguishing it from "ambient horror," noted for its comparative quietness.

Edelstein based his definition of "torture porn" on its extreme nature, its location in mainstream film culture, and the inclusion of appealing and identifiable characters. Lowenstein rejects identification as a dominant means of addressing the spectator in spectacle horror and instead argued that it is more closely aligned to Tom Gunning's notion of the "cinema of attractions," as the spectacle of gore in these films functions as their central site of pleasure. Lowenstein also challenges Edelstein's claim that such films are specific to the contemporary era, placing them in the same historical trajectory as early execution films such as *The Execution of Mary, Queen of Scots* (Alfred Clark and William Heise, 1895) and *Electrocuting an Elephant* (Jacob Blair Smith and/or Edwin S. Porter, 1903). *Hostel* is similar to these films, he argued, in that it utilizes spectacle horror to tap into the viewer's desire to experience horror through emotion and sensation. In terms of the relationship between the horrors of the human rights atrocities in Baghdad at the Abu Ghraib correctional facility and *Hostel*, Edelstein contended the film seeks to act as a justification rather than a criticism of real-world torture. Through the close analysis of particular images, Lowenstein argued strongly this is not the case, and in fact that by utilizing the familiar mechanics of the horror genre *Hostel* places the spectator in the position of both torturer and their victim. In doing so, Roth's movie ultimately demands the audience accept some responsibility for the atrocities at Abu Ghraib.

Regardless of its name, the logic of "torture porn" or "spectacle horror" relies intrinsically upon the excessive visceral exposure of vulnerable bodies. Surely only so much can be seen: There is a limit to how much can be shown and in what contexts in a mainstream-friendly gore film. It is perhaps this that led to the dwindling of interest in Kevin Greutert's later installments, with *Saw VI* (2009) grossing the least of the franchise up to that point (although *Saw VII* [aka *Saw 3D*] saw some improvement), and *Hostel III* (Scott Spiegel, 2011) going straight to video.

So how far can horror film go? The answer seemed to be inescapable: out of the mainstream. Dutch director Tom Six's notorious *Human Centipede* (2010) and *Human Centipede 2: Full Sequence* (2011) only too graphically demonstrate just how far the ultraviolent envelope can be pushed in contemporary horror. Rising in part from the ashes of the mainstream popularity of "torture porn," these films were just as much (if not more) reminiscent of brutal genre entries from the New French Extremity movement, typified by

*Haute Tensio*n (Alexandre Aja, 2003), *Martyrs* (Pascal Laugier, 2008), *À l'intérieur* (Alexandre Bustillo and Julien Maury, 2007), and *Frontière(s)* (Xavier Gens, 2007). The *Paranormal Activity* franchise took up the mainstream box office horror mantle when the *Saw* franchise (and "spectacle horror"-"torture porn" more generally) waned, and the responsibility fell on those working outside the mainstream to experiment with just how far the boundaries of the contemporary horror film could be pushed.

Next to the "spectacle horror" of so-called "torture porn," found footage horror films in most cases eschew the dazzling effects and post-production gloss of movies like *Saw* and *Hostel*. Nevertheless, it is the near-infinite possibilities of what *could* be hiding in these more banal elements that is arguably where contemporary found footage horror gains its strength. In most found footage horror films, it is their quietness that grants the creaking door or the mysterious stick figures hanging from trees the ability to chill audiences. If nothing seems to happen in these films, it does so in strategic ways. The contrast is where the punch of these films is housed, and as Paul Schrodt eloquently noted, the *Paranormal Activity* franchise can be summarized as one where "mundane scenes of suburban life [are] punctuated by extremely un-mundane scenes of suburban life."[21]

Generational territorialism was always going to make it difficult for some critics to embrace as new a trick with which they were already familiar. Just as John Kenneth Muir generously tempered his 2010 review of *Paranormal Activity* by saying, "I don't want to be unkind and call this ... *Blair Witch* for Dummies, but *Paranormal Activity* is certainly ... designed for—shall we say—more mainstream audiences,"[22] a decade earlier Adrian Martin was less delicate in his rejection of *The Blair Witch Project*, calling it "a horror movie for those audiences who have yet to see any classic horror movies."[23] As the following section argues, however, these films may be more complex than they first appear. They were not necessarily critical darlings, but audiences still flocked to these movies in vast numbers. These films may lack the features that experts deem vital for "good" cinema, but it is perhaps their rejection of these traditions that provided *The Blair Witch Project* and *Paranormal Activity* with their powerful cultural lure.

FOUR

Revisiting *The Blair Witch Project*

The awe surrounding the disproportionate finances that fueled the highly publicized rags-to-riches success story of *The Blair Witch Project* (Daniel Myrick and Eduardo Sánchez, 1999)—by one account it cost only $35,000 to make but went on to take $248.3 million globally[1]—has now been redirected to other low-budget independent successes, most notably its subgeneric grandchild, the *Paranormal Activity* franchise. At the time of its initial release, critics appeared interested less in the feature film itself than they did the phenomena surrounding it. As James Keller put it, "[T]he only consistent topic for public discussion generated by the hype over the film was the hype itself,"[2] leaving the feature film's *minutiae* epiphenomenal at best, merely one of many textual curios to support its broader transmedia assault. Now over a decade later, there are new, younger audiences for whom discovering *The Blair Witch Project* is a different experience. For one thing, the brouhaha that marked its initial release has all but vanished. Unless located through Google searches, so too are the *Time* and *Newsweek* magazine covers, the rumors surrounding the actors' deaths, the near-hysterical praise by some and what in other cases was often scathing condemnation. It is therefore with some irony that the most visible relic of the phenomena today is the film itself. This chapter offers a reconsideration of *The Blair Witch Project* fourteen years after the initial phenomenon, without the focus on what was then the inescapable presence of the extradiegetic marketing pizzazz that dazzled so many at the time. With the power of hindsight, these elements are less diverting than they once were, allowing clearer insight into the film that lies at the phenomenon's core.

Keira McKenzie articulately summarized the *Blair Witch*'s plot as "a tale ... of students chasing a mystery that catches them,"[3] simultaneously capturing its tragic hubris and emphasizing the eloquence of its plot mechanics, the latter often ignored in lieu of the surface chaos of its formal aesthetics and ground-

breaking marketing and promotional strategies. The premise of *The Blair Witch Project* is economically stated in its now legendary introductory intertitle:

> In October of 1994, three student filmmakers disappeared in the woods near Burkittsville, Maryland, while shooting a documentary. A year later their footage was found.

Those film students were Heather Donahue, Michael C. Williams and Joshua Leonard (verisimilarly played by actors with the same name), and the subject of their documentary was the mythological figure of the Blair Witch. With her friend Josh responsible for filming and his friend Mike brought along to assist with sound, director Heather had spent two years researching and preparing the shoot in and around Burkittsville (ex–Blair) in Maryland. In their first filmed scene in the Black Woods, Heather reads a section from an antiquarian book titled *The Blair Witch Cult* aloud to camera, telling us about five men in the 19th century who were ritualistically slaughtered there, with implications that the Blair Witch was responsible for this and other gruesome murders that had plagued the town. *Vox pop* interviews with locals tell the legend of local hermit Rustin Parr who during the 1940s lured seven children to his isolated house in the woods where they were killed. As one local explains, Parr would take the children to the basement in pairs and make one face the corner while he tortured and murdered the other. When captured, Parr insisted that he committed the crimes only to appease the ghost of an 18th century witch named Elly Kedward—the Blair Witch—whom he claimed would only leave him alone if he murdered the children. With this basic plot outline propelling one of the most surprising blockbuster successes of the late 20th century, it is futile to completely jettison the significant debates that surrounded the broader *Blair Witch Project* phenomenon at the time. However, this chapter will also explore what the predominant focus on this meta-material allowed us to overlook. Looking back at the film and its critical treatments almost a decade and a half later allows further insight into the subgenre that *The Blair Witch Project* is responsible in large part for launching into the mainstream.

Productive Masochism: "Method Filmmaking" and Authorship

Aside from the preliminary prehistory outlined earlier in this book, *The Blair Witch Project*'s literary and cinematic ancestors have been broadly

Opposite: **Poster for *The Blair Witch Project* (1999) (Artisan Pics/The Kobal Collection).**

discussed. Myrick and Sánchez themselves have acknowledged the influence of films like *The Legend of Boggy Creek* (Charles B. Pierce, 1972),[4] while others have added a diverse range of titles to the list, including the Australian arthouse classic *Picnic at Hanging Rock* (Peter Weir, 1975), the Vietnam War movie *84C MoPic* (Patrick Sheane Duncan, 1989) and the documentary *Paradise Lost: The Child Murders at Robin Hood Hills* (Joe Berlinger and Bruce Sinofsky, 1996). Literary antecedents have also been flagged, such as the Brothers Grimm's *Hansel and Gretel,* Shakespeare's *Macbeth*, Henry James' novella *The Turn of the Screw* (1898) and Samuel Richardson's *Pamela: Or, Virtue Rewarded* (1740).[5] Peg Aloi identified a Gothic sensibility underscoring its basic plot with her observation that its protagonists "sally forth to cerate a film and stumble, lost, into a dark primal place where no help comes."[6] Bruce Alexander also detected elements of the Gothic in the film's treatment of the failures that riddle Heather, Josh and Mike's attempts to bridge the gap between childhood and adulthood.[7]

Considering its success, *The Blair Witch Project* can also be paradoxically viewed as a brutal procession of never-ending failures. Heather fails to finish her movie, while Josh and Mike fail to return their equipment on time. Technology fails to protect them: It does *not* manage to "filter ... reality" as Josh describes it, despite Heather's dedication to that belief. Neither the film's directors nor its cast have yet attained the level of success their fairytale rise suggested.[8] The documentary form fails to capture concrete material evidence of the Blair Witch herself and proof of what happened to the students: As Jane Roscoe noted, "we are left only with the knowledge that we cannot trust documentary form to tell the truth."[9] The supporting extratextual materials—the books, the websites, the *Curse of the Blair Witch* mockumentary, and even Joe Berlinger's 2000 sequel, the box office disaster *Book of Shadows: Blair Witch 2* (discussed in the next chapter)—fail to provide any real information to bridge the narrative gaps. Sarah L. Higley and Jeffrey Andrew Weinstock noted, "[T]he true horror ... of *BWP* is its bleak celebration of a spiritual nothingness which its ancillary texts and wild-goose chases end up confirming rather than denying."[10]

In terms of interpretation, there was arguably also a widespread failure to "read" the film's basic set-up correctly: It was simply so easy to confuse a film *about* amateur filmmaking for an actual amateur film. This of course was the result of the marketing push of the Blair Witch as an authentic, factual document. As Scott Dixon McDowell admitted, it took him numerous viewings to shift his verdict on *The Blair Witch Project* from "cinematically challenged" to "cinematically challenging."[11] The belief that the film's success was purely the result of good fortune rather than good filmmaking is most visible

Four. Revisiting The Blair Witch Project

in Sarah L. Higley's comparative analysis with *The Last Broadcast* (Stefan Avalos and Lance Weiler, 1998), a movie that she champions as superior and that was made before but released after *The Blair Witch Project*. Higley has contended *The Last Broadcast* was unfairly "overlooked"[12] because it was so much "more sophisticated." Higley stated:

> Remarks on the Internet Movie Database reveal that a number of viewers found *The Last Broadcast* "boring." Could this be because what it replicates and satirizes is the "discourse of sobriety"...? Or is it because it expected too much from a popular, teenage audience?[13]

While *The Last Broadcast* is a fascinating film in its own right, it and *Blair Witch* are very different beasts. Most immediately, the former lacks the fundamental experimental confidence of *The Blair Witch Project*. As will be discussed in the next chapter, *The Last Broadcast* also incorporates found footage but is not reliant wholly upon an appropriation of observational documentary codes and conventions in quite the same way that the way *Blair Witch* is. And unlike *The Last Broadcast*, *The Blair Witch Project* is not an amateur film as much as it is an independent production that employs a particular amateur filmmaking aesthetic in its pursuit of making a movie *about* amateur filmmaking.

This difference is crucial, as its ambiguity hinges on significant questions surrounding *The Blair Witch Project*'s approach to authorship. When Alexandra Juhasz referred to "the filmmakers' uncanny ability to look scared,"[14] for example, she is clearly not talking about Myrick and Sánchez but the three actors who play filmmakers: Donohue, Williams and Leonard. Statements like this are not incorrect, however, because of Myrick and Sánchez's technique that they branded "method filmmaking." Myrick described it as follows:

> It's just an approach from both the actors' side and the filmmaking side of reducing the process of the filmmaking technique. Basically, it's when you look around you, there are no filmmakers ... there are no crewmembers ... there are no cameras shooting the actors; they are shooting it themselves, so the process of filmmaking is as much a character as the actors themselves, and that was what our goal was. It was not to make the actors aware of the filmmaking process around them, and then we just kind of dubbed it the method filmmaking approach.[15]

After coming up with a basic script of primary plot points, Myrick and Sánchez spent three weeks scouting locations in the woods. Using hand-held GPS technology they were able to direct their cast between predetermined locations, although it was up to the actors to work out how to get to these points. Without the presence of a crew, the actors were able to remain in character much more than they could with a traditional stop-and-start filmmaking process, and it allowed them to respond more directly with the unknown elements of their circumstances. When arriving at each checkpoint, the cast would find fresh supplies for their cameras and notes from the directors regarding character development and upcoming scenes. The actors would deposit their tapes at these points, and it was through regular viewings of these—as well as by physically following the cast but remaining out of sight—that Myrick and Sánchez directed the film.

When recounting the trajectory of their post–*Blair Witch Project* careers, Sánchez recalled that because their film was so successful in creating a sense of authenticity around the premise that Heather, Joshua and Mike were the makers of the diegetic *Blair Witch Project*, many believed Myrick and Sánchez were little more than bystanders.[16] Obviously the directors consciously chose to obscure themselves behind the public-facing myth that its diegetic filmmakers created the film, but this obscurity also shifted the focus to the directorial and acting methods once the supposed secret was out. As Peg Aloi reminded us, although we are encouraged to believe that what we are watching was the unedited footage from the ill-fated film crew, Myrick and Sánchez carefully cut the final 81-minute product down from over 100 hours of raw footage.[17] Joseph S. Walker also observed that there is ample formal evidence within the text itself—such as the cutting between video and film—that indicates there is an external authority controlling this end product that is not the three student filmmakers whose story it follows.[18]

This rejection of Myrick and Sánchez's directorial imprint undermines the creativity behind employing this approach in the first place. While positioning her work firmly in the realm of experimental cinema, Laura U. Marks' essay "I Am Very Frightened by the Things I Film" provides useful insight into the power imbalances in documentary between filmmakers and their subjects that can be loosely applied to *The Blair Witch Project*, allowing a reconsideration of Myrick and Sánchez's "method filmmaking" technique. Some documentaries, Marks has argued, utilize the struggle between filmmaker and subject by challenging both the subjectivity of the filmmakers themselves and the truth claims inherent to documentary filmmaking—both major conceptual concerns of *The Blair Witch Project*. Marks saw this struggle manifesting in the controversial films of Japanese filmmaker Kazuo Hara, whose work consciously seeks to reverse the traditional relationship between subject and filmmaker. It is the filmmaker whose identity is destabilized, and the world that is shown results from that confusion.

By doing so, Marks noted that Hara willingly surrenders what is the traditionally masculine dominance of the filmmaker role, and he is open about his own personal frailties. Certainly the former is true of *The Blair Witch Project* on a superficial level at least, where male directors relinquish control to a team of amateur filmmakers led (diegetically) by a woman. In both *The Emperor's Naked Army Marches On* (1987) and *Extreme Private Eros: Love Song 1974* (1974), Hara deliberately places himself in a position of weakness next to the subjects of his film. It is this adversarial relationship that propels his films, particularly in the ways that the power struggles feminize the director, and that by actively allowing this to happen he makes his authorial imprint. Identifying a "productive masochism"[19] in Hara's work, Marks refers to Norman Bryson's 1988 essay "The Gaze in the Expanded Field" which uses both Western and Japanese philosophy to place Western assumptions about the gaze into perspective. This allows her to argue that masochism as it plays out in Hara's films need not need to be destructive, bur can be considered constructive.

The fictional world of *The Blair Witch Project* is obviously vastly different from Hara's documentaries, but some of Marks' ideas are applicable to the logic behind "method filmmaking," especially in relation to Myrick and Sánchez's own unique brand of "productive masochism." In this sense, control and authorship function as a loose concept that can be reconceived as a creative—and productive—group experiment. The raw, engrossing performances that "method filmmaking" provoked were so convincing that many were unsure if Heather, Josh and Mike were acting at all. Sánchez at least remained clear: When Lynden Barber asked him outright, "Is it acting ... this is real fear, surely?" his reply was as blunt as it was revealing: "It's real acting."[20]

Intertextual Complicity: Consuming The Blair Witch *Project*

One of the reasons why confusion about *The Blair Witch Project*'s amateur status existed was simply that the idea that it was an amateur film that "made it big" was a major component of its marketing strategy. With so much of its authenticity relying on the implication it was a genuine found artifact, its status as an independent film helped distinguish it from the typical Hollywood product. This independent-underdog-conquers-the-world story was crucial to the marketing machine that was ironically grounded squarely in the commercial Hollywood film industry. James Castonguay's essay "The Political Economy of the Indie Blockbuster: Fandom, Intermediality and *The Blair Witch Project*" explored precisely what the commercial motivations were behind the marketing of *Blair Witch* as a supposed indie marvel, a construction that ignored the vast amounts of cash that Artisan spent in the promotion of the film.[21] Rather than a victory for independent filmmaking, Castonguay contended that *The Blair Witch Project* was instead evidence of how independent filmmaking has been swallowed up by Hollywood, and noted its "political economy ... may ultimately function to propagate a myth of independent cinema by falsely suggesting that this film disproved the rule of New Hollywood's hegemony in an age of unprecedented media conglomeration."[22] For David Banesh, this myth of the supposed indie victory that was peddled so furiously at the time was also a distraction from the film's inherent and extreme diegetic nihilism, where the nervousness surrounding its myriad failures "are repressed and turned into a utopian affirmation of our contemporary moment through the valorization of our imagination (self) coupled with the indie myth of good-old American economic self-reliance."[23] The narrative and thematic bleakness of *The Blair Witch Project* was effectively trumped by a much more digestible and optimistic meta-narrative.

In one of the most well-known critical treatments of *The Blair Witch Project*, J.P. Telotte examined the film's ancillary texts—particularly the official website—and argued that they confirmed the conventional relationship between audience and marketing, and made it virtually impossible to fully engage with the film without these supplementary materials. He suggested that the film itself was simply one of many artifacts offered to support the information given on the website, and not vice versa.[24] Chuck Tryon also argued that it was difficult to separate the marketing and promotional material about *The Blair Witch Project* from the feature film itself,[25] and Keller noted that it was highly unusual because of this, as audiences enjoyed the novelty because they were not commonly asked to seek essential information beyond the film text itself. Like Telotte, Keller argued that the film was a "supplementary text" to this external material, rather than the other way around.[26] Castonguay warned against praising such supposed subversions as they serve the same corporate motives as more traditionally presented cinematic products. He ultimately identified this not as "progressive interactivity" but rather a form "of inter-passivity in which Internet users actively embrace the pleasures of consumerism and celebrate the profit-driven practices of Hollywood film production and distribution."[27]

Examining online discussions about the film's mythology, Margrit Schreier identified a conscious surrendering of rationality and logic as participants allowed themselves to enter Myrick and Sánchez's narrative universe. However, she noted, this was a complex submission:

> There are some recipients who willingly enter into the game of the directors yet do so with a kind of double consciousness: They keep themselves deliberately ignorant of the fictional status of the film, with a view to a higher enjoyment of the ambiguities, yet knowing full well on a metalevel

that keeping themselves ignorant is necessary only because they already know that the film is fiction.[28]

These observations collectively suggest an important point: Many of us participated in the *Blair Witch* "game" because we consciously *wanted* to. Expanding on Jane Roscoe's observation in 2000 that this was the case for many in the United States, Angela Ndalianis noted that because the film was released in Australia over four months later, issues of its authenticity were a moot point. Despite "the cat being out of the proverbial bag," she observed it still had little impact on its box office success. Emphasizing how its marketing functioned as an early ARG (alternate reality game),[29] Ndalianis suggested that for Australian viewers "the eventual experience of *The Blair Witch Project* was a different one in that not many viewers were creeped out by the 'based on real events' hoax." She continued, "[T]he pleasure now circulated around both film and extratextual information being about a game of horror." Even those for whom the issues of authenticity were no longer relevant were still able to actively partake in this "game about participating in the production of horror."[30] We can ask how satisfying a game that was, with as many seemingly titillated as were frustrated by *Blair Witch*'s refusal to provide any satisfactory

In search of *The Blair Witch Project*'s Heather, Josh and Mike (Artisan Pics/The Kobal Collection).

closure. For all the information that circulated around the film itself, there were still no answers or explanations. The marketing may have been viral, but so was the seemingly inescapable sense of futility inherent to the movie's thematic core.

The most insightful critical explorations into *Blair Witch* written at the time of its release tended to strike a balance between form, context and content. As stated previously, however, *Blair Witch*'s status has changed significantly since its initial release and the issues of intertextuality that dominated discourse surrounding it at the time—particularly the information supplied in what was often claimed to be the primary material on the website and/or in the *Curse of the Blair Witch* television special—have today been substantially reduced. Once deemed more important than the film itself, these elements have over time been reduced to mere vapor trails in the popular memory, materially relegated to the ghost town of the DVD extras menu or a small subsection on its Wikipedia page. It is in light of this that the following analysis of the feature film itself is positioned, considering it not as incidental but as a complex and dense text in its own right. It will suspend a fascination with its satellite material briefly to consider what the movie itself can tell us.

"*Did you ever see* Deliverance*?"*

Perhaps the most immediately arresting feature of *The Blair Witch Project* for audiences at the time of its release was its shaky hand-held camera work. Roscoe and Hight have observed that in documentary, this type of camcorder material "serves to heighten the feeling of seeing the world unfold before our eyes."[31] Like viewers of *Cloverfield* eight years later, audiences complained when watching *Blair Witch* of feeling nauseous because the hand-held camerawork evoked a very real biological sensation of motion sickness. "What happens is the camera and the brain mismatch messages," explained clinical audiologist John Risey. "Because you are seated and you are still, your brain gets wrong information that you are in motion," resulting in the widely held complaint of queasiness when watching the film.[32] Heather diegetically shares her fascination with the affective elements of her craft in the film's first few minutes: As the doomed trio share a lighthearted moment shopping for supplies, she playfully zooms in and out of a packet of marshmallows, emphasizing its softness and flagging her awareness that film is capable of engaging the haptic as much as the aural and visual. This consciously flags an understanding of tactility that creates a sense of immersion that will dominate the film, both diegetically and in terms of its broader reception. Striking also is the film's predominant black-and-white cinematography. The importance of this cannot be understated in terms of the linkage of the film with indie horror filmmaking traditions, most notably George A. Romero's *Night of the Living Dead* (1968). Perhaps even more significant is the association between black-and-white photographs and film and video footage in relation to documentary filmmaking codes and conventions. Roscoe and Hight note that in mock-documentaries, footage seems more authoritative if it is black-and-white because it stands as an artifact from a time before the mass manipulation of the image in digitally recorded images that has become so familiar.[33]

Considerations of Heather as a filmmaker have generally focused on her obsession with control: keeping control of the shoot, keeping control of the camera and, despite her best efforts, even attempting to keep control of the reality of their bleak predicament. As the director of the diegetic project, Heather is far more complex than the control-freak "bitch" that she is accused of being. Despite being held responsible by Josh and Mike for getting them lost (her guilt supposedly manifested through her refusal to admit that they have gone off track), Heather was aware of the potential dangers of camping, as illustrated in an early shot in the film of her copy of Bradford Angier's classic *How to Stay Alive in the Woods* (1969); that the book was shown upside down suggests that she inverted its lessons, foreshadowing the events that were to follow. Heather also had a clear directorial vision: She wanted to "avoid cheese" in her documentary, and "to present this in as straightforward a way as possible." Scenes of Heather shooting the documentary in these early stages establish her understanding of her role. Both the scene at the cemetery where she discusses the graves of the children in Burkittsville and atop Coffin Rock where she reads from the antiquarian book *The Blair Witch Cult* align her with expository documentary's authoritative narrator, implying her faith in directorial omniscience. She was condemned by the other characters for this false sense of control, but up to a certain point it was not an illusion: Heather felt she had control over her project simply because as its director, she did.

Of the three, Heather is also the most respectful to their environment and its history. In this light, Josh's carelessness in disturbing a cairn at a makeshift cemetery is a key moment of the story's development because it appears to prompt an increase in unusual activity. In response, Heather gasps and says, "You didn't just knock that over, please tell me you didn't just knock that over. That's not very nice." She rebuilds the pile of rocks and blows it a kiss noting, "You can't be too careful." Heather is in tune with what is and what is not appropriate in this space, and despite her insistence that she is in control and that they are not lost, it is only after the appearance of the film's iconic stick doll figures in the trees—not Josh and Mike's berating of her—

that she finally admits that they are lost and that she does not know what to do. Heather can identify and understands the risks of nature disrupted.

The scale of what is occurring here is arguably much larger than simple character alignment between Heather and the witch. It constructs the wilderness more broadly as a feminine space, standing in opposition to traditions that code it as masculine. There is an important difference here. If the woods are feminized solely because of the witch's dominance over them, there is by default a troubling ideological aspect that suggests the woods are evil *because* they are feminized. However, there is evidence within the film that indicates this is not the only way to read its gendering processes, and that it may be more ambiguous. In terms of gender politics, the very reference to witches in the film's title evokes the often-violent historical mistreatment of women spanning centuries. Barbara Creed has highlighted the presence of witches in the panoply of familiar horror movie monsters, and noted this figure is commonly characterized as a grotesque hag. During the European witch trials between the 15th and 18th centuries, witches were accused of everything from castration to cannibalism, and Creed noted they were even held responsible for phenomena like the plague.[34] *The Malleus Maleficarium* was written by Dominicans Heinrich Kramer and James Sprenger in 1484 for the Catholic Church, and was used by inquisitors as a manual to assist in their persecution of witches. Amongst other terrifying misogynies, this official document details at length why female sexuality was so specifically suited to this particular affront to God. Of the history of the witch more generally, Creed states:

> The witch is defined as an abject figure in that she is represented within patriarchal discourses as an implacable enemy of the symbolic order. She is thought to be dangerous and wily, capable of drawing on her evil powers to wreak destruction on the community. The witch sets out to unsettle boundaries between the rational and irrational, symbolic and imaginary. Her evil powers are seen as part of her "feminine" nature; she is closer to nature than man and can control forces in nature such as tempests, hurricanes and storms.[35]

Tracing the appearance of the witch as a figure of terror in film back to *The Wizard of Oz* (1939) and the Val Lewton–produced *The Seventh Victim* (1943), Creed lists a number of famous horror movies about witches including the Barbara Steele vehicles *Black Sunday* (1960) and *The She Beast* (1966), Dario Argento's *Suspiria* (1977) and *Inferno* (1980), and the film that forms the basis of her case study of monstrous-femininity in horror films about witches, Brian DePalma's *Carrie* (1976). While horror film emphasizes the sexuality of the witch in regard to her monstrosity, Creed noted it simultaneously plays down traditions that link this figure to more positive roles, such as healers.[36]

Four. Revisiting The Blair Witch Project

For Linda Badley, film and television in the 1990s offered a reconfiguration of the witch, responding to a postfeminist reclamation of the figure "as the outspokenly pro-woman woman, the bitch." This reclamation was celebrated in movies such as *The Craft* (1996) and *Practical Magic* (1998) and television series such as *Sabrina the Teenage Witch* (1996–2003), *Buffy the Vampire Slayer* (1997–2003) and *Charmed* (1998–2006). *Blair Witch* can be understood as a denunciation of this updated image, and in their desire "to bring back today's witch's repressed older, weirder sister," Myrick and Sánchez rejected the "postfeminist icon *par excellence*, the witch contained, domesticated." For Badley, this new witch had become "soft, white, liberal, politically correct," and in *Blair Witch* Heather represents all the things this postfeminist witch stands for: the independent, determined, single-minded "bitch." No longer celebrated, she is now punished: representing the witch as she has been "reinvented by feminism," Heather the postfeminist "bitch" is penalized for her deviations. Badley claimed that *Blair Witch* could therefore on one hand be understood as "an anti-feminist response to female power in general." At the same time, she simultaneously acknowledged that in the 1990s, "media witches had gotten too sweet, pretty and complacent" and that the "*Blair Witch* reinvested the horror film with respect for the 'woods'—the power in 'female' nature—for Kali, Medusa and the Crone."[37]

These tensions manifest in *Blair Witch*'s complex construction of gender and its representation in ways perhaps far more fluid than commonly assumed. It flags this by directly encouraging an intertextual parallel with the most notorious American wilderness thriller of the 1970s. When Josh casually asks Heather, "Did you ever see *Deliverance*?" he appears to simply mention John Boorman's 1972 film in passing as a way of illustrating his suspicion that they are being harassed by locals in the woods. However, of the 100+ hours of footage Myrick and Sánchez painstakingly edited down to that final 81 minutes, it is reasonable to assume that even the most casual aside should not be dismissed. This *Deliverance* reference functions as a conceptual key that unlocks how gender and its representation function in *Blair Witch*. Carol J. Clover has included gender politics and *Deliverance* in her discussion of the rape-revenge film, and noted the fictional Cahulawassee River in Georgia where it is set is frequently referred to by the film's male protagonists as a "she." Faced with the looming threat of development, the river itself becomes a symbolically violated feminine figure, mirroring the literal rape of soft, feminized Bobby (Ned Beatty) by local hillbillies in the infamous "squeal like a pig" scene. *Deliverance* effectively presents a film about gender politics in a context where gender representation is a malleable and not ascribed through the biological configuration of its cast; by flagging this film, *Blair Witch* suggests it too may be doing something similar, and opens up new possible interpretations of the film as a whole.

Keeping in mind that it is Josh who makes this reference to *Deliverance*, it is fruitful to summarize the film's broader character development:

- Before leaving on their trip, Heather is excited but calm and in control. Josh appears relaxed and friendly. Mike seems a little distant, and even at their hotel is unhappy with Heather filming "behind the scenes."
- When they first hear noises outside their tent, Mike is scared and hides in the tent while Heather and Josh investigate.
- Mike throws a tantrum when he realizes they will need to stay an extra night camping in the woods. Josh attempts to maintain a calm environment, as he and Heather again discuss what may be responsible for the increasingly unusual occurrences.
- After the map vanishes, Josh loses control and becomes hostile to Heather. When it is revealed that Mike threw the map away, both Heather and Josh attack him verbally and physically. Mike laughs, clearly finding it difficult to deal with their traumatic circumstances.
- After the stick doll figures appear and Josh's belongings are covered in slime, Josh becomes increasingly hostile and upset. He attacks Heather verbally, and now it is Mike who seeks to maintain calm.
- The morning after Josh disappears, Heather and Mike are frightened but quickly begin to cooperate with each other. Although terrified, their interactions are kind and warm.

Combined with the fact that we never actually see the witch, this presents a possibility that is not widely discussed in academic treatments although it is often voiced in fan forums: that Josh fulfills the role of the so-called "witch." The evidence supporting this is ample. Both Mike and Josh suggest the sounds outside their tent at night are locals, which is never shown to be either true or untrue and thus remains a possibility. There is no reason why the cairns and stick doll figures could not have been built by these locals in an attempt to scare the young filmmakers, whose presence townsfolk were aware of from the *vox pops* they did earlier in the movie. As their situation worsens, Josh's calm demeanor becomes hostile to the point of viciousness. It is he who upsets the cairn, thus in his own mind "cursing" himself for disrupting the environment and provoking whatever supernatural aspects he has ascribed to them. While Heather notes that both she and Mike are on the "brink of losing it," Mike recognizes that Josh's sanity has *already* broken, that "he's lost it." If Josh is insane, it is quite reasonable that he may have wandered off on his own volition: that it is he they hear screaming in the night after he has gone missing,

Four. Revisiting The Blair Witch Project

not because he is being tortured by a real-life witch, but because he has (as Mike has already identified) stepped over the brink of sanity, and has now potentially succumbed to his own deranged fantasies about the myth that has led them to getting lost in the first place. It is possible that he has self-mutilated and menacingly left a macabre, bloody parcel of teeth and hair for Heather and Mike to find outside their tent (his hair is long, incidentally: a traditional marker of femininity). It is possible, when Mike follows the sound of Josh's voice down to the basement of the abandoned house, that it is Josh himself who awaits off-camera. It is possible that it is Josh who attacks Heather while Mike stands in the corner with his back to the camera, recalling the story of the Burkittsville local earlier in the film about the Rustin Parr murders. In this sense, it is quite possible that Josh is the Blair Witch "herself."

Obviously, the extratextual material stands firmly in opposition to such an interpretation, and *Book of Shadows: Blair Witch 2* makes it clear that there was no house on the site where Heather, Mike and Josh's tapes were found. However, according to the internal logic of the first film alone, there is strong evidence—supported by allusions to gender fluidity indicated by the significant reference to *Deliverance*—that Josh has gone insane and is responsible for Mike and Heather's deaths or disappearances. This allows two further possibilities: Either Josh has become a Rustin Parr figure, used by the witch to commit her heinous wishes, or—and most rationally if we are not strong believers in the paranormal—*there is no witch*. Josh has simply gone insane and succumbed to the mythology of the witch in a crazed submission to his own insane fantasies, propelling him to maintain the myth by (probably) murdering his peers.

So why does the extratextual information make this interpretation untenable? Why did critics, academics and audiences embrace this external material so enthusiastically? It was new and novel, but it also actively sought to maintain the myth of the witch, keeping the blame directed away from the ambivalent gendering of the film's protagonists. If there is no witch, if there is no supernatural activity behind the events that we see in the movie, then another collapse can be added to the list of *Blair Witch*'s seemingly endless inventory of slippages: not only have the lines between sanity and insanity collapsed, but the very foundations that govern how gender is represented have also become unstable. To protect the integrity of those boundaries we instead cling to the extratextual evidence even over the narrative logic of the film itself. We embrace the supernatural fable of an evil woman and condemn Heather as a control-freak "bitch" who doomed innocent men who were doing her a favor. And we do all this against the film's own internal logic so masculinity can remain intact. We default to blaming women because we have a cultural history that encourages us to do precisely that: It is certainly easier than questioning broader representational constructions of masculinity. Despite all this, however, it is still not an easy task to paint *The Blair Witch Project* as particularly progressive.

Technology, Gender and the Gaze

There is no real mystery why it was so easy to blame the Blair Witch "herself" despite evidence within the film suggesting this alternate reading. Aside from the history of the demonization of witches as outlined by Badley and Creed, an examination of Heather's supposed "crime" leads to the heart of how *Blair Witch* positions gender in terms of technology and the mechanics of the spectatorial gaze. Most obviously, Heather is deemed responsible simply because she admits to it herself in the film's most iconic scene, her fourth-wall shattering confession at the film's climax:

> I'm so sorry for everything that has happened because in spite of what Mike says, now it is my fault. Because it was my project and I insisted on everything. I insisted we weren't lost. I insisted we keep going. I insisted we walk south. Everything had to be my way and this is where we've ended up. And it's all because of me we're here now: hungry and cold and hunted. I love you, Mom and Dad. I am so sorry. It was never my intention to hurt anyone and I hope that's clear.

This self-flagellation indicates a crucial cultural rupture encapsulated by her statement at the end of this soliloquy: "I'm scared to close my eyes and I'm scared to open them." As Linda C. Badley succinctly observed, "as the project's 'tough-minded director in charge,' Heather represents a serious breach in having taken possession of the conventionally male—and often murderous—gaze."[38] Although Heather is not necessarily the person behind the camera on every shot in the film, it is made very clear that she is the project's authoritative directorial presence. Even just by attempting to dominate the traditionally masculine gaze of the camera, the film suggests Heather was engaging in an uphill battle. As Josh famously observed, filming through the camera is "totally like filtered reality, man. It's like you can pretend everything is not quite the way it is." The way it is, of course, is that men film women. Heather challenged these boundaries and—like so many other elements of the film—met with failure.

As discussed elsewhere in this book, this tendency to assume a sadistic and dominant male perspective was established in Laura Mulvey's foundation 1972 essay "Visual Pleasure and Narrative Cinema." Heather fights with every last breath against the tendency of cinema to make her a subject, struggling to master the gaze rather than be its subject. At significant moments in the film when things go askew, when the camera turns on her (both literally and metaphorically), the way that she is shot shows her struggling to escape its gaze. The manner in which she responds and the way she is shot illustrates just how intuitively she has attempted to subvert the cinematic gaze. Out in the woods, Heather frequently wiggles like a worm on a pin when the camera tries to film her: When she admits to Josh on-camera that the map has gone, the camera appears to be incapable of capturing her. She averts her eyes and looks out of frame, and when she finally admits, "I don't have the map," her eyes are completely out of shot. Similarly, while her weeping eyes and famously dripping nose feature centrally in the confession at the end of the film, her mouth is predominantly out of frame. She is simultaneously gagged and speaking, just as she is "scared to close" her eyes and "scared to open them." During Josh's malicious attack where he repeatedly asks her from behind the camera "What's your motivation?" he mockingly zooms in and out from her face pressing for an answer as to why she keeps filming. He mimics her lighthearted shot of the marshmallows at the beginning of the film, emphasizing the instinct of the masculine gaze to reduce female flesh—and a woman's suffering—to a soft, accessible commodity. This assault may not be explicitly sexual but it is framed around the visual language of gender difference. The weeping Heather cannot escape this assaultive gaze, forcing her to confess, "It's all I fucking have left." The camera is more than a device of control for Heather: It is a weapon to deflect the kind of aggressive objectification of women that Josh typifies in this sequence. If Josh and Mike react strongly to her filming them, it is arguably as much because it is a position as men that they simply are not used to and are deeply uncomfortable with. They are threatened that on some level Heather is attempting to demasculinize them.

By blurring the distinctions between gender and its representational mechanics—rendering men as objects and granting herself a subjective,

Heather (Heather Donohue) in *The Blair Witch Project* (Daniel Myrick and Eduardo Sánchez, 1999) (Artisan Pics/The Kobal Collection).

dominant gaze as director—Heather has transgressed a fundamental rule of conventional filmmaking. Thus, when Heather says, "I'm scared to close my eyes and I'm scared to open them," she articulates the paradox of her position as a woman filmmaker: With dominant film traditions intent on keeping her in her place in front of (as opposed to behind) the camera, her failed attempts to thwart these roles render her effectively damned if she does and damned if she doesn't. This does not bode well for the final ideological conclusions of *Blair Witch* in terms of its gender politics, as despite its ambiguous gendering it still can be read as being one where the feminine and female are coded negatively. Josh may be the guilty party, but that is precisely because he has adopted the feminine role of "witch." As for Heather, Christina Lane's reading is as brutal as it is accurate:

> In comparison to the industry support that benefited Sánchez and Myrick, the road for independent women's film looks a lot like the menacing scenery of the low-budget horror flick. Is it any mystery that the Sánchez-Myrick project sustains its own visibility through a singular fetishized image—that of its aspiring filmmaker-female protagonist breaking down into tears as she shines an ominous flashlight on her face and apologizes profusely for ever picking up a camera in the first place? Does she really owe us, or the male members of her crew, an apology? Did we really need to see our indie woman filmmaker reduced to a sniveling, groveling victim?[39]

Whether this is an outright act of misogyny on the part of Myrick and Sánchez themselves is open to speculation. Even giving them the benefit of the doubt, however, the result is still bitter: The best-case scenario means this is just one of many failures in the film as a whole. The only real ideological hope for the film's gender politics is to throw Heather's struggle onto the ever-growing pile of ashes that *Blair Witch* casts in its nihilistic wake.

The alternating between 16mm film and High 8 video is therefore worthy of consideration. Heather makes it clear throughout the film that the material she wishes to use for her final finished documentary will be in black-and-white 16mm, while video is to record the behind-the-scenes, making-of elements of their journey. Throughout the film, she begs Josh to record on film significant moments such as the discovery of the stick doll figures hanging from trees, imploring him, "Please, I've got to get this on 16!" Earlier, she explains this at length after a night where they had been disturbed by strange sounds outside their tent:

> I wake up and all of the sudden shit's going down, and all I can think is I gotta get it. I gotta get it all ... all I wanna get it on sound get it on 16. If we can see anything I want to see it on 16.

Superficially, this is simply Heather striving to have the highest quality footage for her school assignment, but there is a significant underlying assumption: She deems 16mm as more authoritative and valid than video footage. At stake here is a tension between old and new media, but even more importantly, between old and new ways of looking. She is challenging the latter simply by virtue of her directing a film rather than being subjected to the camera's conventional masculine gaze. Despite herself, Heather therefore defaults to similar traditional filmmaking hierarchies as the ones she sets out to challenge.

In her distinction between film and video, Heather also flags crucial technological differences between private and public space. The video footage is for her own records, documenting the "documentary"-making process, while the 16mm records material for public consumption. Like so many other binaries by the end of the film, however, these too collapse: The lines between private and public, "documentary" and "diary," between old ways and new ways of looking are rendered futile. That the final film released in cinemas was a combination of the 16mm black-and-white footage and the color video effectively flattened out the distinctions Heather had made, making the story of their privately experienced horror a publicly digestible spectacle. And as such, like every other aspect of their ill-fated trip, her struggles as a female filmmaker attempting to grapple the gaze out of the hands of the traditional male keepers was also exposed as inherently doomed. For better or for worse, *The Blair Witch Project* exposed the conceptual dangers inherent in making assumptions about the construction of gender, the mechanics of realism, the trustworthiness of technology and the documentary project as a whole. That its conclusions on all counts were so steadfastly bleak and inescapably problematic make it easy to understand why its supplementary materials were so enthusiastically embraced at the time of its release.

Five

The Vanishing of the Real

Between 1999's *The Blair Witch Project* and the cinema release ten years later of the first *Paranormal Activity* film, found footage horror style developed and consolidated. As the introduction to this section already suggested, mainstream attention during this period was in large part focused on so-called "torture porn" horror, typified by the *Saw* and *Hostel* franchises. Post–*Blair Witch*, horror filmmakers therefore had the opportunity for subgeneric experimentation without the pressures of appeasing the box office, which while financially challenging no doubt allowed an autonomy they perhaps would not have had if the intense mainstream attention on found footage horror surrounding *Blair Witch* had been maintained. Some of the films produced in the early half of the period between *Blair Witch* and *Paranormal Activity*'s mainstream cinema release would draw the attention of horror fans, such as *The Last Horror Movie* (Julian Richards, 2003) and *Behind the Mask: The Rise of Leslie Vernon* (Scott Glosserman, 2006), despite them remaining relatively unheard of to broader audiences. Other titles, however—many of which will be discussed in this chapter—may not have been as well received by fans or have attained necessarily wide distribution. The arrival of YouTube in 2005 brought user-generated content and its particular brand of amateur aesthetics to the fore, no doubt responsible to some degree for the noticeable spike in the production of found footage horror from 2007 onwards. The years 2007 and 2008 saw the appearance of more commercially viable found footage horror titles such as *Diary of the Dead* (George A. Romero, 2007), *[Rec]* (Jaume Balagueró and Paco Plaza, 2007), and *Cloverfield* (Matt Reeves, 2008), leading up to the widespread mainstream release of *Paranormal Activity* in 2009.

Found footage horror now formally denotes the ubiquity of this specific subgeneric horror style that developed during this period, rather than necessarily containing a genuine claim of authenticity or "realness." It was in the period between *Blair Witch* and *Paranormal Activity* that this system under-

Five. The Vanishing of the Real

went rapid development, eradicating the threat of the real inherent to ancestors like *Cannibal Holocaust* (Ruggero Deodato, 1980) and snuff-fictions and replacing them with movies understood as adopting this authentic style. In doing so, found footage horror has become a subgeneric playground for audiences who appreciate the pleasures of this "pretending-to-be-real" experience, allowing them to consciously engage with the films on those terms. In her examination of horror texts that successfully utilized viral marketing and transmedia storytelling, Angela Ndalianis concisely identified this fundamental shift between "really believing" and "pretending to really believe":

> Since the release of *The Blair Witch Project*, entertainment media have undergone dramatic transformations that amplify the performative potential of multiple modes of media reception that center on the same narrative premise. The emphasis on playing the illusion that the media fiction is real is central to the performance. The key words in this instance are "play" and "performance": The participant is invited to literally play and become part of a performance *as if it's real.*[1]

This sense of play is crucial to found footage horror, also. Audiences now do not have to believe or even suspect a film is a genuine documentation of something that actually happened to be able to playfully enjoy *pretending* that it might be the case.

In the wake of *Blair Witch*'s phenomenal success, the near-overnight appearance of parodies and knock-offs illustrated how just readily adaptable the signature codes and conventions of Myrick and Sánchez's indie hit were. Comedies such as *The Bogus Witch Project* (Steve Agee, 2000), *The Tony Blair Witch Project* (Michael A. Martinez, 2000), *Scary Movie* (Keenen Ivory Wayans, 2000) and even Cartoon Network's *The Scooby Doo Project* (1999) all brazenly riffed on the original film's form and premise, as did *The Blair Kitch Project* (Georgios Papaioannou, 2002), *Da Hip Hop Witch* (Dale Resteghini, 2000) and *The Black Witch Project* (Velli, 2001). Further indication of just how reproducible the defining features of *Blair Witch* were was the enthusiasm and speed with which it was incorporated into pornography, with movies like *The Erotic Witch Project* (John Bacchus, 2000) appearing almost immediately. The success of Jim Wynorski's *Bare Wench* series is particularly notable as this franchise ironically demonstrated far greater longevity than the original across its four entries: *The Bare Wench Project* (2000), *Bare Wench Project 2: Scared Topless* (2001), *Bare Wench 3: Path of the Wicked* (2002), and *The Bare Wench Project 4: Uncensored* (2003).

Pornographers and comedy directors were not the only people interested in cashing in on the success of the 1999 film. Released for Halloween 2000, director Joe Berlinger's *Book of Shadows: Blair Witch 2* was a commercial and critical disaster and deviated from the original in a number of crucial ways. Aside from the notable increase of gore and nudity, the most jarring feature was its determined move away from the found footage of the original. Satirically addressing the hype that surrounded the first film's release, it followed a group of "*Blair Witch* tourists"[2] in Burkittsville under the guidance of Jeff (Jeffrey Donovan), a *Blair Witch* fanatic with a history of mental illness. While it does not construct verisimilitude in the same way as its predecessor, it still uses diegetic cameras in significant ways and it attempts to attain authenticity through the inclusion of film clips of real-world celebrities such as Jay Leno, Conan O'Brien and Roger Ebert discussing the *Blair Witch* phenomenon. It is densely intertextual, not only in the context of these overt appearances but also by flagging Frederick Wiseman's controversial documentary *Titticut Follies* (1967) and of course through its primary reference to the *Blair Witch* marvel itself. It is more accurate to position *Book of Shadows* as being set primarily in the universe of the original *Blair Witch*'s film release, rather than the fictional universe *per se*. In slipping into horror as the narrative progresses, it attempts to remystify the first film, insisting that even proximal relationships to Burkittsville come under the Blair Witch curse.

Sarah Higley has examined the relationship of *Book of Shadows* to a previous documentary by its director Joe Berlinger about the West Memphis Three case in *Paradise Lost: The Child Murders at Robin Hood Hills* (Joe Berlinger and Bruce Sinofsky, 1996). Having noted parallels between the documentary and *Blair Witch*'s video-packet design, and the fact that Myrick and Sánchez based their original *Blair Witch* website on the *Paradise Lost* one, Higley convincingly argued that *Book of Shadows* is just as closely related to *Paradise Lost* as it is the original *Blair Witch* film in its central interrogation of the unreliability of technology.[3] The climax of *Book of Shadows* relies on a terrifying discrepancy between what the characters experience and what cameras record them doing (often filmed by diegetic hand-held camera or surveillance footage), and as such for Higley *Book of Shadows* "implicates both *The Blair Witch Project* and his previous documentaries in the complex technology of illusion and audience reception." She continued, "[I]t literally brings documentary and Hollywood film fiction together in a movie about the unreliable camera—the malevolent and bewitched camera—and the power of the media to shape the emotional decisions of its viewers and lawmakers."[4]

In many ways typical of the movies *Blair Witch* inspired, *The St. Francisville Experiment* was released in the same year as *Book of Shadows* but to much less fanfare. Director Ted Nicolaou had previously demonstrated an interest in the critical and fantastic potential of audio-visual technology in his joyful cult masterpiece *TerrorVision* (1987), but *The St. Francisville Exper-*

iment—like *Blair Witch*—is tonally lacking in his earlier film's gleeful flamboyance. Unlike *Blair Witch*, however, *The St. Francisville Experiment* is closer structurally to *Curse of the Blair Witch* in its incorporation of found footage with other documentary-style material such as interviews, newspaper clippings, photographs and illustrations. The movie follows four people (a psychic, a history student, a film student and a leader to coordinate the exercise) who investigate a Louisiana house said to be the residence of the 19th century sadist Madame Delphine LaLaurie, thus also sharing the *Blair Witch*'s linkage of American history with monstrous femininity. While experiencing a number of increasingly frightening paranormal encounters (including a crashing light fitting, which would soon become a signature motif across the *Paranormal Activity* franchise), the protagonists of *The St. Francisville Experiment* survive, although traumatized by their experience. In the years between *Blair Witch* and the rise of YouTube, a number of other horror films would appear that— like *The St. Francisville Experiment*—incorporate found footage with codes and conventions appropriated not only from observational documentary film but also from other documentary modes.

The First "Last" Found Footage Horror Films

Even the very titles of *The Last Broadcast* and *The Last Horror Movie* evoke Jeffrey Sconce's description of Orson Welles' *War of the Worlds* 1938 radio broadcast as a kind of "media 'death wish.'"[5] These are films that attempt a conceptual endgame that as I argue in Chapter Seven is continued in found footage exorcism films like *The Last Exorcism* and *The Devil Inside*. Just the name *The Last Exorcism* suggests an awareness of this heritage, stretching back not only to *The Last Broadcast* and *The Last Horror Movie* but to films like *The Last Picture Show* (Peter Bogdanovich, 1971) and *The Last Movie* (Dennis Hopper, 1971), all of which in their own unique ways emphasize the fact that film as a notion is both potentially both finite and volatile. In specific relation to horror, it most directly recalls the cult movie *The Last Horror Film* (David Winters, 1982). This cult horror movie follows New York taxi driver Vinny Durand (Joe Spinell) to the Cannes Film Festival as he monitors scream queen Jana Bates (Caroline Munro). *The Last Horror Film* includes small but significant black-and-white clips of Vinny's own film footage that he records of Jana as part of his grander delusions about being a filmmaker, intercut with scenes from an imaginary film he dreams of making, and the comparatively realistic footage of his increasing list of "real-life" failures. At points these formal styles merge as Vinny's delusions intensify, reflecting his difficulties in distinguishing reality from fantasy. While not a found footage horror film as such, the tension between fantasy and reality is framed in relation to the technical construction of the genre itself.

The Last Broadcast follows an investigation into the murder of members of a public-access cable television crew in the New Jersey Pine Barrens by documentary filmmaker David Leigh (David Beard). These "*Fact or Fiction* murders" were named after the program being filmed by the victims themselves: sound recordist Rein Clacking (Rein Clabbers) and hosts Steven Avkast and Locus Wheeler (played by *Last Broadcast*'s director-producers-writers Stefan Avalos and Lance Weiler). Accompanying them was mentally unstable psychic Jim Suerd (James Seward), who was later found guilty of the murders. The crew are directed to the Pine Barrens to search for the legendary "Jersey Devil" by an anonymous IRC caller to the program, and Avkast suggested they do a live webcast and television broadcast from the woods in a bid to improve ratings. Suerd later dies in prison, rendering the case effectively closed for everyone but David. After he discovers a box of loose videotape, he hires data recovery specialist Shelley (Michele Pulask), whose restoration work reveals that the real killer was in fact David himself. At this revelation, David attacks Shelley on-camera and violently suffocates her. The film ends with David returning to the filming of his documentary, unaffected by Shelley's death.

Although made in 1998, *The Last Broadcast* was only widely available after *The Blair Witch Project*'s success, and its release was based on a desire to profit from the success of Myrick and Sánchez's movie. According to Guido Henkel,[6] *The Last Broadcast* was scheduled to screen at the midnight viewing at Sundance exactly one year before *Blair Witch*'s debut in the same slot but was removed from the line-up for unspecified reasons. Henkel also claimed that Avalos and Weiler used "Missing Persons" flyers similar to those of Myrick and Sánchez. In her championing of *The Last Broadcast* as a critical underdog, Sarah Higley drew other parallels: Both are about film crews who go missing in the woods, both rely on the discovery of found footage, both have an amateur cast who use their real names (or names similar to them), and both were directorial collaborations between two young men.[7]

A defense of *The Last Broadcast* as a potential underground alternative to *Blair Witch* raises further issues, however. Based around the premise of a television program where IRC users can suggest subjects for *Fact or Fiction* investigations, the film recalls the earlier episode of the French found footage television series *Les Documents Interdits* "The Ferguson Case" as discussed in Chapter Three. Additionally, *Blair Witch*'s conclusion remains open, while the revelation at the end of *The Last Broadcast* of its killer removes the bulk of its ambiguity. The most obvious deviation between the two films of course is their formal structure: While *Blair Witch* relies solely on the found footage material (primarily appropriating the codes and conventions of observational documentary), *The Last Broadcast* appropriates those of a number of documentary modes, and is heavily reliant on interviews, voice-overs and the presentation of visual evidence such as maps, newspaper clippings, crime scene photographs, courtroom transcripts and illustrations, animated infographics, and television news reports. It is visibly marked by its post-production, such as the inclusion of non-diegetic music, fast editing, and its non-linear narrative structure. While the film's climactic revelation relies upon the discovery of found footage material, the movie as a whole is formally marked much more by the presence of its diegetic filmmaker, whose to-camera narration and ever-present voice-over link it to expository documentary traditions. Unlike *Blair Witch*, *The Last Broadcast* also relies heavily upon the literary tradition of the unreliable narrator, a term coined in Wayne C. Booth's *The Rhetoric of Fiction* (1961) regarding a narrator whose integrity and truthfulness has been compromised in the telling of their story.

Dominated by its voice-of-god styled narration, *The Last Broadcast* is very much David's story. He makes it increasingly explicit throughout the film that his "documentary" is concerned with *his* experience of the investigation; it seeks to answer the questions *he* wants solved. With his discovery of the found footage material—the missing lost tapes shot by Rein and Locus on the night of the murders—David acknowledges that he has become part of the *Fact or Fiction* murder story itself, and as such foreshadows his involvement in the killings. As his earlier description of the crime as "murders of a hi-tech age" whose victims were "children of a digital age," David's analysis of the case is understood through the role and function of media technology itself. Says David:

> As this journey nears its end, I begin to fully understand the essence of what this is about. The media upon which these events were recorded—the media that *should* have been able to provide a truth more pure than ever before—has somehow become the story. This has become more than a search behind the truth of the *Fact or Fiction* murders. It has become an indictment of how it is viewed through the lens of the media.

After he is shown brutally murdering the unsuspecting Shelley (in the film's only protracted murder scene, heavily sexualized and the victim's suffering shown in close-up detail suggesting like *Blair Witch* it too is far from unblemished in its gender politics), there is a dramatic formal shift in *The Last Broadcast* as a secondary camera film takes over. Filming David filming himself, this *mise-en-abîme* closes the narrative loop of the film. For all the attempts to formally align us with David (most notably via his omniscient, fourth wall–breaking expository-style voice-over), the final moments of the movie add daunting weight to his introductory statement "I came to this documentary with the same assumptions you have." By revealing our primary point of identification with the *Fact or Fiction* killer himself—the very name strategically articulating the film's deliberate blurring of the lines between documentary and mockumentary—we are implicated in David's crimes.

    The Last Horror Movie makes a similar indictment by breaking the fourth wall in a different way. Of all the found footage films discussed in this book, this film offers the most ingenious premise for its central material's discovery: Rather than being police or court evidence or material uncovered in the woods, *The Last Horror Movie* purports to be a first-person encounter with a supposedly "real-life" serial killer who has deliberately taped his story over a video we have supposedly rented called *The Last Horror Movie*. With a near-identical introduction to *The Last Horror Film*, *The Last Horror Movie* opens with a typical slasher movie scene *in media res*. Again it is revealed that we are watching a film-within-a-film, and in *The Last Horror Movie* we are addressed directly by Max (Kevin Howarth), its serial killer protagonist. Max claims his motive for interrupting this standard horror fare is to show us "real" horror, and to interrogate the pleasure we find in watching screen violence as he provides "raw" footage of his comparatively unglamorized murders. David Ray Carter suggested that the finale "takes the found-footage gimmick to its zenith"[8]: Max's reveals that the videotape we are now watching has been deliberately planted, marking us as his next potential victim.

    Along with the obvious reference to *The Last Horror Film*, *The Last Horror Movie* wears its other influences on its sleeve including homages to *Man Bites Dog*, *Henry: Portrait of a Serial Killer* and *Ringu*.[9] Max's first-person address allows him to openly question the spectator, challenging us about the pleasures we find in violent horror movies and going to great lengths to articulate the differences between theatrical violence (typified by the internal slasher film segment at the start of the film that he interrupts) and what by his definition at least is "the

Max (Kevin Howarth) in *The Last Horror Movie* (Julian Richards, 2003) (Prolific Films/Snakelair Prods/The Kobal Collection).

real." Johnny Walker has associated Max's critique of horror film spectatorship with the "Video Nasties" controversy of the 1980s in the United Kingdom, arguing that *The Last Horror Movie* "deals head-on with an array of prominent issues that have continued to surround British horror film criticism since the dawn of VHS: notably, the consumption of violence, and distinguishing between what is real and what is simulated."[10] Significantly, the film clearly wishes to distance itself from broader critical analysis. When explaining the title of the film as it draws to an end, Max jokes that he chose a video called *The Last Horror Movie* to record his story over "because in its self-conscious subversion of horror movie conventions it's kind of the last word on horror," stating that such an explanation might lead us to assume he is "a bit of a wanker." Rather, he offers the more practical—and fantastic—explanation that it is our last horror film because he has possibly followed us from the video store where we theoretically rented it, implying that our fate will be the same as those victims we have just seen him slaughter. "If you're watching this film, you've become very dangerous to me, as I have to you," he warns.

That a film character is openly threatening his audience with violence marks a literal articulation of the broader "threat" of the movie camera itself, recalling Susan Sontag's famous declaration that "there is an aggression implicit in every use of the camera."[11] However, it is a threat worth considering in depth: Today, with the near-total eradication of the VHS format with DVD and digital downloads dominating the home entertainment market on the movie front, the materiality at the heart of *The Last Horror Movie* renders it as little more than a historical curio. As Walker crucially noted, the release of *The Last Horror Movie* occurred at a time where home entertainment was going through dramatic shifts and even at the time of its release it was more than likely that audiences would have seen the film on DVD (thus less open to the material interference upon which the film is predicated)[12]: This was certainly my experience of seeing the film for the first time in the mid–2000s. Consequently, rather than a literal threat to the spectator where we seriously believe Max could appear in our living rooms to torture and murder us as he describes, what *The Last Horror Movie* imparts is a fictional space where we have the opportunity to knowingly indulge in its wildly fantastic horror "what-ifs."

The Evolution of Found Footage Horror

The Last Broadcast and *The Last Horror Movie* were of course not the only notable post–*Blair Witch*, pre–*Paranormal Activity* found footage horror films. These movies were often low-budget independent productions, and as such their distribution networks were often limited. Certainly few reached the levels of success that the subgenre would finally attain with its big blockbuster titles later in the decade, although many became fan favorites and have garnered strong reputations in horror circles. The movies surveyed here are not presented to suggest any widespread influence or to imply their commercial success, but rather they illustrate that while the eyes of the mainstream were on the glossy atrocities of so-called "torture porn," found footage horror was quietly bubbling away in the background. It was here that the codes and conventions of the subgenre were shifting and consolidating the formal and narrative palate that would provide later found footage horror blockbusters with their essential elements.

One of the most intriguing post–*Blair Witch* found footage horror films was *909 Experiment* (Wayne A. Smith, 2000), a film that has in recent years garnered a cult reputation based solely on its appearance on file-sharing sites and YouTube as a rumored uncredited inspiration for *Paranormal Activity*. The film follows college students Alex (Wayne A. Smith) and Jamie (Denise Devlin) and their experiences in a Lake Arrowhead house with a reputation for high electromagnetism, a natural phenomenon that causes LSD-like hallucinations. They are eager for the $150 they will each receive for staying in the house for 72 hours and recording their experiences on the video cameras provided. The property is also rigged up with a number of surveillance cameras that captures phenomena in the house not filmed by the protagonists themselves. The surveillance footage shows poltergeist movement that becomes increasingly apparent to Jamie and Alex. Revealing that she has had psychic abilities since she was a child, Jamie has strange feelings about the house, but her boyfriend Alex is not easily convinced, and initially believes the unusual events are a practical joke that Jamie is playing on him. As Alex begins vomiting blood and is plagued by intense headaches, his behavior becomes progressively more disturbing: He starts sleepwalking, grows more aggressive, and talks about things that he should not know such as Jamie's history of infidelity and, even more disturbingly, about a German soldier who committed suicide in the house. Alex's behavior deteriorates to the point where Jamie locks herself in her bedroom for her own safety, and the next morning he breaks in and drags her to the basement laundry where much of the supernatural activity has occurred. He shoots her in the stomach before he commits suicide.

Jamie's survival after these events is indicated by the fact that retrospective interview footage with her is intercut into the surveillance and hand-held footage of which *909 Experiment* consists. Unlike *Blair Witch* and *Paranormal Activity*, the film appropriates codes and conventions from a number of documentary modes—primarily observational and participatory—rather than relying solely on the former. That being said, it is remarkable just how many significant parallels with *Paranormal Activity* can be drawn with this rare low-budget predecessor: Like Katie, Alex sleepwalks as if seemingly possessed, at one point even getting a kitchen knife and taking it back to bed with him. As in Peli's film, the poltergeist activity seems notably focused on lights, and Alex uses the phrase "paranormal activity" numerous times. The relationship between the hand-held footage and the surveillance footage is also crucial, the latter implying an external presence is ominously watching the events as they unfold (probably at the university that has hired them, the very structure of the film suggesting the movie we are watching has been complied as some kind of research document or report). Thematically, both *909 Experiment* and *Paranormal Activity* at their heart also concern the deterioration of a romantic relationship that ends in domestic violence. Whether these similarities are coincidental or whether some elements of Peli's film were inspired by the earlier film is unclear, but it is worth highlighting the fact that his latter film jettisoned the interview components completely: Peli understood how powerful observational documentary's codes and conventions were on their own merits, and how to successfully appropriate them into a fictional horror film context.

It would take some time for other found footage horror directors to embrace this fact. Following a trend that would continue for many years, *The Black Door* (Kit Wong, 2001) also incorporated discovered hand-held material with other types of supposed "documentary" materials. This film follows a documentary crew's investigation into the mysterious medical condition of Steven (Sergio Gallinaro), a Ph.D. student whose research leads him to the accidental discovery of a group of devil worshippers through mysterious documents and a black-and-white 8mm film. *The Black Door* once again is formally closer to *Curse of the Blair Witch* than it is *The Blair Witch Project* itself through its appropriation of other documentary modes next to found footage horror's predominantly observational one. For example, non-diegetic music and the inclusion of different types of material evidence (interviews, photographs, police files, handwritten documents, etc.) indicate its post-production.

The Internet would also become a dominant feature in many post–*Blair Witch* found footage horror films, and although there were other horror movies that centered on the Internet like *FeardotCom* (William Malone, 2002) and *Suicide Club* (Sion Sono, 2002), found footage horror offered its own unique examples. The German film *Suicide* (Raoul W. Heimrich and Yvonne Wunschel, 2001) incorporated the developing "reality horror" category with Jörg Buttgereit's cult horror film *Der Todesking* (1989) in both its episodic structure and its fascination with death. *Suicide*'s story is simple: A couple offers individuals wishing to commit suicide the opportunity to have their deaths filmed, to be featured on their website. Breaking them into thirteen different suicide scenarios, the filmmakers shift from recording fake suicides to what are effectively consensual snuff films. It was shot primarily through diegetic hand-held video. This brief plot outline does not do justice to the moving and extremely dark nature of the film, one that utilizes its diegetic first person perspective to maximum effect.

Like *Megan Is Missing* (Michael Goi, 2011) and *Vlog* (Joshua Butler, 2008), digital interfaces also form the structural basis of *The Collingswood Story* (Michael Costanza, 2002). Along with *Suicide*, *The Collingswood Story* is one of a number of films that predicted the influence that online video streaming technologies would have on the found footage horror subgenre (and horror more generally) after YouTube's arrival in 2005. The film concerns Rebecca (Stephanie Dees), a student who lives in a house linked to a grisly murder and a history of cult worship. Like Joe Swanberg's *V/H/S* (2012) segment "The Sick Thing That Happened to Emily When She Was Younger," this film unfolds primarily through online video chats with her boyfriend Johnny (Johnny Burton). Unlike *V/H/S*, however, in *The Collingswood Story* the Internet itself is imbued with dark, malevolent powers that lead to the film's climactic revelations. That it is the very medium that is haunted recalls key found footage horror ancestors such as *Ghostwatch* (Lesley Manning, 1992).

The science fiction legacy of Orson Welles' *War of the Worlds* radio broadcast and television mockumentaries like *Alternative 3* (Christopher Miles, 1977), *Without Warning* (Robert Iscove, 1994) and *Alien Abduction: Incident in Lake County* (Dean Alioto, 1998) was also reactivated in this post–*Blair Witch* environment with films such as the *X-Files*–like alien conspiracy *The Wicksboro Incident* (Richard Lowry, 2003) and the darkly comic Werner Herzog film *Incident at Loch Ness* (Zak Penn, 2004). The thriller genre garnered inspiration from this climate, with the John F. Kennedy assassination mockumentary *Interview with the Assassin* (Neil Burger, 2002) and the Australian crime film *The Magician* (Scott Ryan, 2005). As will be expanded in Chapter Nine, found footage is also at the core of much of Japanese filmmaker Kôji Shiraishi's work, and *Noroi: The Curse* (2005) offers an early instance of its application in his oeuvre.

By halfway through this century's first decade, the diegetic inclusion of a camera crew was not uncommon in horror, even though mainstream attention was still predominantly focused on the *Saw* and *Hostel* franchises. Some found footage films made during this interim period struggled to see the light of distributive day until the climate became more responsive after the blockbuster success of *Paranormal Activity* in 2009: Sevé Schelenz's *Skew* is an excellent example, made in 2004–2005 but not released until 2011. However, found footage was less commonly deployed as the primary formal device in the bulk of these interim films, and like *The Last Broadcast*, they continued the tradition of "found" or discovered material being used alongside other types of "documentary" evidence. This is typified by the Italian film *Il mistero di Lovecraft—Road to L.* (Federico Greco and Roberto Leggio, 2005) that follows the investigation of an Italian and American film crew into a manuscript suggesting that despite claims that horror author H.P Lovecraft never left the United States, he in fact visited an unidentified Italian town identified only by the initial "L" in 1926. They discover stories like "Shadow Over Innsmouth" (1936) and "The Call of Cthulhu" (1928) were based on *filò* or folktales from the Polesine region about a water monster that inhabits the Po Delta. Lovecraft's work was a less abstract inspiration for the 2013 (partially) found footage film *The Banshee Chapter* (based loosely on his 1934 short story "From Beyond"), but *The Road to L* is significant because like *The Last Broadcast*, the impact of its final revelation lies within the mysterious appearance of what was until then believed to be missing videotape. The playback of this video discloses the final shocking truth behind the investigation, placing the (diegetic) filmmakers in unresolved danger.

So established by the middle of this decade was the broader horror mockumentary category that its boundaries could be pushed for comedic as well as horrific effect. The influence of *Man Bites Dog* apparent in *The Last Horror Movie* is even more visible in *Behind the Mask: The Rise of Leslie Vernon* (Scott Glosserman, 2005). Recalling the tongue-in-cheek postmodern reflexivity of Wes Craven's *Scream* franchise (1996–2011), this mockumentary features cameos from cult horror figures including Robert "Freddy Krueger" Englund, Kane Hodder who played Jason Voorhees in a number of *Friday the 13th* films, and Zelda Rubenstein from Tobe Hooper's 1982 film *Poltergeist*. In *Behind the Mask,* famous serial killers from iconic slasher films including *Friday the 13th* and *Halloween* are assumed to exist in the real world. The movie follows journalist Taylor Gentry (Angela Goethals) in her investigation into aspiring slasher Leslie Vernon (Nathan Baesel), and—as in *Man Bites Dog*—she and her crew become increasingly involved in Vernon's preparations to face his Final Girl, a key figure in slasher movies. After a change of heart, Taylor not only realizes the seriousness of Vernon's planned killing spree, but also decides to stop him, thus making *her* the Final Girl. In keeping with slasher tradition, despite Taylor's apparent victory over Vernon, the film's final moments show him rising from an autopsy table to presumably continue his murderous activities in sequels.[13] *Behind the Mask* was not alone in its attempt to combine diegetic hand-held footage in a comedy mockumentary about horror; for example, *Brutal Massacre* (Stevan Mena, 2007) concerns a film crew investigating the struggles of fictional horror auteur Harry Penderecki (David Naughton) to salvage his dwindling professional reputation.

A perceptible shift begins to occur around this period, and 2007 in particular denotes a significant spike in the production of found footage horror due in large part to the rise and broad cultural impact of YouTube. In these films, the previous tendency of combining found footage with interviews and other "documentary" materials (interviews, photographs, newspaper clippings, etc.) gives way to films with a more dedicated found footage focus. *Alone with Her* (Eric Nicholas, 2006) contains no contextualizing intertitles to frame its story and instead leaps directly into its confronting hand-held, diegetically shot material. Opening with his foray into "upskirting," cameraman Doug's (Colin Hanks) predatory status is apparent as he focuses his attention on unsuspecting Amy (Ana Claudia Talancón). The audience experiences Doug's harassment through this footage and thus solely from his perspective. As his obsession with Amy increases, Doug films himself buying home surveillance cameras which he installs in her apartment, and the material after this switches from his hand-held camera to surveillance footage to a camera he conceals on his own body. On one level, *Alone with Her* can be considered an exposé of the perverse voyeuristic desires potentially inherent to film spectatorship, but it can also be deemed as deliberately exploiting those desires. That the film is focused on the increasingly aggressive harassment, attempted rape and ultimate murder of its female

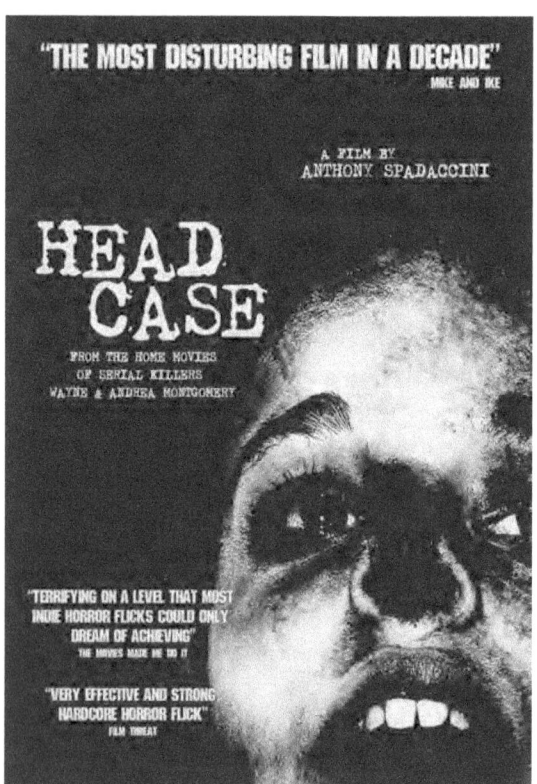

Head Case (2007). DVD artwork (courtesy Anthony Spadaccini/Fleet Street Films).

victim solely from the perpetrator's perspective only adds to this problematic contradiction.

Head Case (Anthony Spadaccini, 2007) is a found footage horror film that relies solely on home video, and like *Blair Witch* eight years before, it is only its introductory intertitles that provide context: "The following film is edited from the home movies of serial killers Wayne & Andrea Montgomery. The footage is being presented in what is believed to be chronological order." This low-budget film follows a superficially ordinary middle-aged suburban couple through a vicious killing spree that culminates in the murder of their own daughter, contrasting the violence of their crimes against what feels like an all-too-familiar replication of middle-class domesticity. For example, the film's lingering focus on details like their floral sofa and lace tablecloths contrast shockingly with images of Wayne force-feeding one victim liquid bleach. Bereft of any complex special effects and with director Spadaccini's obvious appreciation of the strengths of found footage horror, *Head Case* is reliant in large part upon the convincing performances of its main cast members Paul McCloskey and Barbara Lessin. Its horrors stem predominantly from contrasting the supposed normality of Wayne and Andrea's life with their macabre serial killing secret. *Head Case* consciously eschews found footage horror's dominant fascination with the supernatural, turning instead to real terrestrial horrors: Documentary's codes and conventions are not appropriated to explore the paranormal, but rather to underscore the brutal reality of murder itself. Serial killers have appeared in a range of other found footage horror films, be they reliant predominantly upon found footage (like *Head Case* and the sequels *The Ritual* [Anthony Spadaccini, 2009] and *Post-Mortem* [Anthony Spadaccini, 2010], *Man Bites Dog*, and the *August Underground*[14] and *Video X* films) or incorporating it with elements of other documentary modes (such as John Erick Dowdle's 2007 film *The Poughkeepsie Tapes*).

There are earlier micro-budget examples of found footage horror that place hand-held material at the forefront such as *Experiment 909* (Wayne A. Smith, 1999) and *Strawberry Estates* (Ron Bonk, 2001); but during the latter half of the 2000s horror films that drew predominantly from the codes and conventions of observational documentary began to rise. The ascent of YouTube in 2006 indicated just how accepting of UGC–styled amateur filmmaking aesthetics mass audiences had now become. In this climate, films such as *Exhibit A* (Dom Rotheroe, 2007), *Welcome to the Jungle* (Jonathan Hensleigh, 2007) and of course *[Rec]* all looked and felt like they could have been extended YouTube clips. Premiering at the Venice Film Festival in 2007, *[Rec]* played at a number of international film festivals, garnering it and its sequels a reputation as fan favorites. In *[Rec]*, television journalist Angela Vidal

(Manuela Viscalo) believes she is accompanying a local firefighting unit on a typical evening, but when responding to a rescue call from a local apartment block, it is revealed that the building has been infected by some kind of contagion that turns people into zombie-like killers. Along with her cameraman Pablo (Pablo Rosso), Angela is cornered in a top floor apartment where they determine its former tenant worked for the Vatican and discovered that demonic possession could be spread virally. His case study was a young girl called Medeiros (Javier Botet), whom he locked in his apartment to die when he realized the virus was highly contagious. Upon discovering the now monstrous girl, Pablo is violently murdered and the Medeiros girl ominously drags a screaming Angela away from the camera.

[Rec] and *Diary of the Dead* mark a refocus on found footage in mainstream horror, but they also present significant examples of how thin the lines between observational documentary-inspired found footage and mockumentary elements appropriated from the codes and conventions of other documentary modes can be. *[Rec]* includes interviews, which typically mark participatory documentary. Here, however, what is shown is Pablo's raw footage that includes Angela asking the building's trapped residents questions about their experiences. In *Diary of the Dead*, while the internal film "The Death of Death" is predominantly found footage, it is positioned within a framing narrative dominated by a voice-over, a feature typically aligned with expository documentary.

[Rec] and *Diary of the Dead* also rely heavily on zombie horror film traditions. There have been other, lesser known found footage–mockumentary zombie-based films, including but not limited to *Zombie Diaries* (2006) and its sequel *World of the Dead: The Zombie Diaries 2* (2011), *Re-Kill* (Valeri Milev, 2012), *Pretty Dead* (Benjamin Wilkins, 2012), *Killer Shrimps* (Piero Golia, 2004), and *American Zombie* (Grace Lee, 2007). But few have been as widely celebrated by fans as *Diary of the Dead* and *[Rec]*. Both adopted a survival horror model from earlier videogame-inspired zombie films like *Resident Evil* (Paul W.S. Anderson, 2002), and with narrative emphasis placed upon the challenges their protagonists face when confronting zombie or zombie-like threats, both *[Rec]* and *Diary of the Dead* revolve around the fight for survival and are therefore substantially more action-based than movies like *The Blair Witch Project*.

Like *Blair Witch*, *Diary of the Dead* concerns a group of student filmmakers, but in this instance its fictional Hammer Horror–style mummy movie becomes a documentary as its late director Jason (Joshua Close) captures his first-hand struggle to survive a zombie apocalypse. Recalling *The Last Horror Movie*, *Diary of the Dead* is structured as a horror-film-within-a-horror-film, where Jason's girlfriend Deb (Michelle Morgan) explains through voice-over that she has edited together Jason's footage into a final documentary as both a tribute to Jason and to serve as a warning about the bleaker side of human nature when faced with extreme survival conditions. When considering the mummy film footage on top of this, however, what Romero has effectively created is a horror-film-within-a-horror-film-within-a-horror-film. This Russian doll structure for supernatural storytelling has famous predecessors going back at least to Henry James' novella *The Turn of the Screw* (1898), but in this instance it grants Romero the opportunity to reflect on the codes and conventions of the genre itself in particular reference to the relationship between real and fictional horror. *Diary of the Dead* is a noteworthy example of the self-reflexivity of found footage horror in relation not only to filmmaking more generally, but to horror itself.

Because Oren Peli's original entry into the *Paranormal Activity* series was made in 2007 but not released into the mainstream until 2009, there were a number of found footage horror films made after its creation that were most likely untouched by its influence. Some of the movies that appeared in the period between 2007 and 2009 were tightly constructed independent features like *Home Movie* (Christopher Denham, 2008) and *Lake Mungo* (Joel Anderson, 2008), and the comparatively amateur *Chronicles of an Exorcism* (Nick G. Miller, 2008) and *June 9* (T. Michael Conway, 2008). Others like the blockbuster *Cloverfield* (Matt Reeves, 2008) illustrated the broad appeal of found footage horror before *Paranormal Activity* achieved its phenomenal success. Two more films provided further evidence that the codes and conventions of found footage horror were firmly established by the time of the *Paranormal Activity* sensation. The first of these was *Monster* (Erik Estenberg, 2008), one of production company The Asylum's so-called "mockbusters." These quickly made, often straight-to-video titles seek to cash in on upcoming blockbusters by producing films with similar names, such as *Transmorphers* (Leigh Scott, 2007) and *The Da Vinci Treasure* (Peter Mervis, 2006). The Asylum moviemakers have been no stranger to the found footage horror subgenre, with titles including *Paranormal Entity* (2009), *Gacy House* (2010), *Anneliese: The Exorcist Tapes* (2011), and *100 Ghost Street: The Return of Richard Speck* (2012) under their belt. *Monster* was not shy in emphasizing its many overt similarities to *Cloverfield*: It adheres closely to the basic story of a group journeying through a big city while a monster attacks, but also refers to both *Cloverfield*'s internal narrative and its transmedia campaign by placing its action in Tokyo.

A more straightforward original-remake relationship existed between the first *[Rec]* film and its American adaptation by *The Poughkeepsie Tapes* director John Erick Dowdle, *Quarantine* (2008). Aside from major alterations in the ending of the latter (explored in Chapter Nine), these two films are relatively indistinguishable beyond differences in language and culturally specific references. Aside from plot and dialogue similarities, *Quarantine* even uses a near-identical color palette and replicates much of the Spanish film's *mise-en-scène*. Both *Monster* and *Quarantine* illustrate how firmly established the codes and conventions of found footage horror were by the time *Paranormal Activity* was released into the mainstream, so familiar and identifiable that they could be easily replicated. As these more popular found footage horror films made their way to the forefront of the genre, what became important was not that the audience necessarily believed that they were real, but rather that they offered a framework to knowingly indulge in a horror *fantasy* of the real. The solidification of a recognizable found footage horror style meant that horror audiences understood and identified them as such, defining a subgenre where an authentic style (rather than claims of authenticity itself) prevailed.

This development continued after *Paranormal Activity*'s widespread release. Like *Blair Witch,* it inspired a slew of spoofs, homages and outright rip-offs including *Paranormal Effect* (Ryuichi Asano and Teruo Ito, 2010), *Paranormal Whacktivity* (Roger Roth, 2012), *Supernatural Activity* (Derek Lee Nixon, 2012), *Paranormal Proof* (Kevin Kicks, 2010), *Paranoid Activity 2* (Kevin Clark and Manzie Jones, 2011), *Abnormal Activity* (Jason Gerbay, 2010), *Paranormal Entity* (Shane Van Dyke, 2009), *30 Nights of Paranormal Activity with the Devil Inside the Girl with the Dragon Tattoo* (Craig Moss, 2013), and *A Haunted House* (Michael Tiddes, 2013). The first *Paranormal Activity* film included intertitles that implied it was "true" but as the series progressed it demonstrated a lack of interest in such claims. Despite this, the *Paranormal Activity* franchise still employs the authentic style typical of found footage horror in its construction of a diegetic universe that at times appears to be as dense as *The Blair Witch Project* itself.

Six

Approaching
Paranormal Activity

Like *The Blair Witch Project* a decade earlier, *Paranormal Activity* became a genre high water mark, but for very different reasons. In 2006, videogame programmer Oren Peli was inspired to make a self-funded low-budget horror film after hearing noises in his San Diego home. Actors Katie Featherstone and Micah Sloat had very little experience but appealed to Peli, and they set to work over one week in October 2006, using the director's home as the set. With its script almost completely improvised, Sloat also doubled as the primary cinematographer.

Peli was hoping to attract attention in a manner similar to *The Blair Witch Project*. Initial interest was low. After receiving some very limited notice in 2007, in 2008 it came to the notice of DreamWorks. They felt it would be a good film to remake, and offered a hesitant Peli $350,000. However, the film's producer convinced DreamWorks to release Peli's version after Steven Spielberg became one of its most vocal champions. It was his suggestion that the now-famous end scene be added, and with this the film was eventually released on a limited theatrical basis. Paramount utilized social media to create demand, and Senior Vice-President of Interactive Marketing Amy Powell used the online Demand It! Service where audiences could vote for certain films to play in their region, granting *Paranormal Activity* the "grassroots, do-it-yourself support ... from the bottom up" that she felt it required.[1] While the $11,000 it cost to make the film[2] is a more famous statistic in the original movie's now legendary ascension than the $2 million it cost to promote it, even with this figure added it was still a remarkable financial success: As early as January 2010 it had cleared over $90 million.[3] By 2013, the franchise has by one account grossed over $700 million internationally,[4] with another suggesting that with DVD sales it reached close to the $1 billion mark.[5]

Compared to the reaction to *The Blair Witch Project*, critical debate

Oren Peli (Blumhouse Productions/The Kobal Collection).

surrounding *Paranormal Activity* has been subdued. By 2009, the marketing strategies, issues of authenticity and audience hysteria surrounding found footage horror were old hat. Despite the comparatively reduced number of scholarly treatments on *Paranormal Activity* at present, a few insightful critics have noticed that in the fine grain detail some things *are* different this time around. Leslie A. Hahner, Scott J. Varda and Nathan A. Wilson's essay "*Paranormal Activity* and the Horror of Abject Consumption" suggested that the first two titles in the franchise have been broadly viewed as either morality tales about a middle-class living beyond their means, or as a successful experiment in cinematic minimalism. While so-called "torture porn" is linked to post–9/11 America and the supposed "War on Terror," the *Paranormal Activity* franchise has moved on to the drastic collapse of the U.S. housing market during and after the Global Financial Crisis and "the public's fear of and fascination with materialism and consumption."[6] The authors contended that consumption itself becomes abject in these movies, both repulsing and attracting audiences with stately homes under siege by unseen forces. Linking the trope of demonic possession with a broader conception of ownership and the possession of commodities, the films are marked by out-of-control consumerism, reflected by the audience's own desire to consume the franchise itself.

Sébastien Lefait has focused on the surveillance footage in *Paranormal Activity* and *Paranormal Activity 2*, suggesting that these films offer "a reflection on the state of cinema in a surveillance world."[7] While this surveillance footage is responsible in large part for their verisimilitude, the significance of the first film especially transcends this by exposing how in this climate horror itself must adapt to the changes in spectatorship that surveillance culture has brought. "Thanks to its numerous metacinematic moments, the film shows that the rise of surveillance societies impairs the traditional efficiency of the supernatural horror films, and makes it necessary to correct the rules of the genre," Lefait said. "The spread of surveillance changes the viewing contract of any type of audiovisual material, and inevitably amends how revelations can be staged."[8]

A 2011 roundtable discussion between Julia Leyda, Nick Rombes, Steven Shaviro, and Therese Grisham on the release of *Paranormal Activity 2* considered how shifts in technology pertain to Shaviro's notion of the "post-cinematic." While cinema was broadly considered the dominant medium in the last century, it has now lost that position to digital media. It is in this scenario that Shaviro has posed a number of crucial questions:

> What happens to cinema when it is no longer a cultural dominant, when its core technologies of production and reception have become obsolete, or have been subsumed within radically different forces and powers? ... How do particular movies, or audiovisual works, reinvent themselves, or discover new powers of expression, precisely in a time that is no longer cinematic or cinemacentric?[9]

The first two *Paranormal Activity* films address these questions in a significant way for Shaviro, through not only being produced with but also diegetically focusing on low-cost digital technology. These movies riff on the fundamental spatial and temporal foundations of the traditional horror film—invasions of space from a supernatural force, and the temporal tensions between action and inaction—but convert them into something much more specific to the new digital technologies that dominates them both formally and narratively. As Nick Rombes observed, at their core these films "tackle the question of how to navigate the private spaces of this new media landscape."[10]

Terms of Engagement

As noted in the previous chapter, the *Paranormal Activity* franchise indicates a significant shift away from overt claims of authenticity. The first movie opens with an intertitle: "Paramount Pictures would like to thank the families of Micah Sloat and Katie Featherston and the San Diego Police Department."

This statement positions the consequent action both with a self-reflexive awareness of itself as a film released by a major studio, and as supposed police "evidence" in keeping with the manner that the film material itself was to be considered authentic documentation of a "real" event in *The Blair Witch Project*. As the *Paranormal Activity* series progresses, however, it becomes less reliant upon pseudo-truth claims. The fact that the first film includes characters who use the real names of the actors who play them as *Blair Witch* did is self-explanatory in regards to its desired sense of authenticity, but this is notably not deployed in later series entries.

An early title screen in the second film informs the audience that "Paramount Pictures would like to thank the families of the deceased and the Carlsbad Police Department," but unlike the first film it seeks to retain a degree of mystery by not revealing here who those "deceased" might be, and how many of them there are. By the third film, it appears to have become redundant to justify where the tapes came from, and aside from a brief prelude with Katie, Daniel (Brian Boland) and Kristi (Sprague Grayden) finding the videos in a box Katie has inherited from her grandmother Lois (Hallie Foote), the recordings that make up the bulk of the film are mere devices. This decreased interest in claiming their own factuality across the franchise reveals much about shifts in the subgenre more generally: As these dwindling claims of authenticity suggest, the "hook" of actuality is needed less to maintain audience interest as the series has unfolded. What *was* central, however, was what always has been at the heart of successful horror: frights, and lots of them. The *Paranormal Activity* franchise is an old-fashioned ghost train ride, and its success stems from its playful invitation to indulge in a fantasy of the real.

The *Paranormal Activity* series is all about this game. As such, its story arc and underlying mythology provide only a bare minimum of information to propel its demon's seemingly non-stop onslaught with his signature tricks: shaking light fittings, pulling back sheets, and hurling limp bodies across rooms towards cameras. These films are marked by their hand-held and surveillance camera technologies (security cameras, webcams, etc.), the latter of which are crucial in constructing the broader sense of presence (both supernatural and technological) that dominates the franchise. That its spaces are haunted as much by the demon as they are by surveillance cameras is of no minor importance. David Lyon has emphasized that "surveillance concerns the mundane, ordinary, taken-for-granted world,"[11] and each film goes to some length in their respective introductions to emphasize precisely the everyday, business-as-usual aspects of their protagonists' lives through the camera's presence. Lyon suggested that simple, banal tasks like using a library card or an ATM are often undertaken with little to no consideration for the data stains they leave behind.

Six. Approaching Paranormal Activity

They create metaphorical ghosts that haunt the shadows of our day-to-day lives without us thinking twice about them. These data fragments together construct a biography of sorts, providing enough information to cobble together the comings and goings that construct our life stories. In these films, those data stains captured on surveillance cameras in particular morph into a literal ghost story: The protagonists are watched as closely and as ominously by the surveillance cameras as they are by the demon that torments them. As Nick Rombes observed, the *Paranormal Activity* films therefore "reflect deeper anxieties about reality TV and how it reflects the super-abundance of surveillance itself in American society."[12]

The franchise begins with *Paranormal Activity* in 2007, and follows Katie and her boyfriend Micah who are tormented by a demonic entity that has been plaguing Katie since she was a child. The film ends with Katie becoming possessed by this demon and killing Micah. *Paranormal Activity 2*, an immediate prequel, focuses on Katie's sister Kristi and her family: husband Daniel, stepdaughter Ali (Molly Ephraim), and baby Hunter (Jackson Xenia Prieto and William Juan Prieto). The same demon from the first film is also tormenting them, and when Kristi appears to become possessed, Daniel performs a ritual to transfer the supernatural attention to Katie. At the film's conclusion, the demonic Katie appears, murders Daniel and Kristi, and abducts Hunter. The third film extends back to Kristi (Jessica Tyler Brown) and Katie's (Chloe Csengery) childhood and follows their first contact with the demon who Kristi calls Toby, mistaken by her mother Julie (Lauren Bittner) and to a lesser extent her boyfriend Dennis (Chris Smith) to be an imaginary friend. It outlines the events that lead up to the girls' pact with the demon, and indicates that their grandmother Lois is a member of a coven that has encouraged the union. *Paranormal Activity 4* returns to present-day 2011, and relocates Katie and her supposed son Robbie (Brady Allen) to suburban Nevada, where mysterious events plague their neighbors: teenage Alex (Kathryn Newton), her younger brother Wyatt (Aiden Lovekamp) and their parents Holly and Doug (played by real-life couple Alexondra Lee and the late Stephen Dunham). As Robbie becomes increasingly involved in their lives, it is revealed that the coven is again behind the eponymous activity, seeking to abduct Wyatt (Hunter under an adopted name).

Although the series has yet to be completed at the time of writing, there is already significant information that offers a range of insights into the formal, thematic and ideological concerns of the franchise: it functions around a basic mythological framework to which each new film contributes. In the first film, Katie tells the psychic Dr. Fredrichs (Mark Fredrichs) that her first supernatural experience was when she was eight and her sister Kristi was five: They were visited by a "mass," a "shadowy figure" that frightened them. They managed to escape a house fire but lost all of their possessions. These occurrences began again when Katie was thirteen. In the second film, Ali suspects that "Kristi's grandmother made a deal with a demon so she could get rich," and notes that as Hunter was the first male born in Kristi's family since the 1930s, the paranormal events happening in her house may be the demon seeking to collect his payment—the soul of the first-born male. Ali's boyfriend Brad (Seth Ginsberg) reads aloud the following from a website:

> It has been said that if a human makes a bargain with a demon for wealth, power or any other benefit, they must forfeit their first-born male. If the debt is not honored, the demon will follow the defaulter and his or her brood until its soul of an infant is collected.

This line of thought is expanded in the third film, and Dennis studies a book called *Malevolent Entities* in his attempt to discover what is happening to Julie's children. He tells her that a coven would wait until girls could get pregnant, have ceremonies and then remove their sons, brainwashing them so they would forget. Lois' involvement in this conspiracy appears to be validated by her attempt to coax Julie into having a son. Following this, Kristi makes some kind of unspecified deal with the unseen Toby if he promises to stop tormenting Katie. Alex's research in the fourth installment links Katie and Robbie to the Hittites. Her revelation that virgin blood must be spilled for the demon to enter its host (combined with her confession that she is a virgin) implies that her future is far from rosy. That Katie and Robbie finally capture Wyatt/Hunter for the coven suggests Toby's debt is finally close to being repaid.

Performance and Dominance: Paranormal Activity *(2007)*

Even leaving aside the supernatural focus of the first *Paranormal Activity* film, it stands as an unflinching rendering of the collapse of a fictional relationship. It is a break-up that is propelled by psychological abuse and ends in domestic violence. Few films have captured the everyday casualness that dominates a relationship breakdown quite like the original movie. The emotional intensity that normally dominates end-of-the-affair melodrama is deflected off the relationship and onto the external and unapologetically hyperbolic distraction of the titular paranormal activity. Katie and Micah cling to anything that can divert their attention away from the reality of their crumbling relationship, making the film's conclusion deeply ironic: that distraction not only exposes the couple's trust issues, but those very issues provoke and empower the demon, leading to the relationship's violent termination.

Gender politics play a crucial role in the first *Paranormal Activity* film. It is nothing less than a battle for dominance and the literal possession of Katie between her boyfriend and a male demon, Toby. The power imbalances between Katie and Micah are clear from the outset. Working as a day trader, Micah gloats to Katie that the camera he has purchased only cost him half a day's pay, positioning him in a financially superior position to his student girlfriend (she is an English major at college, studying to become a teacher). Micah's sense of ownership of Katie can be understood as an extension of this fact, and their relationship issues are both based on and stem from their respective financial situations. Micah's job in the financial sector is historically significant: A *Newsweek* article, released early in the same year that the film hit mainstream cinema screens, noted a growing trend where "the global financial meltdown has given rise to a newly reinvigorated scapegoat, at least on stage and screen: the evil financier."[13] With the bursting of the U.S. housing bubble leading to the worldwide financial crisis that began in 2007, the instability of "McMansions" like Micah's are tied to the ethical shakiness of a job he personifies. By positioning him as a representative of his industry, the volatility that inflicts Micah's house in some ways acts as fictional revenge for the uncertainty that the financial sector has brought to many homeowners. *Paranormal Activity* was not unique in being a horror movie addressing these concerns: The found footage horror film *Exhibit A* (Dom Rotheroe, 2007) also had the financial crisis on its mind, although it explores it in a different way.

Micah's problematic gender politics become apparent with the arrival of Dr. Fredrichs. Threatened by another male potentially taking control of his domestic situation, Micah undermines Katie's description of events and denies that anything unusual is happening. His sense of ownership over Katie is discernible in a number of other ways. Taking a scientific approach to establish the presence of the demonic entity in their household, Micah sprinkles talcum powder over their floor and declares, "I'm taking care of this. Nobody comes into my house, fucks with my girlfriend, and gets away with it." Despite Katie's horrified reaction—shocked, no doubt, that he fundamentally sees the haunting of Katie as a property crime committed against him because it threatens his assumed ownership—he repeats these sentiments again, equating his control of "his house" with "his girlfriend" (instead of "our house" and "Katie") and asserting his idea of masculine power with the blunt and posturing declaration, "I am going to fucking solve the problem."

As Katie's fear and the supernatural occurrences increase, so too does her impatience with Micah's masculine bravado: She openly mocks his claims to

Katie (Katie Featherstone) and Micah (Micah Sloat) in *Paranormal Activity* (Oren Peli, 2007) (Blumhouse Productions/The Kobal Collection).

be in control of the situation by saying, "If you think you're in control, you're an idiot. Not a single thing you've done has helped." However, it is too late for Micah, both literally and figuratively: He appears to find it impossible to listen to Katie. By Night #18, with flashing lights and loud banging plaguing the house, Katie implores Micah not to leave her alone in the bedroom and not to open the door, but he does both without faltering. Finding a photograph of the smiling couple smashed on the floor, Katie notes, "It's getting worse," and her observation applies not only to the haunting but also to her and Micah's relationship. As the film concludes, Micah still refuses to take Katie and her fears, her beliefs and her capacity for violence seriously. Even as she sits catatonic on the floor, clutching a crucifix until her hands bleed, he removes the one thing she thinks will protect her and burns it. By doing so, he unhesitatingly demonstrates just how threatened he is by anything—person, demon, or even object—he considers a threat to his masculine authority over her. It is therefore little surprise that this is the last straw for Katie, and she appears to realize her option is not liberation from male oppressors, but rather which male presence—Toby or Micah—will ultimately possess her. Calmly telling Micah to "trust me" and that "I think we'll be okay now," she appears to surrender herself to what she believes is the better of two misogynist evils: that it is Toby and not Micah speaks volumes about the oppression she has felt at the hands of the latter. As John Kenneth Muir noted, Micah "possesses control over her life. And so, accordingly, when her body stands to be possessed, literally, by a demon, it hardly looks like an effort. Once you lose control of your life, control of your spirit isn't far behind."[14] Todd Ford takes this a step further and has convincingly argued that *Paranormal Activity* is an outright "allegory representing a case study in domestic violence."[15]

Framing the first *Paranormal Activity* film as a triangle of sexual possession between Toby and Micah over Katie's body in this way is supported by the constant focus on the bedroom and the bed itself as a site of horror. Katie tells Dr. Fredrichs that her and her sister Kristi's first experience with the demon was when she was eight, and again when she turned thirteen—an age when young girls typically begin sexual maturation. This flagging of her sexuality as significant to Toby is underscored by her observation to Dr. Fredrichs that most of the supernatural activity occurs in their bedroom. Indeed, many of the film's biggest frights center around the bed, such as an invisible shape getting under the covers with her, and her being dragged out of bed by what is assumed to be the same unseen entity. Through these actions, Toby physically seeks to remove Katie and Micah from the site of sexual union while simultaneously positioning himself in bed with her. At numerous points throughout the film, Katie gets out of bed in a somnambulistic trance and ominously stares at Micah for what the onscreen clock indicates is many hours. However, it was Micah who initially tainted this space as early as Night #1, the evening Dr. Fredrichs first visited them. In attempting to film himself and Katie having sex, Micah tells her that the record light was in fact only the standby light. The fact this conversation was recorded reveals he was lying: He consciously sought to exploit Katie by filming them having sex without her knowing. As a symbolic space where both Micah and Toby have attempted to sexually dominate Katie, it is meaningful that it is here where the film's most dramatic action occurs. Before attacking him off-camera, Katie removes Micah's sheet and thus doing so literally exposes him. That she had to surrender her very subjectivity to a malign male demon to enact her vengeance against the misogynistic Micah rather than doing it herself suggests the gender politics of the first *Paranormal Activity* film would be difficult to hail as particularly progressive.

Micah's control of technology unravels as quickly as that of the domestic situation he seeks to document. This is typified nowhere more strongly than after the fight he and Katie have when he uses a Ouija board after she has asked him specifically not to do so. Katie demands he make an oath not to her but to the camera itself, and by doing so, she attains a brief moment of empowerment as technology becomes *her* witness, not his. Micah begrudgingly states that he will abide by Katie's rules regarding the camera, that he will stop trying to provoke the entity, and that he will "not to betray Katie's trust." The role of the surveillance footage is crucial here as it directly challenges Micah's perceived sense of alignment with it: He may control the camera during the day, but at night it records without him. He may need the camera, but it does not need him. By the end of the film, the camera shifts from working *for* him as a tool propagating his self-image as alpha-male, to working *against* him, becoming a witness not only to his failures as a partner, but ultimately to his murder. Micah employs technology as an instrument of control, but it retaliates against him and literally becomes a witness to—and a weapon in—his death.[16]

Monstrosity Unleashed: Paranormal Activity 2 *(2010)*

Paranormal Activity 2 maintains this relationship between technology and performances of masculinity. Katie's brother-in-law Daniel anthropomorphizes technology in a playful yet consistent way, and often with demonic overtones suggesting that so great is his masculine power, he has tamed the monstrous. He refers to his television set as his "50 inch monster," and at one point feigns an attack by the pool cleaner that he later refers to affectionately as his "little buddy." The association between monstrous technology and performances of masculinity is continued when he and Kristi have sex in the bathtub and he jokingly says, "Release the Kraken," referring to his penis in the same spirit of monstrous personification as he did his television. The casual manner with which Daniel lightly throws around these comments in the lead-up to the film's action distracts from their significance, but it cannot be understated. Daniel aligns both his masculinity and technology with the monstrous and, through joking, implies a casual confidence that he has mastered both. Taken in relation to his character's behavior throughout the film, this position will be seriously challenged.

Like Micah, Daniel associates masculinity with control and dominance. He consistently mocks and dismisses Kristi's increasing fears of a supernatural and malign entity in their house, going as far as rejecting her concerns with the old-fashioned misogynistic chestnut that she is merely "hormonal." Again like Micah, he deliberately ignores Kristi's clearly stated wishes: On Night #12 she says that she does not want to leave Hunter, but Daniel passive-aggressively tells her he misses his "fun wife," giving her no choice but to ignore her instinct and to go out, allowing Toby to use the time to torment their children. When the parents return to Ali's traumatized story of a supernatural visitation, an angry Daniel says, "I don't want to hear any more of this haunted house crap." Up until this point, Daniel believes that he can control what is and what is not true and what is or is not happening by simply stating so. However, unlike Micah, Daniel shifts from this position when he sees his partner in crisis. He then goes to the other extreme, effectively sacrificing Katie so that Kristi can be rid of the demon. Daniel switches from self-obsessed masculinity into protective of his immediate family at any cost, including the damnation of his wife's sister. Katie can therefore in some way be considered as partially justified in seeking revenge against Daniel: He may have ceased acting selfishly towards his wife, but he simply transferred that negative, misogynistic energy towards Katie.

The gender politics of the second *Paranormal Activity* film become more complicated and compromised. It is here that Katie settles into her role as what Barbara Creed has defined as the monstrous-feminine. Creed states:

> I have used the term "monstrous-feminine" as the term "female monster" implies a simple reversal of "male monster." The reasons why the monstrous-feminine horrifies her audience are quite different from the reasons why the male monster horrifies his audience. A new term is needed to specify these differences. As with all other stereotypes of the feminine, from virgin to whore, she is defined in terms of her sexuality. The phrase "monstrous-feminine" emphasizes the importance of gender in the construction of her monstrosity.[17]

Until Creed's influential book *The Monstrous-Feminine: Film, Feminism, Psychoanalysis*, the critical view of the representation of women in horror films was primarily as victims, according to the model offered by Laura Mulvey's identification of a dominant and sadistic male gaze. Employing Julia Kristeva's notion of abjection, Creed argued that woman-as-monster has a long and cross-cultural history, expanding beyond the parameters of screen cultures. Katie—and, as shall be soon discussed, other key female figures in the *Paranormal Activity* franchise—can be understood as demonstrating this kind of female monstrosity.

Katie's homicidal behavior seems at times almost zombie-like, and this is no coincidence: She is a killer controlled by a male power. That she has monstrosity forced upon her is foreshadowed at the beginning of the second film when she jokingly tells her niece Ali that she is an "evil step aunt ... well, I'm not really evil but I can be evil is my point." Katie's moral trajectory is established in other ways. At one point, she pressures Kristi into not speaking about the supernatural horrors that they experienced as children. Because of this, Kristi later tells Ali that she is not "allowed" to talk about what is happening, as she is nervous about disobeying her older sister. Katie's words come back to haunt her, as Kristi later parrots Katie's own advice back to her about repressing what is happening when strange occurrences begin in Katie and Micah's house. If Katie had encouraged Kristi to talk openly about her experience leading up to the point she lost her memory, Katie may have received vital information that could have assisted her when Toby turned his attention to her and Micah under Daniel's direction.

Kristi is pushed around not only by Katie but also by her husband. The opening of the third film even implies that Daniel overrode Kristi when naming their baby (Daniel wanted Hunter, Kristi wanted Tyler). Crucially, the only two people Kristi can talk to about her experiences and concerns are their housekeeper and nanny Martine (Vivis Cortez) and Ali. Martine appears to have some experience with the sort of activity that is afflicting her employer's household, and puts her knowledge to use as she seeks to protect Hunter by chanting and smudging the house. Despite firing her for this behavior, it is Martine and her knowledge that Daniel later relies on when he realizes Kristi is in danger.

Martine's power and knowledge are problematically framed through her ethnicity: As a racialized Other she is supposedly granted access to "primitive" knowledge that the film regressively implies the more sophisticated middle-class Caucasian suburban family are not privy to. Julia Leyda identifies the traditions of such a relationship in the Val Lewton–Jacques Tourneur horror collaborations of the 1940s, where once again "a wealthy white male rejects the atavistic knowledge of a female Other character, followed by his acceptance and reliance on her knowledge."[18] As John Kenneth Muir suggested, today such a stereotypical treatment is at best anachronistic: "It's a bit old and a bit silly to see this ancient idea played out again in 2011; the non-white ethnic as 'keeper' of the real faith while materialistic, grounded white Americans are blind and deaf to all the strange things occurring around them."[19] To its credit, the recent official Latino spin-off *Paranormal Activity: The Marked Ones* (Christopher B. Landon, 2014)—like *Paranormal Activity: Tokyo Night* (Toshikazu Nagae, 2010) before it, discussed further in Chapter Nine—to some degree defuses the simplistic representation of race in the primary films.

Less clumsy is the depiction of the film's other strong female character, Ali. In many crucial regards, her plucky self-reliance is a nod to the tradition of the slasher film's Final Girl as outlined in Carol J. Clover's foundational book *Men, Women and Chain Saws: Gender in the Modern Horror Film*. She deviates in important ways, however. She is not particularly tomboyish, and unlike the Final Girl, she does not "become if not the killer of the killer then the agent of his expulsion from the narrative vision"[20] simply because Ali is absent from the house when Katie goes on her killing spree. And unlike Clover's Final Girl who is sexually inactive, Ali has a boyfriend. Brad assists Ali in her investigations, but he is second-in-command to her. Ali is in control, and she is also willing to stand up to her father and argue with him when others are not. Even more significantly, it is she who urges Daniel not to follow Martine's advice by partaking in a ritual to shift the curse from Kristi to Katie. This may have been the primary factor in Ali's survival, as the film's end credits inform us that Ali was absent from the house when her parents were killed and her brother abducted, and she makes a significant cameo in *The Marked Ones*. But can Ali's survival be considered a triumph? If the best that women in the *Paranormal Activity* franchise can hope for is coming home to find their parents murdered, brother kidnapped and beloved aunt responsible for these horrors, then Ali's "victory" is far from enviable.

Origins: Paranormal Activity 3 *(2011)*

By *Paranormal Activity 3*, it appears Ali is merely a glitch in the franchise's otherwise seemingly immobile system of representing women. Again, attention is paid early in the film to establishing Katie's monstrosity; her mother Julie's boyfriend Dennis tells her to "take it easy" because the piñata she attacks at her birthday party is "already dead," affectionately calling her a "little monster." While an otherwise disposable comment, in light of the films that have preceded it, this statement is laden with significance, and suggests that Katie's future villainy was predestined. In a broader consideration of gender in the *Paranormal Activity* franchise, the third installment introduces two crucial characters, Katie and Kristi's mother Julie, and their grandmother Lois. Revealing Lois as the leader of a mysterious coven that lies at the heart of the series, evidence of Lois' malevolence riddle the film. Lois typifies Barbara Creed's description of the witch traditionally as "an old, ugly crone who is capable of monstrous acts"[21] and like Katie, the representation of Lois relies on the tradition of monstrous-femininity in horror.

This begins early in the third movie, where video footage of Katie's eighth birthday party shows Lois asking Dennis if the heavy video camera hurts his back, foreshadowing her snapping his spine at the film's conclusion. Kristi even tells Dennis that there is a direct relationship between her grandmother and Toby:

DENNIS: Is he old like Grandma or young like you?
KRISTI: He's old, like Grandma.

Superficially, young Kristi's reply suggests that she simply is equating one elderly person with another, but the double meaning contained within her statement aligns Lois and Toby on a much more significant level. The film's climax shows Lois dressing her young grandchild in bridal attire for what Kristi claims is her wedding to Toby, making Lois' involvement explicit and rendering the final revelation of her links to a coven logical. The coven itself of course emphasizes the series-wide commitment to monstrous-femininity: A male demon may wield the power, but elderly monstrous women are to blame for both summoning and serving him.

Less tangible is the ethical status of Julie in the series. In this film, she is presented as a dedicated single mother who acts in a kind although understandably skeptical manner. One of the unanswered mysteries of the series—and one that may be addressed in the upcoming *Paranormal Activity 5*—is how Julie went from the likable, sympathetic character we see in *Paranormal Activity 3* to a woman whom Micah describes in the first film as "mean," and who apparently has other significant yet vague issues: Katie threatens Kristi in the second movie by telling her that if she does not ignore the strange occurrences in her house, then she is "going to end up just like Mom." It is impossible at this stage to lock down precisely what is meant here, but one can speculate that after Dennis' death, Julie quite plausibly reacted negatively (particularly if she had any inkling—conscious or otherwise—of the involvement of her mother and daughters in her partner's death). Either way, Julie's future (off-screen) monstrosity is concretely foreshadowed in the scene where she wears a monster mask and leaps out of a closet to frighten Dennis and his colleague Randy (Dustin Ingram).

If Julie is a difficult character to pin down, then even less tangible is Katie and Kristi's father. The only time he is mentioned is when Lois tells Julie that the "girls miss their father." Whether he died or left Julie and the children is unclear, but his absence offers one possible reason why both Kristi and Katie ended up in relationships with overbearingly "present" men. Crucially, however, they are not without a male role model and Dennis is one of the franchise's more fascinating characters in terms of how he both deviates and conforms to the pre-established patterns of masculinity across the series up to this point. Revisiting a scene from the first movie, Dennis wants to film him and Julie having sex, but unlike Micah—who lies to Katie on the subject—Julie is a willing participant. Her equality in this sequence is demonstrated by her wearing a man's shirt. Julie is aligned with the masculine in other ways in this film, too, and her blunt statement "There is no Toby and there is no ghost" echoes Daniel's denial in the second film, suggesting a belief that their own word is gospel and so powerful that it can confirm their own version of events.

Dennis also takes on an active role in the children's lives. He plays with them, and takes note of small details that Julie does not appreciate, such as the nuances of Kristi's relationship with Toby. At the same time, Dennis also repeats many of Daniel and Micah's less positive character traits. Julie asks Dennis to delete their attempt at making a sex tape, and not only does he not do so, he shows it to Randy. After setting up surveillance equipment throughout the house, when unusual events begin occurring he decides not to show

Six. Approaching Paranormal Activity 143

Katie (Chloe Csengery) and Kristi (Jessica Tyler Brown) in *Paranormal Activity 3* (Henry Joost and Ariel Schulman, 2011) (Paramount Pictures/Blumhouse Productions/Solana Films/The Kobal Collection).

Julie because she would "flip out" and make him stop filming. More and more he keeps information from Julie for this reason until he finally tells her what he has discovered, and she accuses him of neglecting her in preference to his demon-hunting video project. For Julie, the supernatural activity and Dennis's use of technology are inherently linked: "No more cameras. No more ghosts. This ends tomorrow," she tells him at one point. When Dennis tells her he can sense something happening in the house, she draws parallels between his camera surveillance and the paranormal presence: "I feel something, too. It's a camera." Even at Lois' house at the film's conclusion, she asks when he will stop filming. Dennis directly associates the technological and the demonic as being intertwined when he answers, "Not until this thing is over."

Blurring the Boundaries: Paranormal Activity 4 *(2012)*

Doug in *Paranormal Activity 4* offers yet another version of masculinity, one that extends the absent father motif suggested by the notable absence of Katie and Kristi's father from the narrative. This film's opening scene offers typical home movie footage of young Wyatt's soccer game as his mother Holly and teenage sister Alex look on. Doug and Holly argue when Doug arrives late, putting the onus on Alex to distract Wyatt from their bickering. Mirroring the unraveling relationship of Micah and Katie in the first film, rather than providing the emotional intensity that feeds the demonic activity, in *Paranormal Activity 4* the domestic unrest distracts the parents from the horror that has invaded their household. While Micah, Daniel and Dennis embrace technology and align their own performance of masculinity with the video camera, Doug is a Luddite who openly confesses to having little idea of or interest in technology. Compared to the other men across the franchise, Doug's inability to engage in the same rituals of masculinization as his counterparts in the other movies goes to the other extreme, castrating him symbolically by rendering his patriarchal authority impotent.

Doug's diminished sense of masculine control is linked to the collapse of his marriage. While this deterioration does not take center stage as it does in the first film, it is equally as realistic: The sighs, silences and looks of disappointment between the couple are often as powerful as Katie and Micah's vocal hostilities. In one of the film's most memorable scenes, a knife flies up to the ceiling while Holly prepares dinner. It falls dramatically back down when Doug is in the kitchen, leaving him confused and disoriented. When Holly asks him what is wrong, she misinterprets his shock as hostility, and storms off. The paranormal activity that dominates this film falls off the parental radar because they distracted by the reality of their deteriorating marriage.

Their children are not immune to the breakdown of their parents' relationship, and Alex comments at numerous points that she is affected in a negative way. At a silent dinner table, she asks them, "Don't you want to talk about what's happening?" referring to the supernatural events in the house but also implying that there is a notable inability to articulate the obvious fact that her parents' relationship is crumbling. She talks to her boyfriend Ben (Matt Shively) about it, and again tends to focus on the family's failure to discuss openly issues such as Wyatt's adoption. After she is almost killed in the family garage (she is mysteriously locked in with a running car spewing out carbon monoxide), Doug takes her out to dinner to talk but she argues that it is a waste of time because she is never listened to when she does speak. Wrapped up in their own problems, Doug and Holly do not notice those of their children. This neglect is most dramatically demonstrated when Holly leaves Wyatt in the bathtub to talk on the telephone: He is pulled underwater by a mysterious invisible entity (assumed to be Toby). It is here that Wyatt undergoes his supernatural transformation similar to that of Kristi and Katie in the first and second films.

That Doug deviates so notably from the other adult men in the franchise thus far does not mean *Paranormal Activity 4* is totally bereft of adult masculine power, and it fills this gap in a creative way. The significance of next-door neighbor Robbie is twofold in terms of its gender politics: On one hand, he most obviously functions as an abandoned child figure. This is clear in the opening moments as he watches Wyatt's soccer game and walks home by himself. When Robbie appears in their garden, Alex learns that he is supposedly the child of their busy single mom neighbor Katie, and that he is left to fend for himself much of the time. When the family discovers that Katie has been hospitalized, they take Robbie in and he develops a close relationship with Wyatt. Early in the film, Robbie is linked to an adult sexuality inappropriate to his apparent "abandoned child" status, and it is this in part that makes him so strange to Alex and Ben. When Robbie first appears in the backyard playhouse and Alex returns him home, Ben comments, "Thanks for cock-blocking me," implying the child intentionally sought to prevent Ben's sexual advances towards Alex. More obviously, Robbie enters Alex's bedroom and sleeps next to her in her bed in a manner eerily reminiscent of the invisible Toby in the first and third film.

These adult aspects of Robbie's character are evidenced in a number of other tangible ways. Alex makes fun of him wearing socks and sandals (a fashion combination linked traditionally with elderly men), he has a strangely formal, old-fashioned manner, and Robbie himself mentions that he has a special soft toy that is 100 years old, implying his age may be more ambiguous than his physical youth suggests. Robbie recalls the traditional figure of the witch's familiar, assisting Katie in her pursuit of Hunter-Wyatt. Seen in this light, Robbie's adult features usurp his physical child form and he becomes the film's central figure of masculine (adult) power.

The principal female character in *Paranormal Activity 4* is Alex herself, who in many ways reprises the key traits of *Paranormal Activity 3*'s Ali: She is assertive, curious, and fearless when it comes to standing up to the perceived failures and misjudgments of her parents. Alex adheres more closely to the typical Final Girl figure in that, despite the fact she has a boyfriend, she is a virgin. She deviates from the Final Girl tradition because it remains unclear whether she survives at all (the movie ends as she is attacked by the coven of elderly female witches at Katie's house). These similarities and differences between Alex and Ali raise significant questions. Firstly, why was it essential for both Alex and Ali to have boyfriends at all? Why could a female friend not have fulfilled this function, or why would Alex and Ali not be enough by themselves? Are the films suggesting through this trend that girls can only be resourceful, courageous and assertive if they have the support of and are deemed attractive by a male counterpart, or is it merely coincidence?

The latter seems unlikely when considering that Ben repeats what has by this point in the series become the recurring motif of sex tape production. He confesses to Alex that he recorded her sleeping, and at one point even asks her to show a "boob" to the camera. The second question concerns why Alex's status at the end of the film so ambiguous. What did she do that was so different from Ali to warrant such narrative ambivalence? The answer to this appears to be fundamentally ethical: While Ali fought for Katie against Daniel's ritual damnation, Alex has no comparable act. Alex also made the decision to spy on her family via surveillance technology (webcams) without their permission; this is the first time in the franchise this occurs, as up until then all participants (except, of course, for baby Hunter) were aware that they were being recorded. Is this why Alex is (probably) punished at the film's conclusion?

Despite this, *Paranormal Activity 4* is the entry that is the least concerned with linking technology and gender. Rather, it focuses on the double meaning of the word "possession" as identified by Hahner, Varda and Wilson in terms of both the demonic forces at work and notions of consumption and ownership. Far from simply a desire to fill a need, they have argued that in late capitalism consumption is the "drive for possession, the unending pursuit of that which might fulfill the subject's want."[22] By locating the films in suburban "McMansions," the *Paranormal Activity* franchise places consumption at its thematic core because its spaces are marked by this desire for consumption, and in this way Hahner, Varda and Wilson contend that "the homes mirror the motivation of the demon: Both exhibit the drive for more, the very ambiguity of want that seeks possession."[23]

Paranormal Activity 4 is so laden with brand names and logos that, of all the films thus far, it makes this link between spiritual and consumer possession the clearest. There are repeated references to Microsoft's Kinect gaming console, and the regular appearance of Mac logos suggests this gratuitous product placement is little more than a marketing attempt to cash in on a multi-million dollar franchise. However, aside from underscoring the historical specificity of the economic context of the series, these products are also creatively deployed to deal with some of the practical problems that having an invisible villain entails. For instance, the use of the Kinect's night vision dots to "show" the presence of paranormal entities without resorting to enigma-killing reveals is not only inventive, but also is one of the most visually rich features of the entire franchise (*The Marked Ones* also employs the iconic *Simon* electronic game during a séance to create a similar link between game technology and supernatural presence). It also corresponds to a trend in horror video games where media technology is used as a tool to reveal, locate and even potentially destroy the supernatural, such as in *Fatal Frame/Project Zero* and the *Siren* series.[24] While this provides a curious intertextual aspect to the film, it deviates notably from the way that the first three films negotiate gender politics through technology.

A brief concluding observation regarding the franchise's most recent entry—the spin-off *Paranormal Activity: The Marked Ones*—must note how insightfully it critiques the franchise itself. With a first hour that feels more like a Latino *Chronicle* meets *Jackass* than a traditional *Paranormal Activity* film, *The Marked Ones* crucially refuses to privilege the white middle class family at the heart of the franchise's primary films. Like *Tokyo Night* before it, it acknowledges that there are other equally spectacular stories beyond the realm of this white middle class demographic. *The Marked Ones* is also notable for its comparatively radical conclusion as it exposes a number of wormholes between its 2012 present, the 2007 of the first film and the 1988 setting of *Paranormal Activity 3*. By doing so, *The Marked Ones* does not *add* to the revelations of the broader increasingly coherent story arc like the other films do, but rather it *destablizes* it by both spectacularly corrupting its spatial and temporal logic, and also by introducing new stories specific to its characters alternate racial, cultural and class-based contexts and experiences. This diversity necessarily challenges the logic of the dominant white middle-class narrative that had governed the primary franchise up to this point.

At the time of writing, it remains unclear what direction the *Paranormal Activity* franchise will take in the as-yet unreleased additions to the series, and if the many issues and questions explored in this brief analysis will be clarified. Like *The Blair Witch Project*, the franchise thus far shows a complex and at times problematic manifestation of the relationship between gender and technology.

PART 3
Further Discoveries: 2007–2013

As the previous examinations of *The Blair Witch Project* and the *Paranormal Activity* franchise have suggested, found-footage horror both preserves and expands the genre's status as a forum to consider the broader domain of gender politics. Maintaining the historical narrative that has structured the book thus far, Part 3 turns its attention to post–2007 found footage horror to sample the thematic and subgeneric diversity that has flourished in a category often falsely accused of narrowness in these areas.

Chapter Seven turns to the enduring exorcism trope, *The Devil Inside* (William Brent Bell, 2012) and *The Last Exorcism* (Daniel Stamm, 2011) both revealed in a mainstream found footage horror context the complex—and often contradictory—elements that this resilient horror subgenre relies upon, exposed in large part due to their diegetic dependence on technology and documentary filmmaking practices. Likewise, the family has long been a source of often-perverse fascination in horror movie history, and Chapter Eight turns its attention to a number of found footage horror films that place the domestic sphere under the microscope, including *Exhibit A* (Dom Rotheroe, 2007) from the United Kingdom, *Home Movie* (Christopher Denham, 2008) from the United States, the Spanish movie *Apartment 143* (Carles Torrens, 2011) and from Australia, Joel Anderson's *Lake Mungo* (2008). Chapter Nine looks beyond the walls of the family home to the world outside with an emphasis upon notions of nation and national identity, exploring a range of ways that a number of found footage horror films from around the globe have utiliized the subgenre's codes and conventions to reflect on everything from 9/11 to the Australian history wars to the rise of J-pop. Movies such as *Cloverfield* (Matt Reeves, 2008), *[Rec]* (Jaume Balagueró and Paco Plaza, 2007), *Shirome* (Kôji Shiraishi, 2010), *Trollhunter* (André Øvredal, 2010), and *The Tunnel*

(Carlo Ledesma, 2011) all reveal in sometimes surprising ways the capacity for found footage horror to engage with a number of diverse socio-political elements when produced across different national and cultural contexts.

Before we begin, however, it is worth emphasizing that the following three chapters offer merely a sample of a much larger number of possible avenues for further critical investigation offered by found footage horror. By no means are exorcism films, the role of the family and the subject of national identity implied to be the only—or even the major—paths deserving of this kind of critical attention. Even the most cursory glance, for example, suggests found footage horror has a curious relationship with the adaptation of literary texts: on the one hand, both *The Frankenstein Theory* (Andrew Weiner, 2013) and *Frankenstein's Army* (Richard Raaphorst, 2013) have explored the subgenre's unique capacity to develop and expand the ideas of Mary Shelley's classic horror novel, while *Il mistero di Lovecraft—Road to L.* (Federico Greco and Roberto Leggio, 2005) and the semi-found footage film *The Banshee Chapter* (Blair Erickson, 2013) offer equally intriguing adaptations of the work of cult horror author H.P. Lovecraft. Even within the following three chapters themselves are a vast number of possibilities for more focused interrogations: most immediately, the found footage horror films of Japanese director Kôji Shiraishi briefly considered in Chapter Nine are arguably deserving of a book in their own right. To rely on an overused expression, Part 3 is perhaps best viewed in the spirit of "getting the ball rolling" towards further examinations of these films (and many others), rather than attempting anything as futile as a final word.

Seven

Exorcism Films

The demonic possession trope is not uncommon in contemporary found footage horror, as demonstrated by some of its biggest titles like *V/H/S* and the *[Rec]* and *Paranormal Activity* franchises. Nikolas Schreck has traced the origins of demonic forces in film back to the earliest days in movies such as *Le Manoir Du Diable* (Georges Méliès, 1896) and *Der Student von Prag* (Paul Wegener and Stellan Rye, 1913), celebrating it as an enduring cinematic trope.[1] Exorcisms have proven to be particularly powerful in terms of both their visceral effect on audiences and their box office lure, demonstrated by the blockbuster success of William Friedkin's *The Exorcist* (1973). While *The Exorcist* is considered widely to be the starting point of the exorcism subgenre and places it firmly within a Roman Catholic tradition, many of its signature features appeared over thirty years earlier in the Jewish exorcism movie *The Dybbuk* (Michał Waszyński, 1937).

The Last Exorcism (Daniel Stamm, 2010) and *The Devil Inside* (William Brent Bell, 2012) illustrate how the formal and narrative features of found footage horror intersect with these traditions. Aside from these films and the short entry in the found footage horror anthology *V/H/S* "10/31/98" (Radio Silence, 2012), there are a number of lesser-known micro-budget found footage exorcism horror films such as *Back from Hell* (Leonardo Araneo, 2011), *Anneliese: The Exorcist Tapes* (Jude Gerard Prest, 2011), *Chronicles of an Exorcism* (Nick G. Miller, 2008) and *Exorcist Chronicles* (Will Raee, 2007). However, it is in the two recent mainstream examples where these concerns most clearly manifest through their diegetic filmmakers' faith in both technology and the documentary project itself to reveal an intrinsically moral "truth" about the existence of good and evil.

In *The Devil Inside*, this link between vision and technology is privileged by the repeated use of retinal camera footage. Crucially, the revelatory promise in both of these films is actively thwarted to varying degrees by their notoriously difficult endings. In *The Exorcist*, technology stands as a symbol of science and reason, the very forces that exorcism films typically place at odds with religion and faith. Exorcists step in where scientists fail. This failure of technology is granted a visceral intensity in *The Exorcist* in early scenes where Regan's (Linda Blair) body is prodded and probed by a number of gadgets and machines to discover the cause of her condition. The failure of science and technology to provide insight leads her mother Chris (Ellen Burstyn) to the Church, resulting in the eponymous ritual executed by Fathers Merrin (Max von Sydow) and Karras (Jason Miller). Technology is even more central to its much-maligned sequel, *Exorcist II: The Heretic* (John Boorman, 1977), whose narrative in large part concerns a potential technological solution to demonic possession.

When the exorcism trope is deployed in contemporary found footage horror, filmmaking technologies themselves are granted an additional divination quality to expose the "fact" of demonic possession. In different ways, technology fails its mission to provide clarity on the subject of demonic possession and exorcism that its diegetic inclusion might otherwise suggest in both *The Last Exorcism* and *The Devil Inside*. These films rely on an appropriation of documentary codes and conventions then in turn expose their desire to expose a hidden "truth." However, filmmaking technologies in both cases obscure rather than reveal. The vocal public discomfort with this fact suggests that moral vision—what Peter Brooks has called the "moral occult"—active within mainstream found footage exorcism films is contentious at best.

Exorcism Films and the Moral Occult

The Exorcist opens with Merrin discovering an amulet of the demon Pazuzu in Iraq. Merrin had some time earlier defeated Pazuzu, and this discovery acts as a portent of a future encounter. In Georgetown, Karras struggles with his faith after the death of his mother and is approached by single mom Chris about her daughter Regan. Regan was previously a happy and healthy child but her condition has become increasingly serious and her numerous doctors are incapable of providing any answers. These doctors refer Chris to the Church, and by the time she meets Karras she is desperate. As the signs of possession become more apparent, Karras and Merrin unite to exorcize Pazuzu, leading to Merrin's death. To save Regan's soul, Karras invites the demon into himself and leaps to his death out of Regan's bedroom window as the demon attempts to take control of him. Karras' friend Father Dyer (William O'Malley) grants last rites to the dying Karras, leaving Regan to be happily reunited with her mother.

Regan's bodily trauma is central to both the narrative and spectacle of *The Exorcist*. It is the site where the film's battle between good and evil takes place, and both sides of this showdown are personified by masculine figures. The male spirit Pazuzu and the two priests struggle for control of the out-of-control female body (one marked as doubly volatile due to her age as she transitions from girlhood to womanhood). Regan's suffering is spectacularized in an unambiguously moral way: Her tortured body is literally the forum where masculinized good and evil duke it out, as each seeks dominance. The historical context of the film's initial release is vital to understanding exactly why *The Exorcist* caught the public imagination the way it did. Much of its impact lies in its poignant encapsulation of its zeitgeist, capturing the paranoid sociopolitical climate of North America in time where it was dominated with news of Charles Manson, Altamont, the Vietnam War and Watergate.[2] The tensions within *The Exorcist* also reflected the more intimate concerns of those living in a decade that saw radical shifts in family life, with the increase of divorce paralleling a drop in birth rates. The post-hippie generation carried a deep mistrust of traditional values into their adult lives.[3]

Although it was one of *the* defining Hollywood blockbusters of the 1970s,[4] its origins were personal. It was based on the 1971 novel by Jesuit-educated William Peter Blatty; he found in the story of the real-life exorcism of a 14-year-old Maryland boy in 1949 a validation of his own Catholic faith after his mother's death.[5] Regardless of whether this early real-life event was a genuine supernatural phenomenon or something with a scientific explanation, its impact on Blatty was substantial. The influence of *The Exorcist* on later found footage exorcism films is undeniable, and it is significant that Blatty's novel had originally been intended as a factual account of the Maryland exorcism but he was forced turned his project towards fiction when the boy's family refused to assist with his project.[6] However, these documentary origins still influenced both Blatty and Friedkin tonally, and much attention has been lavished upon Friedkin's vigilante-style directorial techniques that included assaulting actors to garner authentic reactions.[7] These histrionics were not restricted to the film's production, and rumors circulated that some screenings provoked fits of vomiting, fainting, crying, and even suicides, murders and miscarriages. Evangelist Dr. Billy Graham publicly declared this was because "evil was embedded in the celluloid of the film itself."[8] That the materiality of filmmaking was granted a specifically ethical quality is significant not just to found footage exorcism films, but to the category more broadly, where there is commonly a tangible relationship between filmmaking technologies and supernatural activity.

The ethical spectacle of Roman Catholicism that manifests in *The Exorcist* functions in two parallel yet overlapping ways, which continue through later found footage exorcism movies such as *The Last Exorcism* and *The Devil Inside*. Many rituals of Roman Catholic faith such as the Eucharist can be understood as spectacular moral gestures, the performances of which in part defines the practice of "being" Catholic. Roman Catholic rituals (in exorcism films, at least) are also powerful signs in the broader non–Catholic cultural imagination that symbolize a less theological and more melodramatic notion of "good" (one defined by its direct opposition to "evil"). The very mechanics of this religious ritual on film is an ethical apparatus that propels narrative, thematic and even stylistic components. More than any other feature, this is in large part what has rendered the exorcism trope so enduring.

The binaries that construct the moral framework of good versus evil in exorcism films are compatible with the same ethical framework as melodrama. Peter Brooks wrote in his foundational 1976 book *The Melodramatic Imagination: Balzac, Henry James, and the Mode of Excess* of its eponymous vision of a world "subsumed by an underlying Manichaeism," where "the narrative creates the excitement of its drama by putting us in touch with the conflict of good and evil played out under the surface of things."[9] Melodrama's dependence upon easily identifiable characterizations is defined along a clear moral trajectory between good and evil. This is symptomatic of its semiotic nature, and Brooks' notion of a symbolic melodramatic "language" finds a parallel in the exorcisms in *The Exorcist, The Last Exorcism* and *The Devil Inside*: "[M]elodramatic good and evil are highly personalized: They are assigned to, they inhabit persons who indeed have no psychological complexity but are strongly characterized."[10] Like the ritual of exorcism, "the ritual of melodrama involves the confrontation of clearly identified antagonists and the expulsion of one of them."[11] Central to Brooks' argument is the "moral occult," or "the hidden yet operative domain of values that the drama, through its heightening, attempts to make present within the ordinary."[12] This moral occult is the main feature of melodrama, as it "strives to find, to articulate, to demonstrate, to 'prove' the existence of a moral universe which, though put into question, masked by villainy and perversions of judgment, does exist and can be made to assert its presence and its categorical force among men."[13] Melodrama's play of moral signs is a dual strategy of occlusion and revelation, its defining excesses constructing spectacular narratives with ethical content hidden within.

Melodrama from this perspective may be considered less a genre as it is a broader tendency of contemporary storytelling. Christine Gledhill posited that melodrama is a "genre-producing machine,"[14] calling it "an organizing modality of the genre system (that) works at Western culture's most sensitive cultural and aesthetic boundaries, embodying class, gender, and ethnicity in a process of imaginary identification, differentiation, contact, and opposition."[15] Consequently, exorcism films like *The Exorcist, The Last Exorcism* and *The Devil Inside* may be fruitfully assessed in relation to how they function melodramatically even if they are not immediately identified as "melodramas" *per se*. In exorcism films, the potential for the moral occult's revelation is contained in the very moment where the horrors that preceded it are finally articulated and contextualized (although not necessarily resolved). What is so fascinating about *The Last Exorcism* and *The Devil Inside* is just how spectacularly they failed—or refused—to do this. In these movies, technology and the documentary project are exposed as fundamentally incapable of clarifying the moral terrain of the exorcism film.

The Last Exorcism *(Daniel Stamm, 2010)*

Both *The Devil Inside* and *The Last Exorcism* rely predominantly upon an appropriation of observational and participatory documentary codes and conventions. Interviews form the basis the earlier sections of both films, implying a sense of formal control over their so-called "documentary" investigations. These interviews are overtly intercut with other types of visual evidence, such as photographs (*The Last Exorcism*), home movies (*The Last Exorcism* and *The Devil Inside*) and television news stories (*The Devil Inside*). In both cases, this sense of formal control increasingly gives way to more observational documentary-style material, its hand-held haphazardness reflecting the growing powerlessness of the investigators in their respective narrative contexts.

The Last Exorcism begins with a hand-held image of the Reverend Cotton Marcus (Patrick Fabian) shaving in a mirror. Presented on screen are three different angles of the Southern evangelist (two in angled mirrors and one of his back as he faces the mirrors), and the significant positioning of this image at the opening of the movie underscores the thematic centrality of divided and split identities to the film. Non-diegetic titles appear on the screen providing location details—Baton Rouge, Louisiana—and along with the appearance of non-diegetic music in key places, this acknowledges from within the film itself that it is a construction. Despite the feeling of immediacy resulting from its heavy reliance on immersive, diegetically shot hand-held footage, the final film we see wears signs of its post-production overtly. Considering the filmmakers in the movie—director-producer Iris (Iris Bahr) and camera operator Daniel (Adam Grimes)—are (probably) killed at the end, this opens up a number of questions: Who edited this footage together? How did they get it? Does this imply that the "finished" movie we are watching acts as evidence that the satanic conspiracy at the heart of the film was in fact exposed? And if so, can this in itself be considered some kind of resolution (at least, a more satisfactory resolution than the highly ambiguous and obscured footage we see in the last five minutes?).

The "documentary" investigation at the heart of *The Last Exorcism* is a character portrait of Cotton, a disillusioned evangelist who after a career of performing exorcisms without believing in them—but telling himself he was providing a necessary service to clients who believed their family members were possessed—decides that the dangers of someone getting hurt are too great, and wants to stop. The film's title refers to a randomly selected plea for assistance he responds to so he can show documentary director Iris the charlatanism inherent to his profession. As they approach the isolated farmhouse where the potential client lives, Cotton and the film crew encounter strange teenage boy Caleb, who tells them to "go back to where you came from." They discover that the request for an exorcist came from Caleb's fundamentalist father, Louis (Louis Herthum), a simple farmer mourning the recent death of his wife. Louis introduces Cotton and the documentary crew to his teenage daughter Nell (Ashley Bell), and his belief that she is possessed by a demon and is killing his livestock stands in sharp contrast to the polite and naïve adolescent they see before them. As they spend more time with the family, Cotton discovers that both Nell and Caleb have suffered greatly with the loss of their mother. Louis is an alcoholic who has isolated Nell by home schooling her, even removing her from Sunday School because it did not appeal to his fundamentalist beliefs and "didn't seem right."

Caleb discovers quickly that Cotton is a fraud and consequently tones down his hostilities, telling the preacher, "We don't have any problems now." The supposed exorcism begins, and cuts between Cotton performing the ritual over Nell's shaking bed and him showing the camera the different props he uses to create the effects, exposing the procedure as fraudulent. Afterwards, Cotton, Iris and Daniel leave the family believing the job is complete. Iris compliments Cotton and tells him the performance was "more than I expected." The film's first half-hour plays out precisely how Cotton believed it would, but its business-as-usual tone ends when Nell mysteriously appears in his motel room that evening. They rush her to a hospital; when her physical tests come back normal, Cotton urges Louis to consider psychiatric treatment for the girl, a suggestion that Louis greets with hostility. Desperate to help in some way after the "failure" of his fake exorcism, Cotton and Iris visit Louis' ex-pastor Joseph Manley. He tells them he is unable to help the family because Louis was adamant in his rejection of the local church when he left two years previously because their teachings were "not sufficiently medieval." Manley adds, however, that if Louis changes his mind, he is happy to assist them, and even offers to recommend a psychiatrist if Louis wishes to accept his help.

While the intensity of the film's action increases from this point, formally it still includes signs of post-production constructedness. Non-diegetic music is still apparent with the repeated appearance of a screechy violin musical motif that recalls *The Exorcist*. After they leave the hospital, Cotton and the crew return to the farm to find Louis yelling for the camera to be switched off as he angrily drags Nell inside and straps her to her bed after she has attacked Caleb. Louis takes Caleb to the hospital, and after she is released, Nell implies that Louis is abusing her. Iris and Cotton take this even more seriously when a call from the hospital informs them that Nell is pregnant. Iris's predominant role as a behind-the-scenes observer now shifts, as she argues strongly with Cotton that they should effectively kidnap Nell before any more harm comes to her. The relinquishment of any directorial objectivity on Iris's part can be pinpointed to this revelation. "There you have it, your underlying trauma," she angrily declares, believing Nell to be an incest victim. While Cotton is hesitant to leave with Nell without talking to Louis first, Iris angrily declares, "You're going to keep exorcizing her while her dad is raping her upstairs in the bedroom?"

It is at the same moment that Iris's directorial presence shifts from objective to subjective that her tangible control over the project begins to wane. Re-enacting a painting of a bleeding cat, Nell steals the camera and takes it into the barn, filming herself bludgeoning a cat to death with the camera itself. This is a significant moment because it is the first time the violent intensity of Nell's behavior is exposed, simultaneously demonstrating Iris's loss of control over her own film. Iris's relationship to Nell is not a focus of the film but is a fascinating one nevertheless. The first time Iris's actions show her as a character rather than an anonymous off-camera presence is when she gives Nell her boots after the teenage girl shyly admires them.[16] These boots are symbolic of some kind of empowerment or connection for Nell, as she wears them in later scenes with her white night dress regardless of how inappropriate to her outfit they are. Most importantly, she wears them during a later exorcism (discussed further shortly) where she uses the phrase, "I don't have any control over what happens to me" to Cotton in describing the feeling of being possessed. However, this statement has far greater significance considering her broader plight. Like Regan in *The Exorcist*, Nell loses all sense of her own agency as her body becomes a symbolic terrain for male conflict to be enacted: between men (Caleb, Louis and Cotton) and patriarchal institutions (Christianity and science/medicine). That the film's finalé exposes Pastor Manley as being behind Nell's strange behavior, the centrality of gender and the battle for masculine dominance over female bodies is made explicit even in his very name: *Manley*.

Iris's boots are a small gesture in contrast with the excessive scale of the film's more hyperbolic action, but they remain important tangible evidence of a potentially empowering female solidarity that Nell herself on some level appears to comprehend. That this unexplored potential is not just coded through a stereotypical cliché about women's interest in fashion but extinguished in the film's climax offers some uncomfortable realities about the overall gender politics of *The Last Exorcism*. This of course must be considered in relation to the fact that Iris is one of the rare instances in found footage horror where a woman has authorial control of a diegetic filmmaking project. Like Heather's project in *The Blair Witch Project*, Iris's project can be considered far from successful considering she does not survive the movie. As discussed in Chapter Four, the diegetic inclusion of female directors on its own cannot be hailed as necessarily progressive.

During the night that Nell returned from the hospital, there is a notable tonal shift in the formal construction of the movie as its non-diegetic features and interviews decrease. This creates a growing sense of immersion and immediacy, adding to the building suspense. Additionally, the activities during this

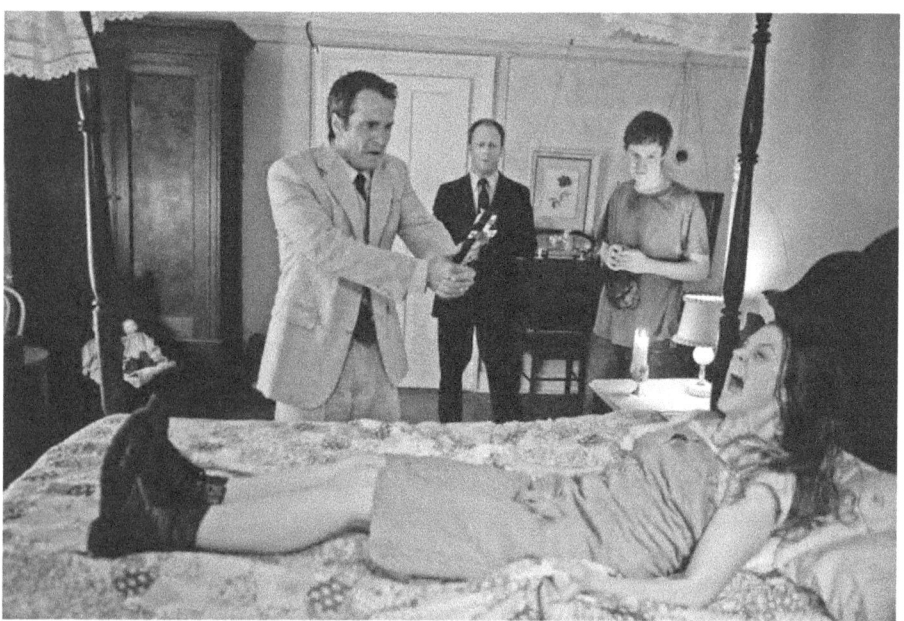

Nell (Ashley Bell) in her boots in *The Last Exorcism* (Daniel Stamm, 2010) (Strike Entertainment/The Kobal Collection).

night are shot in almost total darkness, making it difficult to see what is happening. This enhances the ominous tone and provides a spooky focus on features like Louis' glowing eyes, glistening in the darkness as he implies that he will kill Nell when he tells Cotton, "Reverend, if you can't save my daughter's soul, I will." This literal darkness obscures much of the film's action that we want to see. Emotions reach fever pitch as Nell attacks Cotton, and Louis pulls a gun on them, with Cotton finally agreeing to do another exorcism.

The next day Cotton admits to camera that he is in a "no-win situation" and that by trying to save Nell he has risked getting her killed. Non-diegetic music plays through a brief montage of Cotton preparing for the second exorcism, to take place in the barn. Shot in high contrast and edited quickly to enhance the sense of action, this sequence includes some of the film's most memorable moments of horror such as Nell breaking her own fingers and her torso bending backwards. However, it is her clumsy, childish way of talking about sex that leads Cotton to conclude that the entire possession is an act on Nell's part. When faced with this accusation, Nell breaks down crying. In her bedroom, she confesses that she is pregnant to local boy Logan (Logan Craig Reid). Cotton, Iris and Daniel leave Louis praying at her bedside with Pastor Manley, and as soft acoustic guitar plays in the background, a non-supernatural conclusion is implied. Seemingly tying up loose ends, Cotton and Iris visit and are shocked to hear that Nell's story is untrue because he is gay. Iris and Cotton believe that both Nell and the pastor lied to them, and their desire to find out why sees them returning to the farm.

A menacing soundtrack accompanies them as they rush through the house and find it defaced with satanic graffiti. Cotton hears strange chanting and runs out of the house. He tells Daniel to turn off the light on his camera to help hide them, and therefore much of the action that follows occurs in almost total darkness. Adding to the sense of immediacy and urgency that has been increasing throughout the film, in this climactic sequence the video is also heavily distorted; combined with the fact that the camera's light is switched off, the action is doubly obscured. The group sees a large fire and approach it, and in the light of its flickering flames they see a chained-up Lewis and other images in brief flashes, leading Iris to suggest they contact the police. Cotton disagrees. There is screaming as Cotton explains that Nell has given birth to something that appears not to be human. The sounds of screaming and noises similar to a pig can be heard, and in the bursts of firelight they familiar faces and people walking around in dark cloaks. It is revealed that Pastor Manley himself is overseeing the satanic ritual. Daniel suggests they should run but again, Cotton refuses. He holds up his crucifix and walks towards the fire reciting Biblical verse. It is unclear what happens to him, but like the cat earlier, this image recalls one of Nell's paintings and implies that Cotton meets his death at this time. Iris and Daniel flee, and from the perspective of Daniel's camera the sound of Iris screaming and the sound of her being attacked are heard. The film ends with Daniel running through the darkness until he is confronted by Caleb, who appears to kill him. The screen cuts dramatically to black and the credits roll.

The Devil Inside *(William Brent Bell, 2012)*

With audiences already shaken by the ambiguities of *The Last Exorcism*'s ending, it is surprising that *The Devil Inside* opted for a less and not more intelligible conclusion. Paramount paid only $1 million for the movie; it took $34.5 million in its first weekend, but the second weekend takings dropped a staggering 76 percent once the negative feedback from reviewers and early audiences spread.[17] In the wake of the exceptionally poor critical response— *Rolling Stone*'s Peter Travers labeled it the worst movie of 2012 as early as January that year[18]—its creators (director William Brent Bell, co-writer Matthew Peterman and producer Morris Paulson) scrambled to save face in the post-release press coverage. Some of these interviews suggest that the film was conceptually misfiring from the outset. For instance, taken on its own merits the film's introductory intertitle suggests a firm authorial grasp on the power of denial: "The Vatican does not authorize the recordings of Roman Catholic exorcisms / The Vatican did not endorse this film / nor aid in its completion." The logic of the statement implies that by virtue of the Vatican's lack of endorsement, what we are about to see *is* in fact an actual exorcism. It is therefore disappointing that the intertitle literally referred to a direct request by the filmmakers that the Vatican turned down.[19] The film's oft-cited promotional slogan "The film the Vatican doesn't want you to see" also recalls that of the found footage horror film *Exorcist Chronicles* five years earlier ("The film the Church doesn't want you to see"), suggesting that *The Devil Inside*'s claims of innovation were slightly overstated,[20] and linking it to traditional exploitation film marketing strategies.

Like *The Last Exorcism*, *The Devil Inside* appropriates familiar documentary modes, and begins by intercutting interview footage with home video, archived television news footage and photographs. It retraces the story of Maria Rossi's (Suzan Crowley) murder of three people during a "church meeting" in her house on October 31, 1989, in South Hartford. Rossi's daughter Isabella (Fernanda Andrade)—now an adult—fills in the details, saying that she noticed when she was six years old that her mother began changing, and

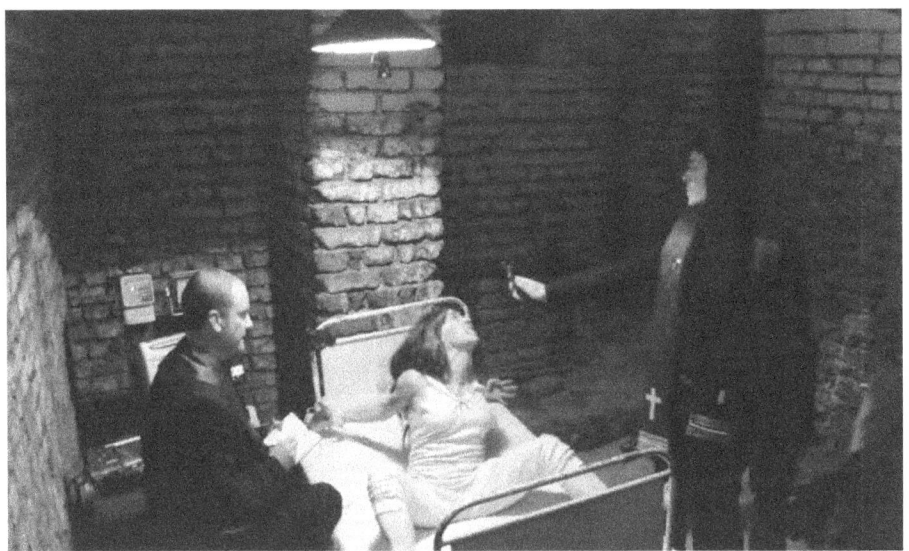

Rosa (Bonnie Morgan) is exorcised in *The Devil Inside* (William Brent Bell, 2012) (Insurg Pictures/The Kobal Collection).

that her father told her as an adult that the killings occurred during an attempted exorcism. Isabelle tells documentary filmmaker Michael Schaeffer (Ionut Grama) that she wants to make a film with him so she can begin to understand what happened to her mother. Further interviews and television news clips indicate that Maria was found not guilty by reason of insanity, and after a period of incarceration at the South Hartford State Asylum, she was transferred to the Centrino Mental Hospital for the Criminally Insane in Rome, Italy.

Like *The Last Exorcism, The Devil Inside* relies heavily on interviews in these early stages, intercut with Michael's raw hand-held footage. Michael and Isabella arrive in Rome to investigate a newly instigated "exorcism school" at the Vatican, as Isabella's curiosity was sparked by the Church's official denial that her mother ever had an exorcism. They meet Father David Keane (Evan Helmuth) and Father Ben Rawlings (Simon Quarterman), whose disillusionment with Church bureaucracy has led them to perform unauthorized exorcisms on individuals they believed to be possessed, but who had not met the Church's strict criteria for such a diagnosis. Up until this point, Michael is ambivalent about exorcism: "I guess now we'll see if it's bullshit or not," he says to-camera before his first eyewitness encounter. This occurs as he and Isabella watch Ben and David's exorcism of Rosa (Bonnie Morgan), who supplies one of the film's most spectacular images as she contorts her body into terrifying shapes without the assistance of special effects. Convinced that her mother is possessed, Isabella urges the renegade priests to accompany her and Michael to visit Maria in a hospital where they covertly execute a successful exorcism. Ben has previously identified that Maria is possessed by multiple demons, and the latter half of the film suggests they left her to inhabit first David and then Isabella. This is illustrated through a number of sequences, including David's attempted murder of a baby during a baptism and his suicide, and Isabella having seizures and violently attacking people in a hospital emergency ward.

The controversial final moments of the film suggest that the demons leave Isabella and possess Michael, as Ben attempts an on-the-fly exorcism as they frantically drive from the hospital to get help from exorcism expert Father Robert Gallo (Claudiu Trandafir). Physically rocked by the demonic presence, Michael loses control of the car and it crashes, destroying the automatically activated cameras attached to the car and ending the film. Effectively finishing *in medias res*, this conclusion is often pinpointed as the cause of *The Devil Inside*'s failure. After the commercial nose-dive of the film after its debut weekend once word of mouth spread, interviews by its creators did little to assuage audience's fury. Rejecting the criticism, they argued that the film's ending in fact has many fans, and those who did not appreciate it simply did not appreciate their conscious rejection of traditional Hollywood norms. The bravado underlying this dismissal (repeated on numerous occasions[21]) is perhaps a natural response in the face of the scathing public attacks the film received from both audiences and critics.

The intensity of this negativity does raise interesting questions, however. Critics such as Isabel Cristina Pinedo,[22] Tania Modleski[23] and W.H. Rockett[24] are three of many who have argued that the open-endedness of horror is not just common, but one of its defining features. From *The Birds* (Alfred Hitchcock, 1963) to *Carrie* (Brian De Palma, 1976) the big slasher franchises (*Halloween*, *Nightmare on Elm Street*, *Friday the 13th*, etc.), there is ample evidence of the ubiquity of open-ended horror. So what precisely was it about *The Devil Inside* that went so wrong?

One accusation lobbed at the film was that the conclusion simply maintained the weaknesses that permeated the film from its opening moments. Others felt that audiences more generally were becoming increasingly tired of found footage horror as a whole, desensitized to its once-shocking tactics. As Mark Olsen at the *LA Times* said, so clichéd was *The Devil Inside* that it "plays like a horror film conceived on graph paper."[25] Actor Simon Quaterman also admitted there was some nervousness when making the film that *The Last Exorcism* shared its subject matter, despite his insistence that the final products were notably different.[26]

While the film has been interpreted as being merely bad, the hostility towards it stems from something more complex. Even more than *The Last Exorcism*, *The Devil Inside* takes the idea of technology-as-failed-witness to its most logical and extreme conclusion. In horror, the refusal-to-show tradition stretches back at least to Val Lewton, and *The Blair Witch Project* provides perhaps the most famous example in found footage horror. *The Last Exorcism* reconfigures this refusal-to-show by literally filming in darkness: It is almost impossible to tell what is going on in its final sequence without the guidance of its characters voices.

However, *The Devil Inside* does much more than simply occluding vision at the moment where we most desire it: *It extinguishes the entire film*. The extent to which audiences felt so vocally disappointed in *The Devil Inside* spoke well beyond mere subgeneric over-familiarity. The tone of its angry fans was closer to outright betrayal. The intensity of this suggests there was a genuine sense of fury at being handed on a proverbial platter what found footage horror had been coyly suggesting ever since *The Blair Witch Project* opened up its nihilistic abyss: Not only is technology and the documentary project incapable of fully acting as a reliable, omniscient recording of a singular, unified "truth," but if we accept this then all we are left with is a black screen—unembellished eternal nothingness.

This ending literally cuts off any places for occulted moral messages to hide, be they ambiguous or otherwise. While *Blair Witch* and *Paranormal Activity* rely heavily on a refusal-to-show for their frights, their endings do not eradicate the possible presence of a malign entity upon which a moral spectrum of good and evil can be mapped. In the context of the exorcism film where the binaries of good and evil form such a large part of the narrative and thematic dynamic, *The Last Exorcism* pushes the limits of expectation by physically obstructing the climactic details so that we cannot be altogether clear on what the rules of engagement are for its ethical battle. We are only vaguely aware who the heroes and villains are, and what may (or may not) have happened to them.

The Devil Inside does not have a twist ending like *The Last Exorcism*, but rather has an *anti*-ending. These two mainstream found footage exorcism films therefore adhere closely to Jeffrey Sconce's identification of Orson Welles' 1938 *War of the Worlds* radio broadcast as a type of "media 'death wish,'"[27] but it is *The Devil Inside* that stretches this to its extreme by denying any possibility of a comprehensible ethical framework. By finishing at this point in this manner, it denies even the most basic plot information necessary to make such a judgment. Acting in defiance of films like *The Exorcist*—and, interviews suggest, even against the conscious intentions of the film's creators themselves—the ending of *The Devil Inside* renders good and evil ultimately incomprehensible. In an interview in 2012, director Bell stated, "I think it's showing as realistic a portrayal of the battle between good and evil, or God and the Devil ... as possible. And that the battle is out there, so don't think that it's not."[28] Ironic, then, that the film's morality remains so spectacularly and eternally unfathomable, forever occluded.

Eight

The Family

Alfred Hitchcock's *Psycho* (1960) saw horror's site of monstrosity shift from "outsiders" like Bela Lugosi and Boris Karloff to something far more familiar. Norman Bates' infamous horror story played out not only in the domestic sphere, but also at its core sought to expose the dark side of the family itself. In his 1996 book *Hearths of Darkness: The Family in the American Horror Film*, Tony Williams identified the importance of the family as one vital to many cultures and societies as they play a crucial role in the formation of individuals, and the significance of this role means they can adapt to shifting historical and political contexts. Williams suggested that family horror films are not by definition necessarily ideologically reactionary or progressive, and this can be seen in family-oriented found footage horror. Many family horror films can even demonstrate conflicting ideological leanings, and Williams noted that these contradictions mirror the same ones that are active in society more generally. The films are part of a much broader tradition that Williams suggested crosses a wider category of American film and literature that seeks to challenge the constraints of the domestic sphere. Peaking with films like *Rosemary's Baby* (Roman Polanski, 1968), *The Exorcist* (William Friedkin, 1973), *The Omen* (Richard Donner, 1976) and *It's Alive* (Larry Cohen, 1973)—but with evidence of its roots stretching back as far as some of the Universal monster films of the 1930s and Val Lewton's horror films of the 1940s—the horror genre has offered visions of the family that oppose the ideal image of the American family as depicted broadly in film and television programs like *Leave It to Beaver* (1957–1963).[1]

For Vivian Sobchack, the post–1960s horror and science fiction film is a space where patriarchy itself comes under fire. In these movies, "figures from the past and the future get into the house, make their homes in the closet, become part of the family, and open the kitchen and family room up to the horrific and wondrous world outside this private and safe domain." She continued,

A man's home in bourgeois patriarchal culture is no longer his castle. In the age of television, the drawbridge is always down; the world intrudes. It is no longer possible to avoid the invasive presence of Others—whether poltergeists, extraterrestrials, one's own alien kids, or starving Ethiopian children.[2]

Children play a crucial role as a gateway for both literal and metaphoric intruders into the domestic space, challenging the masculine control of the father. For Sobchack, much contemporary horror film seeks to dramatize precisely the "patriarchal impotence and rage"[3] that result from such challenges to this authority, undermined by a broader sense during the 1970s and 1980s in particular that the traditional American nuclear family was crumbling. She stated, "[T]he contemporary horror film dramatizes the terror of a patriarchy without power and refuses or perverts parental responsibility when it is not rewarded with the benefits of patriarchal authority."[4]

In found footage horror, the diegetic appearance of filmmaking technologies—whether in the context of home movie production (Dom Rotheroe's 2007 *Exhibit A* and Christopher Denham's 2008 *Home Movie*), supposedly professional "documentary" productions (Sean Tretta's *Death of a Ghost Hunter* [2007] and Joel Anderson's *Lake Mungo* [2008]), or as one of many tools utilized in an investigative context (*Apartment 143*, Carles Torrens, 2011)—can add new dimensions to the way that family horror explores its internal power dynamics. At the same time, it creates an increased sensation

Exhibit A (Dom Rotheroe, 2007) (courtesy Bigger Pictures http://biggerpictures.co.uk).

of intimacy as we experience the otherwise hidden domain of the family through the formal invitation of the diegetic camera's first person gaze.

Evil Children? Home Movie *(Christopher Denham, 2008)*

The meaning of "childhood" diverges throughout history and across different cultures. Gill Valentine has observed that in the West, the image of the child has typically been cast along an angel-devil binary. The 19th and 20th centuries were dominated by visions of childhood drenched in innocence, but particular contemporary events such as the 1993 murder of Jamie Bulger in the United Kingdom by two ten-year-old boys radically challenged this stereotype. As Gill suggested, fluctuations between visions of children as angels or devils hinge on Othering processes: We believe our own children to be innocent, while it is other people's children who are out of control and dangerous. Films such as *The Bad Seed* (Mervyn LeRoy, 1956) and *The Good Son* (Joseph Ruben, 1993) challenge such assumptions, placing sociopathic or "evil" children in the center of dramas where parents come to grips with the monstrosity that lives in their very homes.[5] William Wandless has argued that "evil children" horror films like *The Exorcist*, *Godsend* (Nick Hamm, 2004) and *Grace* (Paul Solet, 2009) deflect attention from the moral complications of these so-called evil children onto a super/natural condition that causes their monstrosity. In contrast, Rob Zombie's 2007 remake of John Carpenter's 1978 slasher *Halloween*, *Joshua* (George Ratliff, 2007) and *Home Movie* construct plausibly evil children through the sheer glut of their bad behavior. These are not simply naughty children—that is a charming, although sometime grueling, aspect of normal development. In these films, there is something much darker going on.[6]

Home Movie begins with a seemingly random shot of flies devouring road kill, a gruesome image that is interrupted by a sudden cut to the film's title, a generic titles offered in-camera by the home video camera that supposedly shoots the film's events. It cuts to David (Adrian Pasdar) and Clare Poe (Cady McClain) in Halloween costumes, celebrating both the holiday and the birthday of their twins, Emily (Amber Joy Williams) and Jack (Austin Williams). This is the first of many festive occasions performed in front of—and for— the camera, where the parents' excessive enthusiasm overcompensates for the mute withdrawal of the twins. Jack and Emily have a clubhouse with a "no parents allowed" sign on it, which is rendered ominous through the children's increasingly hostile behavior. Jack throws a rock at his father with a clear intent to hurt him, they throw their food off the table during Thanksgiving dinner, and their unruly behavior rapidly escalates to animal torture (Jack makes a goldfish sandwich, Emily kills a frog in a vice, they crucify their cat and behead the family dog). This behavior worsens when they attack a boy at school, biting him violently. The children are expelled.

As a pastor, David's approach to helping the obviously troubled children is markedly different from the approach of child psychiatrist Clare. The latter refers to the children as "subjects" and medicates them heavily, while David opts for an exorcism to cast out whatever unholy spirit is forcing them to behave so terribly. They congratulate themselves on the successful rehabilitation of Jack and Emily; by Easter it appears the twins have returned to normal, chatting and playing. The film's climax, however, reveals that this has been a ruse: They attempt to murder the boy they previously attacked at school, tying him to a table in their clubhouse and torturing him. David and Clare are granted custody of the children overnight until they are charged with attempted murder the next day. Now in charge of the video camera, Jack and Emily gleefully reveal their plan to murder their parents. This culminates in the image of David and Clare strapped to the kitchen table being tortured by the children, who wear strange masks as they bash their cutlery on the table, ready to devour their parents.

The revelation that Jack and Emily have edited the previously seen footage together as part of what they call "The Jack and Emily Show" allows retrospective insight into the traumas and secrets that lie at the heart of *Home Movie*. The reliance on generic default credits on their video camera implies ubiquity, not only of the technology itself, but also to the potential prevalence of its events. *All* home movies, it suggests, can become horror movies. This is not a horror film stemming from supernatural fantasy, but rather a more terrestrial explosion of visceral and violent energy as the Freudian repressed seeks its return. "The Jack and Emily Show" is the children's attempt to expose the family secrets that lie at the core of their frenzied violence. Through their parents' (particularly David's) near-hyperactive fascination with performing parenthood for the camera, the twins through mimicry alone understand the remediation potential of home video. They understand that they can construct their own version of reality, but their story is strikingly different from the upbeat version that David has presented.

This becomes apparent on subsequent viewings of the film: What elements do the children highlight? Why have they included certain scenes in this particular order? Why do they on numerous occasions use the in-camera rewind function to repeat certain phrases or moments? The answers hold the secrets of both the Poe family tragedy and of *Home Movie* itself. In short, the children seek to dominate not only their parents but, through technology, to dominate the narrative of their family history. One of the first significant moments from this perspective is when a grumpy David turns the camera off after Jack has thrown a rock at him. Seemingly unhappy with the camera recording the shift from contrived family hijinks to the hint of domestic violence to come, David stops recording because it is not a narrative in keeping with his ideal vision of their family life. The children choose footage throughout the film that highlights the often-hyperactive display of performative parenting, particularly on David's part.

Why? This becomes clear when Clare discovers David in bed one evening with the twins, and finds the children's bodies covered with deep bite marks. Combining David's drinking problem with Clare's admission that he was abused as a child—both facts that the children go to lengths to highlight in their "documentary"—it is reasonable to assume that David has been abusing Jack and Emily. Initially shocked and angry, Clare curiously has no trouble believing this to be true, and at one point even insists on taking the children to her mother's house. However, after the attack on the boy at school, Clare convinces herself that David did not bite the children at all but rather they bit each other. Relations with David then return to normal, but while Clare is convinced of his innocence, the audience remain skeptical: This does not answer, for example, why David was in bed with the children and why this was hidden from Clare. More significantly, the children emphasize through their careful editing that the bulk of their bad behavior occurs as a direct response to David's performative parenting for the camera: praying at the Thanksgiving table, teaching Jack how to tie knots, playing baseball, etc. Jack and Emily seek to expose David as an abusive parent, but because they are effectively silenced through his performance of loving father, wacky husband and diligent local pastor, their repressed trauma bubbles up in other ways.

Most unsettling of these is their growing fascination with cannibalism. Before the discovery of their schoolmate's tortured body in the twins' clubhouse, David and Clare discover a number of grisly drawings pinned to its walls articulating Jack and Emily's obsession with eating people. William Wandless has emphasized a continuing interest in dragons in the film, typified by the masks the children wear both at Halloween and when they attack Clare in the climax. The children also include in their video a relatively long sequence where David reads them a story about a two-headed dragon that places a paper bag over his head to convince children that he is one of them so he can eat them. This story is important, as in the final reel Jack and Emily wear paper bag masks when they sit at the table with cutlery waiting for their parents to die. The children are also careful to emphasize the importance of food at other points. Again, many of the rituals David seeks to "stage" for the camera involve food. Birthday cakes, Thanksgiving turkeys, and ice cream—these are all important aspects of the rituals that David and Clare use to construct their fantasy of their idealized family, a vision that the children's documentary implies stands in sharp contrast to the abuse they have suffered. That cannibalism and home movie–making technology are the two aspects that intersect at the shocking conclusion is therefore only fitting: mimicking their parents, this is the way Jack and Emily have been taught that new histories are written.

The symbolic and literal disintegration of the Poe family, just like their namesakes in *The Fall of the House of Usher* (1839), forms the foundations of *Home Movie*. What on the surface appears to be a straightforward "evil child" film undermines this subgeneric assumption through a complex formal subtext that recasts David and Clare's dominant historical narrative of domestic bliss as closer to what Jack and Emily have experienced: a horror story. "The Jack and Emily Show" therefore argues that home videos are not a straightforward documentation of reality. They can construct a range of realities, which in the hands of different authors present diverse narratives about what are sometimes incomprehensible secrets.

Falling Apart: Exhibit A *(Dom Rotheroe, 2007)*

A family falls apart in a different way in the British found footage horror *Exhibit A*. As discussed in Chapter Six, *Paranormal Activity* (Oren Peli, 2007) has been understood as reflecting on the recent global financial turmoil, and the notion of "possession" deliberately links on its dual meanings as both supernatural control and a product of capitalist consumption. *Exhibit A* is a financial horror film of an altogether different type. Rejecting supernatural metaphor, *Exhibit A* follows the disintegration of the King family as the father Andy (Bradley Cole) psychologically collapses under the financial burden of keeping up the appearance of a successful, affluent family man. Like the Poe parents in *Home Movie*, King is jovial to the point of aggression. Unlike Clare and David, Andy is not overcompensating for his detached children but presents this forced persona as a way to disguise a much darker side to his personality. The intensified visibility of this repressed paternal violence provides the film with its central narrative trajectory.

Like *Cloverfield* a year later, the home video footage of which *Exhibit A* consists—the eponymous piece of evidence in the Yorkshire Police investigation into the murders we see mentioned in the introductory intertitle—is supposedly taped over previous footage of the Kings' pleasant beach trip before Andy's murderous breakdown. This trip is narratively crucial, as it introduces discussion of a new house the family wish to purchase on the back of Andy's assumed promotion at work. When the promotion does not come through, Andy finds himself trapped in an increasing cycle of deception and debt as he tries to live up to what he believes are his family's expectations. It is in this context that some of the film's most shocking revelations are far from those typically expected in horror. For example, the discovery of a large trash bag full of discarded scratch lottery cards powerfully demonstrates in one image just how far Andy's desperation has stretched.

While *Exhibit A* focused on Andy's breakdown, it is told predominantly from the perspective of his teenage daughter Judith (Brittany Ashworth). Her self-consciousness as she grapples with identity-forming crises of her own (most notably, her developing sexuality as she realizes she has a crush on the girl next door) marks her as a refreshing change from horror's frequent stereotypical representation of smug adolescent heteronormativity. Much of the film's earlier sections focus on genuinely happy family moments, but they become increasingly tense as Andy's situation becomes more apparent. For instance, his quixotic obsession with installing a swimming pool becomes the source of many of the film's most awkward and terrifying moments, beginning when he embroils Judith and her older brother Joe (Oliver Lee) in the construction of a *Funniest Home Video*–style clip. This sequence begins with the light-hearted tone that such a production warrants, but turns ugly when Andy grows frustrated, angry and ultimately violent with Joe for not performing how he wants. As in *Home Movie*, domestic-grade video technology offers Andy a potential eyewitness to his performance of his idealized family image, but his delusions and detachment from his bleak reality means that what it ultimately captures is the exposure of his true self, one that stands in stark opposition to this fantasy.

Judith is not alone in found footage horror in her status as a young woman in charge of the camera, and stands alongside Megan and Amy in *Megan Is Missing*, Ali in *Paranormal Activity 2* (and, to a lesser degree, Alex in the fourth installment of the franchise), Heather in *The Blair Witch Project*, Abi (Abigail Richie) and Ashley (Ashley Bracken) at the end of *Evidence* (Howie Askins, 2011), and *Diary of the Dead* as a whole can be considered Deb's (Michelle Morgan) film even though she compiles it from material shot by her deceased boyfriend. Judith's control of the camera's gaze does not necessarily place her in a position of power; rather it acts as a device that helps her struggle to gain control of a situation that is spiraling dangerously out of control. Her heartbreaking video-diary recordings where she addresses the camera illustrate that

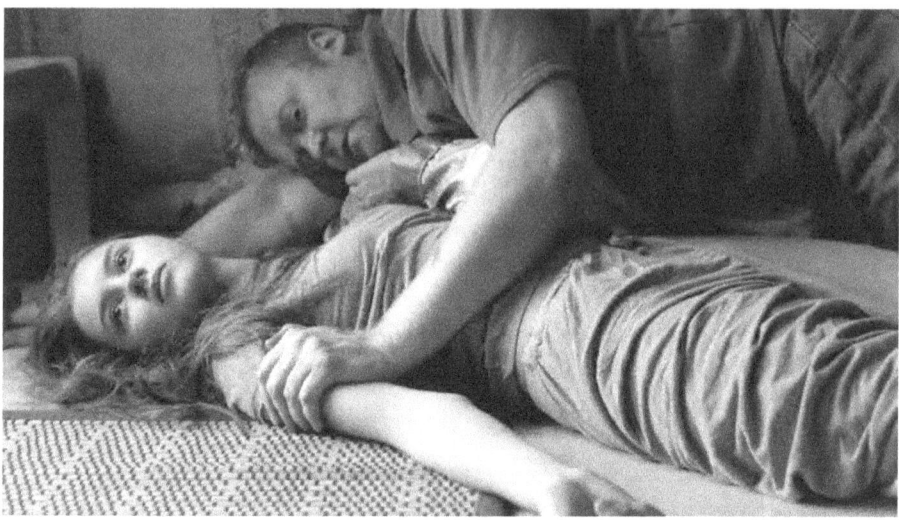

Andy King (Bradley Cole) and his daughter Judith (Brittany Ashworth) in *Exhibit A* (Dom Rotheroe, 2007) (courtesy Bigger Pictures, http://biggerpictures.co.uk).

she talks to it because she simply cannot say these things directly to her father: "I don't know what's going on any more, Dad," she says desperately at one point. Andy too treats the camera as another character, particularly when he gains control of it after a disastrous barbeque with friends and neighbors exposes the extent of his unraveling. "Now you're going to put things right," he says. "No more secrets, and now you're working *for* us." What follows is a manic rampage as he trashes the house looking for evidence of his wife and children's secrets, but in doing so uncovers a truth much more shocking than he imagined. This particular revelation pushes Andy over the edge, leading him to murder his wife Sheila (Angela Forrest), Joe and—if the twist in the final seconds of the film is to be understood correctly—to at least attempt to murder Judith.

Exhibit A is a horror film about domestic violence taken from the perspective of both its victims and its perpetrator. Its climactic murder spree is far from the glossy festival of slicing-and-dicing seen elsewhere in the genre. Rather, it is an inescapably sad affair. Drunk and on pills, Andy weeps as he smothers Judith in front of the camera, and there is a real focus on his shock and shame when he realizes what he has done. Even as he kills his family, however, he still struggles to maintain appearances and utters phrases like "It's all going to be fine," whispering to their bodies "We're all together." Andy's desperation and the real tragedy (and implied ubiquity) of his situation are thus far more palpable than his villainy. However, the film's moral integrity remains intact by allowing him sympathy but forbidding any justifications of or excuses for his actions, as the fear of his children and anger of his wife is depicted just as intensely and sympathetically. Patriarchy does not merely collapse in *Exhibit A*; it issues a swan song under the weight of the very real external pressures that continue to devastate families just like the Kings.

Buried Secrets

Not all found footage horror films address the notion of family secrets in the complex and insightful manner as *Home Movie* and *Exhibit A*. The Spanish film *Atrocious* (Fernando Barreda Luna, 2010) finds teen siblings Cristian (Cristian Valencia) and July (Clare Morelda) in their family's mysterious and isolated summer house with little to do, so they decide to film an episode of their web series "Paranormal Investigations" scrutinizing the disappearance of a girl called Melinda in the 1940s; Melinda is now believed to haunt the woods near the house. While committed to their hobby, they are aware of its scale and at one point even joke sarcastically about being "professionals." Their inquiry becomes more serious when their dog goes missing and is found dead, which is soon followed by the disappearance of their younger brother José (Sergi Martin). Along with their frantic mother Debora (Chus Pereiro), Cristian and July run through the woods searching for him until they are separated. When Cristian finds July, she has been ritualistically tortured; returning to the house, they discover the burnt remains of their younger brother. Cristian hides July in the kitchen and rushes upstairs to his room when an axe-wielding attacker breaks in the front door. The next morning, Cristian finds July's hiding place now soaked in blood, and as he looks for her, he finds a videotape playing in the basement showing Debora in a psychiatric hospital. This tape reveals that not only does his mother have a history of schizophrenia, but that she also murdered another child in the throes of post-partum depression. As he watches, Debora approaches him from behind and kills him. One of the film's most formally interesting moments is a strange non-diegetic break before its climax where crime scene photographs of Cristian, July and José's dead bodies are shown, along with a television news story outlining the case. The film then "rewinds" back to the climactic reveal of Debora's villainy and Cristian's death. This aside, the clumsy deployment of its monstrous-mother-crazed-by-post-partum-depression twist is so thinly supported by an otherwise serviceable film that *Atrocious* breaks down at this point.

Even more confused is *Death of a Ghost Hunter* (Sean Tretta, 2007). The titular paranormal investigator, Carter Simms (Patti Tindall), is offered a three-day job investigating the supposedly haunted Masterson home, and is joined by cameraman Colin (Mike Marsh), journalist Yvette (Davina Joy) and uptight fundamentalist local church representative Mary Young (Lindsay Page), apparently at the request of the home's current owner. Riddled with overwhelming evidence of supernatural activity linked to the murder of minister Joseph Masterson (Tim Wadhams) and his children and the subsequent suicide of his wife Mary Beth (April Hinojosa) at the discovery of her slaughtered family in 1982, it is revealed that Mary Young was not authorized to be in the house. Growing hostilities between the investigative team and the young Christian see her evicted from the premises. Returning to enact revenge, Mary Young murders Carter, Colin and Yvette. A lengthy coda reveals the convoluted backstory: Masterson was a sexual sadist and religious egomaniac who tortured and raped wayward girls in a specially designed chamber above his garage to "cure" them of their sins. One girl refused to confess and was kept pregnant in the chamber until Mary Beth—abused herself and crazed with jealousy—murdered her family and the girl, and attempted to kill the recently born baby. This baby survived, and grew up to be Mary Young.

Death of a Ghost Hunter purports to be based on Simms' journal, and through this logic, the bulk of the film appears to play out as one long re-enactment, suggesting the material we watch is not found footage as such, but a constructed, polished product, complete with voice-overs and non-diegetic music. Formally, however, the film does not maintain this conceit, as other narrators interrupt and at times it breaks into hand-held aesthetics. Most of all, of course, its final scene is supposedly Carter's ghost trying to make contact from "the other side," which makes little sense in practical terms, for how was this based on diaries she wrote after she died? Gaping plot holes aside, the sensational and exploitative revelation of Masterson's history as a sexual abuser seems at best clichéd, and the demonization of his wife and Mary Young in particular provoke some serious ideological questions about the implication that Masterson's victims (and not he himself) are the source of horror, actively responsible for the terror that haunts the house.

Suggestions of sexual abuse underscore the familial tensions at the heart of other found footage horror films including *The Last Exorcism* (Daniel Stamm, 2010), *Paranormal Entity* (Shane Van Dyke, 2009) and *Apartment 143*. The latter focuses on supernatural events in the eponymous apartment, where Alan (Kai Lennox) lives with his two children, teenage Caitlin (Gia Mantegna) and her four-year-old brother Benny (Damian Roman). Paranormal investigators Paul (Rick Gonzales) and Ellen (Fiona Glascott) and psychologist Dr. Helzer (Michael O'Keefe) respond to Alan's report of increasingly disturbing events that have plagued the family in their last two places of residence. The investigators install cameras throughout the apartment, and the movie consists of a combination of this surveillance footage and handheld material.

Alan informs the team that the strange occurrences began after his wife Cindy died, and combined with Caitlin's increasing hostility toward her father, there is an implication of a sexually abusive relationship. During a séance, Caitlin asks the spirit, "Who killed you?" The supernatural presence turns its attention toward Caitlin with overt sexual overtones, at one point lifting her skirt while she sleeps. A medium reveals that Cindy has possessed Caitlin, and the mother is angry with Alan because supposedly he sexually abused their daughter. However, Dr. Helzer's declaration that Caitlin is schizophrenic contextualizes these accusations. Forced to reveal the truth about his marriage, Alan confesses that his wife suffered from a severe mental illness that when left unmedicated made it impossible for her to be left alone with the children. When Caitlin discovered her mother in bed with a stranger one day, Alan's temper broke and he hit his wife and threw her out of their family home, and she died soon after. "Things couldn't go on like that," he said. At this revelation, extreme poltergeist activity begins and Caitlin floats above her bed in a scene reminiscent of Linda Blair in *The Exorcist* (William Friedkin, 1973). In the climactic scene, the spell is broken when Caitlin calls for her father's help and their hands touch: All supernatural activity ceases at the very moment that Caitlin and her father are reunited. In the twist ending, the one remaining camera left by the investigators captures the image of the monstrous Cindy appearing on the ceiling and crawling menacingly toward the camera.

While the team congratulate themselves for the apparent victory of their scientific approach, this does not address the lingering tensions that placed Caitlin in the firing line between Alan and his estranged, undead wife. While the film seems to unequivocally dismiss the abuse claims as part of Cindy and Caitlin's mental health issues, that Caitlin's sexuality was evoked at all speaks of some degree of sexual exploitation. The problem, therefore, is this: If (as unlikely as it is) Cindy was right, then Caitlin was the victim of sexual abuse at her father's hands. If this was untrue and merely the result of Cindy's delusional fantasies, then Caitlin is still a pawn in this vicious domestic battle. Dr. Helzer's emphasis on science's superiority over superstition therefore suggests that a much broader set of binaries dominate the film: good-evil, pure-corrupt, honest-deceitful. From Caitlin's perspective at least, mother-father must also be added. She cannot have both: She is forced to cut one loose if she is to bond with the other. Her supposed happily-ever-after at the end of the film should therefore be considered a far from total victory.

Hidden histories of sexual abuse feature in the horror mockumentary

Lake Mungo, but as part of a much broader thematic interest in gender and family relationships. At its core, it is an exploration of a mother and daughter who—after the death of the latter—struggle to resolve their relationship issues in an environment defined by masculine attempts at control (especially through the use of home video technology). Unlike *Apartment 143*, *Lake Mungo* does this without relying on demonizing any particular character. Instead the source of its horror lies in the mysteries that concern its protagonist.

Recalling David Lynch's cult television series *Twin Peaks* (1990–1991) in a number of ways (including the family's surname), *Lake Mungo* begins with the death of seemingly wholesome teen Alice Palmer (Talia Zuker). It is in the fallout from this tragedy that her dark secrets are exposed, prompting serious reflection by both her family and, more broadly, her community—the small Australian country town of Ararat. After her drowning in a local dam, both strangers and her family members see Alice on numerous occasions, and her brother Mathew (Martin Sharp) installs cameras around their house in the hope of capturing these supernatural appearances. The evidence he finds brings national media attention to the family and their unusual plight. Along with local psychic Ray (Steve Jodrell), Mathew, his father Russell (David Pledger) and mother June (Rosie Traynor) not only work through their grief by investigating Alice's troubled last months, but they are also forced to address the notion of "truth" on a more fundamental and personal level.

Mathew provides the bulk of the material of which *Lake Mungo* consists. Crucially, the choice to record these events is his: He is a confused teen who is both mourning the sudden death of his beloved sister, as well as dealing with his parents' grief. In one of the film's first major twists, it is exposed that Mathew has faked the initial footage showing Alice's ghost in an attempt to give his parents a tangible link to his sister's memory. Although his motives are benign, Mathew seeks to control his sister and her memory through technology. His attempt to do this fails through the exposure of his fraudulent footage, and while he inadvertently succeeds in capturing evidence of a flesh-and-blood intruder in their house (a discovery that leads to the exposure of one of Alice's most shocking secrets, her sexual relationship with her adult neighbors), regardless of how well-intentioned his hoax it ultimately distracted the family from the fact that Alice's real ghost had returned with its own mission.

Technology plays a crucial role in this pursuit of repairing the bond between Alice and her mother, the central relationship that the film seeks to explore. Despite Mathew's best intentions, then, male actions and motives must necessarily take a back seat. Curiously, Ray's video interviews with both

June and Alice before she died, where the women are allowed to speak honestly for themselves, hold valuable information that propels the female healing at the heart of the film. Ray does not control these interviews as much as he facilitates them: He provides the women with an intimate space to voice their fears and concerns. When considering the gendering of technology in this way, it is significant that the film's revealing climax at Lake Mungo draws a distinct parallel between Alice holding the camera, and the chilling exposure of the mystery that haunted her to her early grave. Alice understands that technology can expose things best not seen, and rather than seeking to dominate it, she instead chooses to reject it—to literally bury it. Likewise, the found footage family horror films in this chapter all speak in a number of different ways of things irretrievably lost, be it relationships, hopes, futures or entire identities. The diegetic inclusion of video technology in the construction—and destruction—of these features are fundamental to how they address their particular thematic sites of interest, albeit with varying degrees of success.

Alice's mother June Palmer (Rosie Traynor) during an interview in her kitchen in *Lake Mungo* (Joel Anderson, 2008) (courtesy Mungo Productions Pty. Ltd.).

NINE

Nation, History and Identity

As demonstrated by the recent global success of J-horror, K-horror, and the New French Extremity, horror audiences have voraciously consumed genre films from around the world. Books like Steven Jay Schneider's *Fear Without Frontiers: Horror Cinema Across the Globe* (2003) and Pete Tombs' *Mondo Macabro: Weird & Wonderful Cinema Around the World* (1998) illustrate that national borders have not been an impediment to horror fans in their pursuit of fresh and interesting takes on a genre that can too readily default to clichés. While its myriad tropes and iconographies have found little difficulty in crossing national borders, horror is also uniquely positioned to reflect upon national history, culture and identity. Examining the relationship between horror movies and the real-world horrors that have plagued history, Adam Lowenstein convincingly argued that the affective intensity of this particular genre allows it to be defined as a "return to history through the gut."[1] Lowenstein expanded upon Walter Benjamin's idea that representations of historical trauma are allegorical as they "honor ... representation's promise that trauma can be communicated—its commitment to the image of death is simultaneously a commitment, however conflicted and provisional, to the past's value to the present."[2] This "allegorical moment" became crucial to Lowenstein's broader argument in his book *Shocking Representation: Historical Trauma, National Cinema, and the Modern Horror Film* and he defines it "as a shocking collision of film, spectator and history where registers of bodily space and historical time are disrupted, confronted and intertwined."[3] Although horror has previously been discounted as a space where representations of historical trauma could meaningfully manifest, Lowenstein offers a reconsideration of how horror confronts the representation of historical trauma, particularly in national contexts.

Lowenstein addressed these ideas by identifying links between certain horror films and major historical traumas such as *Last House on the Left* (Wes Craven, 1972) and American involvement in the Vietnam War; the Holocaust and the films of French director Georges Franju such as *Eyes Without a Face* (*Les yeux sans visage,* 1960); and the bombing of Hiroshima in 1945 and *Onibaba* (Shindo Kaneto, 1964). In terms of found footage horror, *Cloverfield* (Matt Reeves, 2008) gives further credence to Lowenstein's argument. *Cloverfield* is presented as personal film material that has been discovered and archived by the United States Department of Defense. What begins as a memento of a farewell party for Rob (Michael Stahl-David) before he moves to Japan, turns into an immersive first-hand recording of what initially appears to be an earthquake, but is later revealed to be a large, terrifying monster on a destructive rampage. Some of New York City's most recognizable landmarks are destroyed; the Statue of Liberty's head is knocked off; the Woolworth building collapses; and the Brooklyn Bridge is demolished. Along with fellow party guests Lily (Jessica Lucas), Marlena (Lizzy Caplan) and Hud (T. J. Miller, who films the bulk of the proceedings), the group searches for Beth (Odette Annable), with whom Rob is romantically involved. They are told by a soldier that there is to be a mass evacuation and offers them details so they are not left behind when the "Hammer Down Protocol" destroys Manhattan completely in order to destroy the monster. A number of dramatic events reduce their numbers until only the reunited Beth and Rob remain. Unable to leave the city, they hide in Central Park as the bombing of Manhattan begins; there they record their parting words to camera. *Cloverfield* is bookended by footage that has been supposedly recorded over, following Rob and Beth at Coney Island a month earlier on their first date, thus framing the monster film as a romantic tragedy.

Unlike the marketing surrounding earlier found footage horror films like *The Blair Witch Project*, there was little intent to present *Cloverfield* as a genuine found footage artifact. No one thought it was real, but then again no one had to. Its central allegory was easily decipherable, pointing to a traumatic reality that the American national psyche still understandably struggles to grasp in terms of its sheer scale and horror. Geoff King noted, "Even while it was still unfolding, the [9/11 attacks were] described on numerous occasions as like something 'from a movie.'"[4] Despite the inescapable fact that these events were really happening, the 9/11 attacks were only comparable in their scale with epic Hollywood spectacles. King drew parallels between 9/11 and moments from the Hollywood blockbusters *The Matrix* (Larry and Andy Wachowski, 1999), *Armageddon* (Michael Bay, 1988), *Die Hard* (John McTiernan, 1988), *Independence Day* (Roland Emmerich, 1996), *Deep Impact* (Mimi Leder, 1998), *Fight Club* (David Fincher, 1999) and *Godzilla* (Roland

Emmerich, 1998). As King emphasized, these of course were just movies, not real events. Regardless, we tend only to be able to conceive the scope of the attacks through the hyperbolic spectacle of the Hollywood blockbuster.

Many critics have commented on the obvious parallels between *Cloverfield* and 9/11,[5] and these links are not difficult to locate in the spectacular images of chaos and destruction in Lower Manhattan: People run screaming down streets filled with smoke and dust as buildings explode around them. The film's first major special effect is the sudden smashing of the Statue of Liberty's head. This scene does not explicitly reference the Middle East, but the fact that this symbol of freedom has been beheaded implies a threat from that region as it is still a legal judicial method of execution on many Middle Eastern nations. Also evocative of 9/11 are the numerous shots of deserted, destroyed New York streets and the makeshift military and medical bases. Of course, the numerous close-ups of news reports that spread misinformation and confusion as the scale and intensity of the assault is digested also recall 9/11 reflected in the film with news headlines like "New York Under Attack" and "Panic in Manhattan." This is a $25 million film strategically designed to feel like it has just been uploaded to YouTube to create a sense of immersion and immediacy. Despite the gloss of its special effects, *Cloverfield*'s overt amateur moviemaking aesthetics replicate the all-too familiar footage of the terrorist attacks on the World Trade Center that were played and replayed on television news and online. As David Ray Carter has observed, "[E]ach act of destruction in the film purposefully evokes memories of the real event, and though never mentioned, the specter of 9/11 is present in every scene."[6]

The parallels between *Cloverfield* and 9/11 were not accidental, and director Reeves openly admitted that he studied YouTube videos of 9/11 at length when researching the film's aesthetic.[7] Daniel North noted that producer J.J. Abrams wanted to construct a national monster for the United States akin to what Godzilla was to Japan. Just as Godzilla "embodied (and revisited) fears of atomic destruction, then *Cloverfield*'s monster might be seen to give head, limbs and torso to a morass of nightmares about terrorist attack ... ruptured borders, and the fracturing of America's military dominance."[8] Crucially, North added that what makes *Cloverfield* unique to the post–9/11 North American context is that there is no clear way to slay the aggressor and restore the status quo. Rather, the fact that the limitations of hand-held camera technology prohibit Hud from fully showing the monster on film symbolically suggests this invader cannot be wholly comprehended. Taking the relationship between *Cloverfield* and 9/11 even further, Emanuelle Wessels persuasively argued that rather than simply playing out national trauma through horror, Reeves' film can be understood as having specifically political intent. Emphasizing the widespread encouragement for civilians to be on their guard against unusual activities that could potentially be linked to terrorism, *Cloverfield* for Wessels demonstrated how "self-militarization becomes intertwined with the consumption of particular technological commodities and mobilization of a surveilling gaze."[9] As such, Wessels suggested that the film contributes to the positive branding of the citizen-as-surveillance-operative.

There are other instances where the contemporary American political climate is rendered into allegory in found footage horror. *American Zombie* (Grace Lee, 2007) is as darkly comic as it is frightening, and masterfully presents an exploration into the lives of "high-functioning zombies," who look like everyday people but who happen to be undead. These include passionate scrapbooker Judy (Suzy Nakamura), and aspiring installation artist and florist Lisa (Jane Edith Wilson). This horror mockumentary is heavily reliant on the appropriation of observational documentary codes and conventions as it tracks the growing zombie rights movement, providing a powerful allegory for racism and identity politics in the contemporary United States. Similarly, *The Bay* (Barry Levinson, 2012) examines the role and function of mainstream news and social media in environmental emergencies, and the attitudes Americans often have towards the environment more generally. While these examples demonstrate how found footage horror responds to Lowenstein's definition of "a return to history through the gut," it is worth underscoring that not all examples are American, nor are they necessarily as consciously executed.

The Tunnel *(Carlo Ledesma, 2011) and the Australian History Wars*

In the Australian found footage horror film *The Tunnel* (Carlo Ledesma, 2011), young and ambitious journalist Natasha Warner (Bel Deliá) finds herself under increasing pressure in her new job on a current affairs television program to come up with an impressive story. This is compounded by sexual harassment from a number of her male work colleagues. She is deemed to be a pretty face but with little professional ability to back it up; the added complication of a recent unexplained failure now puts her job at risk. Natasha sees an investigation into the New South Wales government's mysteriously shelved plans to turn the railway tunnels under the Sydney CBD into a water reservoir as the scoop she needs to save her career. Desperate and alienated from her colleagues, she lies to her already-suspicious male crew—cameraman Steve (Steven Miller), producer Pete (Andy Rodoreda) and sound recorder Jim "Tangles" Williams (Luke Arnold)—telling them they have permission from their boss to enter the tunnels to investigate rumors that many of the homeless people who live there have mysteriously vanished. Natasha's lie is dramatically exposed as a mutant terrorizes her and the crew, leaving only her and Steve as survivors.

A surface glance at *The Tunnel* may not indicate just how uniquely Australian it is. Far from *Wolf Creek*'s (Greg McLean, 2004) subversive reconfiguration of the *Crocodile Dundee* "Aussie bushman" image, Australia in this film is intrinsically urban. For non–Australian audiences in particular, outside of the recognizable accents and references to Sydney there is seemingly little in *The Tunnel* that flags it as particularly specific to the Australian context. However, this film hinges upon the exposure of a hidden alternative history that is literally buried underneath the city. This central conceit of *The Tunnel* flags it as a powerful allegorical reaction to the frequently tense and emotionally charged Australian history wars. In this context, the attempt to re-write Australian history (and the suppression of alternative histories) at the heart of *The Tunnel* can be seen as fundamentally political. The schism that polarized political discourse since the early 1990s in Australia was so fixated upon the challenge of constructing a historical narrative to white Australia that it defined the ideological differences between the country's two major political parties. While these history wars were concerned with the subjective writing of Australian history in relation to European settlement and the treatment of Indige-

Poster for *The Tunnel* (Carlo Ledesma, 2011) (courtesy Distracted Media, www.distractedmediaonline.com).

nous Australians, these debates often expanded to encompass issues of national identity and the nature of "Australianness" itself.

Before further analyzing how *The Tunnel* engages with the Australian history wars, a brief overview of the latter is required. While the history wars are steeped in the fallibility of written history, there is little debate that 1992 was a defining moment for Australia. For Felicity Collins and Therese Davis, the High Court's judgment in *Mabo and Others vs. The State of Queensland (No. 2)* (1992) (the "Mabo decision") was a watershed political event that triggered a broader crisis in the national psyche. This case was the culmination of years of legal and social debate concerning the land rights of Indigenous Australians. The belief of *terra nullius*—that Australia was empty land when European settlers arrived—provided the foundations of how white Australia viewed its presence in the country for over 200 years. This assumption was usurped by the landmark *Mabo* decision. For non–Indigenous Australians, the "story of Australia" was predicated upon a narrative spawned from the fact that the land was discovered, not invaded.[10] The *Mabo* decision shattered the foundations of white Australia's comprehension of its own past.

While the *Mabo* decision triggered debate regarding the rewriting of history, the roots of the history wars stem back to the late 1960s when Professor W.E.H. Stanner identified a "Great Australian Silence" as dominating Eurocentric writing of Australian history. It was post–*Mabo* that the history wars began in earnest. In 1993, historian Geoffrey Blainey accused colleagues such as Manning Clarke of swinging too far in the extreme, toward a "black armband view of history" as a knee-jerk reaction against the Euro-positive, "three cheers" approach. Nevertheless, the history wars—like other national culture wars— were not quarantined within academia. They were immediately politicized after the *Mabo* decision, and in 1992 Labor[11] Prime Minister Paul Keating activated its rhetoric in his powerful Redfern Park speech: "We failed to ask— how would I feel if this were done to me? As a consequence, we failed to see that what we were doing degraded all of us."[12]

While rousing, the speech was far from unanimously hailed. Beyond the spirit of charity it purportedly espoused, Keating's opponents—particularly the conservative Liberal leader of the Opposition, John Howard—viewed the speech as an attempt to politicize history with the intent of allowing the *Mabo* decision and its entanglement of histories to inform what Collins and Davis defined as "the broader context of Keating's Republican agenda." They continued, "Keating's aim, indeed his personal passion, was to shift Australia's identity away from a British-centric past to a history grounded in Australian experience."[13] It was in this climate that Blainey's description of a "black armband view of history" became a powerful weapon in Howard's political lexicon.

With the nation's leading political figures mobilized on opposing sides, by the mid–1990s the history wars had terraformed the Australian political landscape almost completely. History was no navel-gazing exercise confined to behind the creaky doors of the nation's elite tertiary institutions. Rather, it affected the day-to-day construction of policy that governed life in contemporary Australia.

Howard became the 25th prime minister of Australia after defeating Keating in a landslide election in 1996. He then defined the debates within the history wars as an academic indulgence of an elite class of "middle-class do-gooders and intellectuals,"[14] who stood in direct opposition to Howard's "Aussie battlers" (so-called "ordinary" people). Keating may have opened the door to the politicization of history at Redfern Park in 1992, but it was Howard who transformed public anxieties about history into potent political cannon fodder. In 2007, after eleven years of Howard's Liberal government, Australian politics shifted again. Lumbered with unpopular industrial relations laws or simply just ready for a change, the Australian voting public demanded a new direction in ideological leadership as they elected Labor's Kevin Rudd, who remained in power until internal party politics saw him replaced by his deputy Julia Gillard after only two and a half years. Seventeen years Howard's junior, Rudd heralded a generational shift in the history wars when as his first official act of government he apologized to the Stolen Generations, the children of Australian Aboriginal and Torres Strait Islanders who Federal and State governments forcibly removed from their families between roughly 1909 and the 1970s. While debate still rages about whether or not this marked the end of the history wars as such,[15] what is apparent is that the construction of any version of Australian history that stands in contrast to a dominant one reflects in some way the tensions played out in the Australian history wars.

Whether consciously or not, it is in this context that *The Tunnel* can be understood as articulating ideas around competing historical narratives and official government involvement in them, and as such presents a fertile example of the Australian history wars' conceptual mechanics being rendered into horror-based allegory. It too deals with repressed histories: the desire of some to expose them, and the conflicting denial of others who steadily maintain that these alternatives do not even exist. The film makes clear on a number of occasions that the government is directly responsible for the conspiracy designed to hide the truth of what lies buried under the center of the most populous city in the country. However, its critique stems back much further than the specific government officials it shows in a selection of news bites in its opening scenes. That the titular tunnels are located underneath Hyde Park highlights the importance of colonization on its internally conflicting histories.

Nine. Nation, History and Identity 185

In the opening credits to *The Tunnel* the image of contemporary Sydney peels back to reveal an archival photograph of the tunnels that lie beneath Hyde Park. *The Tunnel* (Carlo Ledesma, 2011) explores buried histories under the Sydney CBD. Still from the opening credit sequence (courtesy Distracted Media, www.distractedmediaonline.com).

Named after London's Hyde Park, this colonial playground was a favored recreational space for white Australians and British authority figures such as Governor Macquarie.

The Tunnel does not directly address issues of race, but it does engage with class. The rumor that homeless people had gone missing in the underground tunnels was what initially interested Natasha in the story from the outset, and these forgotten people—like the convict labor that built the tunnels—are implied to be an awkward reality behind the Government's glossier ambitions. Crucially, an intertitle at the film's conclusion indicates that "the police investigation was closed due to 'contradictory evidence,'" and that "despite several requests, no State Government or police representative agreed to be interviewed for this film." This latter statement exposes the film itself as a political mechanism that has sought to reveal the literally buried histories underneath Hyde Park—a space linked to a sanitized vision of colonial history imbued with pleasure and recreation. *The Tunnel* is an investigation into the demons that lurk in Australia's history, a history that has been rejected because of its inability to fit into a dominant, authorized historical narrative.

It is therefore hugely significant that what terrorizes Natasha, Steve, Tangles and Pete is not a zombie or a vampire or Lovecraftian sea monster, but rather a mutant. For Robin Wood, horror hinges on a Freudian "return of the repressed," where "what is repressed must always strive to return."[16] This repression is embodied externally in the figure of the Other whose "psychoanalytic significance resides in the fact that it functions not simply as something external to the culture or to the self, but also what is repressed (but never destroyed) in the self is projected outwards to be hated and disowned."[17] If the return of the repressed lies at the heart of the horror film, then what reaches out to torment white Australians in *The Tunnel* is the very mutation of the perceived official public imagination's desire to bury unwanted, unflattering histories. The appropriation of observational and participatory documentary modes that *The Tunnel* appropriates underscores the fact that historical narratives are constructed. For a nation that has a long-documented—and if its current and past few governments' treatment of refugees and asylum seekers is any measurement, a sadly continuing—history of overtly racist policies, *The Tunnel* is a powerful and fascinating instance of allegorical self-reflection, again typifying Lowenstein's definition of horror as "a return to history through the gut."

International Incidents

While *Cloverfield* and *The Tunnel* provide concrete examples of narratives of national crisis, there is a range of contemporary found footage horror films that address less traumatic aspects of national identity. The first and second entries in the hugely successful *[Rec]* franchise are found footage horror films whose core mythology is strongly imbued with aspects of Roman Catholicism, a predominant religion in Spain. *Trollhunter* (André Øvredal, 2010) offers a playful re-imagining of the Norwegian folklore figure of the troll in an environmental horror scenario where government corruption and media compliance are placed in opposition to the bountiful natural heritage Norwegian folklore recalls. Found footage horror films have been popular in Japan, and an alternate sequel to Oren Peli's 2007 blockbuster *Paranormal Activity 2: Tokyo Night* (*Paranōmaru Akutibiti Dai Ni Shō: Tōkyō Naito*, Toshikazu Nagae, 2010) incorporates uniquely Japanese aspects into the original American story. The many found footage horror films of Kôji Shiraishi offer further evidence of how particular aspects of Japanese culture have been creatively integrated into the found footage horror subgenre, and the focus in *Shirome* (2010) on Japanese pop idol culture offers a clear instance of this.

Of course, whether filmmakers are based in the United States, Australia or elsewhere, one of the primary appeals of found footage horror for directors working outside the Hollywood context is cost. This was the case for Jaume Balagueró and Paco Plaza, who wrote and directed the first two *[Rec]* films. Plaza recalled that the idea was spawned when he and Balagueró discussed a mutual desire to return to their filmmaking roots without having to worry about the complex financing issues that surround major film production. "We began to think about a film we could shoot with a video camera and a few friends," he said in a 2011 interview, "and that was where we became more and more obsessed with the idea of doing something ... small, something we could control one hundred percent."[18] Influenced to some degree by films like *The Blair Witch Project*, Plaza has identified Ruggero Deodato's *Cannibal Holocaust* (1980) and the *Cops*-style episode of *The X-Files*, "X-Cops" (2000), as inspiring them more directly. Plaza noted the influence of low budget "on the ground"– style reporting common to Spanish television, the same style of program as *While You're Sleeping*, the fictional news program whose production grants the first entry its justification for recording its unfolding horrors. *[Rec]²* (Jaume Balagueró and Paco Plaza, 2009) expands this religious conspiracy with even more shocking consequences for Angela. *[Rec]³: Génesis* (Paco Plaza, 2012)— which relies only partially on found footage and then jumps to more traditional cinematography—leaving the Vidal-centered narrative and focuses instead on the events after the infection ravages a wedding party. As of this writing, Balagueró is slated to release a fourth installment in the series, *[Rec]⁴: Apocalipsis* (Jaume Balagueró, 2013), which departs completely from found footage.

[Rec] was remade in America by John Erick Dowdle as *Quarantine* (2008), on the strength of his previous found footage horror film *The Poughkeepsie Tapes* (2007). Initially, there appears to be no notable deviation from its Spanish source, suggesting the film is directly culturally translatable to American audiences. The final scenes of *Quarantine*, however, indicate this is not the case: Rejecting the Vatican-possession revelation of the original, the remake locates the source of its outbreak in a more secular explanation involving chemical weapons and a doomsday cult. Balagueró has disparaged the remake for this very reason: "It's exactly the same, except for the finale," he told Roberto E. D'Onofrio of *Fangoria* magazine. "It's impossible to enjoy *Quarantine* after *[Rec]*. I don't understand why they avoided the religious themes; they lost a very important part of the end of the movie."[19] Balagueró crucially implied that the Roman Catholic subplot of *[Rec]* is the precise feature that made the film so uniquely suited to Spanish audiences, while not considered as relevant to those in the United States: Recent studies noted that 70 percent of Spanish people identified as Catholics, while only 25 percent in America defined themselves in the same way.[20]

Region-specific folklore lies at the core of the Norwegian found footage horror film *Trollhunter*. In the tradition of *Blair Witch*, *Trollhunter* follows three college students making a documentary about bear poachers. Their investigation leads them to Hans (played by comedian Otto Jespersen), the "trollhunter" of the film's title. Although initially amused, the students increasingly realize trolls do in fact exist. Hans is a government employee whose job it is to maintain the mythic status of the creatures. With growing concerns as to the increased aggression and tendency of trolls to move towards populated areas, Hans is asked to attain blood samples to aid the government's investigation into the unusual behavior. A number of spectacular encounters peak when Kalle (Tomas Alf Larsen) is eaten: Trolls can smell Christian blood, and Kalle had lied to his peers about his religious status. Hans finally discovers that the trolls have been infected with rabies, but the mysterious disappearance of the film's protagonists stems not from a rabid troll attack but from the government itself. Officials seize the students to get their tapes, and although the footage cuts out it is implied that a passerby has rescued the camera (hence how the film we have just seen survived). The film concludes with an actual clip of Norwegian Prime Minister Jens Stoltenberg denying the existence of trolls, edited carefully together from a real-life press conference about the Troll Field natural gas and oil field in the North Sea.[21]

Inspired by *Man Bites Dog* (Benoît Poelvoorde, Rémy Belvaux, André Bonzel, 1992) as much as more obvious ancestors like *Ghostbusters* (Ivan Reitman, 1984) and Steven Spielberg's *Indiana Jones* movies, Øvredal emphasized the fundamental link between trolls and Norwegian national identity: "We've had the trolls since the Viking age, so I think it's part of our being, practically."[22] *Trollhunter* frames its protagonists' encounter with trolls through an investigation into environmental issues that are explicitly thwarted by government corruption. By allowing the filmmakers to record him at work, Hans therefore makes a conscious ideological decision to expose the lies the Norwegian government is telling the public about their own history. By evoking the folkloric figure of the troll, Øvredal pits two versions of history against each other: one where trolls do not exist, and one where they do. The film's deadpan and often charming construction of the latter creates a contrast between the environmental destruction that marks it with the magical imaginary of Norse trolldom itself, filled with figures who in Ethan Gilsdorf's words "haunt and inhabit Norway's folkloric consciousness, a still-pristine landscape of woods, mountains, and fiord lands."[23] Carrying the spirit of the stories he was told by his grandparents when he was a child, Øvredal offers a poignant and creative reflection on recent environmental damage. The very status of *Trollhunter* as a found footage horror film serves to emphasize just how powerful the media have been in the eradication of such a perspective, one that he and his diegetic filmmakers seek to redress.

Japanese found footage horror has not received the same international attention enjoyed by J-horror predecessors like *The Ring* (*Ringu*, 1998–2000), *One Missed Call* (*Chakushin ari*, 2003–2006), and *The Grudge* (*Ju-On*, 2003–

2009) franchises, but this does not make it any less fascinating. The director of *Ring 0: Birthday* (*Ringu 0: Bâsudei*, 2000), Norio Tsuruta employed found footage in his recent horror film *P.O.V: A Cursed Film* (*POV: Norowareta firumu*, 2012) in its tale of two school friends who encounter a series of terrifying supernatural events at their school while producing an episode of a web series. *Paranormal Activity 2: Tokyo Night* offers an alternative narrative trajectory for the original American franchise, based on the premise that after fleeing her house after killing Micah in the first film, Katie was hit by a car and killed by Japanese student Haruka (Noriko Aoyama). Haruka takes the possessing spirit back to Japan with her, with equally violent results. Although based on a Western source text, *Tokyo Night* is notable for its fusion of Western and Japanese cultural references. A Buddhist spiritualist-exorcist plays a crucial role in the film, and even more impressive is the logical manner in which it introduces the indigenous figure of the *onryō*, a female vengeance-seeking spirit, marked through her long flowing white garments and black hair that covers her face.[24]

Just as Oren Peli took found footage and made it his own in the United States, Japanese director Kôji Shiraishi can be considered a key J-horror found footage auteur. Although better known in the West for the low-budget horror films *Carved: The Slit-Mouthed Woman* (*Kuchisake-onna*, 2007) and *Grotesque* (*Gurotesuku*, 2009), Shiraishi has experimented with found footage on numerous occasions such as *Noroi: The Curse* (2005), *Occult* (*Okaruto*, 2009), *Shirome, Chō Akunin* (2011), and in *Bachiatari Bōryoku Ningen* with co-director Akihiro Kasai (2010). The cultural specificity of Shiraishi's uniquely Japanese take on the found footage subgenre is demonstrated clearly in *Shirome*. The film follows actual J-pop idol girl group Morimo Clover (or "Momoclo" for short) who, as part of a promotional television program, are taken to an abandoned school which the god Shirome is said to inhabit. Urban legend holds that anyone who can locate a drawing of a butterfly in a building where Shirome is said to dwell can make a wish. This will be granted if it stems from pure intentions, but if those intentions are less wholesome, Shirome will damn the requester through suicide, insanity, or a number of other punishments. The girls enter the building along with the film crew and two spiritualists, and after a number of supernatural encounters, they finally discover the drawing. After singing one of their hit songs for Shirome, they make their request to appear on the popular television show *Kōhaku Uta Gassen* to consolidate their fame. The wish is seemingly granted, but not before a spirit at the film's conclusion seemingly possesses one of the girls, adding weight to rumors that Momoclo are now cursed.

Shirome's sense of authenticity is heightened by its use of diegetically filmed footage, rendered all the more believable because the role of the director in the story is played by Shiraishi himself. *Kōhaku Uta Gassen* is also an actual program, and Momoclo are a well-known idol girl group who existed long before the release of the film. In terms of the latter, *Shirome* can also be considered alongside other fictional feature films about real world rock bands, such as The Ramones in *Rock n' Roll High School* (Allan Arkush, 1979), The Monkees in *Head* (Bob Rafelson, 1968), The Beatles in *A Hard Day's Night* (Richard Lester, 1964) and—in the context of J-horror in particular—Japanese punk band Guitar Hero in the zombie film *Wild Zero* (Tetsuro Takeuchi, 1999). However, Momoclo's status as a J-pop idol band renders them a uniquely Japanese phenomenon. Produced out of the explosion of consumer activity as part of the Japanese postwar economic boom of the 1960s and 1970s, J-pop idol culture stems from a tightly woven corporate structure spanning media and retail industries, and is notable for its emphasis upon its performers' cuteness (*kawaii*), a prominent feature of contemporary Japanese pop culture. The cross-media promotional dynamics of J-pop idol culture is typified by the appearance of Momoclo in *Shirome*. Although the film itself can hardly be described as *kawaii* as such, the performance of the girls themselves—in their school uniforms, cries and shrieks of terror, and songs about skincare—embody Japanese ideals of cute girlhood. As Larissa Hjorth noted, "[T]he use of *kawaii* features to familiarize new commodities or technologies has been common practice in the material culture of post-war Japan."[25] In *Shirome*, the technological savviness of the Momoclo girls (in terms of filming themselves, each other, and performing for the professional film crews cameras) is simply an extension of this association.

This chapter has only scratched the surface of the global reach of found footage horror, and the vast range of international additions to the subgenre suggests its durability. Beyond Japan, there have been a number of Asian found footage horror films including *No. 32, B District* (Jianmin Lv, 2011) from China, the Filipino movie *Darkest Night* (Noel Tan, 2012), *Penunggu istana* (Wan Hasliza, 2011) from Malaysia, Singapore's *Haunted Changi* (Tony Kern, 2010), South Korean efforts such as *Record* (*Zzikhimyeon jukneunda*, Gi-hun Kim and Jong-seok Kim, 2000) and *The Haunted House Project* (*Pyega*, Cheol-ha Lee, 2010) and of course the "Safe Haven" entry in *V/H/S/2* (2013) by Indonesian-based directors Gareth Evans and Timo Tjahjanto. Added to this list of international found footage horror movies are the Brazilian *Desaparecidos* (David Schürmann, 2011), the U.S.-Belize co-production *Hombre y tierra* (Christian Cisneros, 2011), *Incidente* (Mariano Cattaneo, 2010) from Argentina, and the Costa Rican film *El Sanatorio* (Miguel Alejandro Gomez, 2010). Germany has made movies such as *The Dark Area* (Oliver Hummell, 2000) and *Cam—Fürchte die Dunkelheit* (Andreas Arimont 2010), Italy has to its credit *Closed Circuit Extreme* (2012) and *The Gerber Syndrome* (Maxì Dejoie, 2011) and Greece has produced *Subconscious* (Chris Petropoulos, 2010) and the *Blair Witch*–inspired *The Blair Kitch Project* (Georgios Papaioannou, 2002).

Additional European entries include *Haunted Poland* (*Nawiedzona Polska*, Pau Masó, 2011), the Belgian mockumentary *Vampires* (Vincent Lannoo, 2010), the Russian film *Paranormal Yakutsk* (Konstantin Timofeev, 2012) and *Frost* (Reynir Lyngdal, 2012) from Iceland. Aside from *Lake Mungo* and *The Tunnel*, other Australian found footage horror films are *Last Ride* (James Philips, 2011) and *Muirhouse* (Tanzeal Rahim, 2012). India has also produced a number of films in this category including *Case No. 666/2013* (Venkat Siddareddy, Purnesh Konathala, 2013), *The Lost Tape* (Rakshit Dahiya, 2012), *?: A Question Mark* (Allyson Patel and Yash Dave, 2012), *Hotel Hollywood* (Param Gill, 2010) and *Ragini MMS* (Pawan Kripalani, 2011).

Whether these films manifest evidence of national trauma like *Cloverfield* and *The Tunnel*, or reflect on particular aspects of national folklore, religion or pop culture like *Trollhunter*, *[Rec]* and *Shirome*, they all emphasize the increasing saturation of consumer-grade video technology as a particularly fertile terrain to experiment with cultural, political or social concerns.

Conclusion: The Specter of Commercialism

When contemporary found footage horror films like *Cloverfield*, *[Rec]*, *The Devil Inside*, *The Last Exorcism*, *The Blair Witch Project*, *Paranormal Activity* and their myriad sequels hit multiplex screens, the gap between amateur and professional film production was rendered visible in the commercial arena. In many cases, aggressive promotional campaigns by the major studios that snapped up low-budget productions converted the budgetary weaknesses of some of these movies into their strongest virtue. The commercial value of many of these films is built on verisimilitude and their signature deployment of specific amateur filmmaking aesthetics.

Like *The Blair Witch Project* before it, the 2012 film *V/H/S* was thrust into the limelight after it debuted at the Sundance Film Festival. This found footage horror anthology consists of five separate short films and a framing story, directed by independent horror filmmakers Adam Wingard, David Bruckner, Ti West, Glenn McQuaid, Joe Swanberg, and the directing quartet Radio Silence. Between them, these directors had already attained a reputation in cult circles with earlier projects. Wingard directed *A Horrible Way to Die* (2010), Bruckner was involved with the remarkable collaborative horror–science fiction experiment *The Signal* (2007), West made *The Innkeepers* (2011) and *The House of the Devil* (2009), McQuaid directed the horror black comedy *I Sell the Dead* (2008), mumblecore auteur Swanberg developed a reputation for his low-budget productions, while Radio Silence found success with their earlier online filmmaking experiments.

Wingard's framing narrative "Tape 56" contextualizes the five short films of which *V/H/S* consists. If *V/H/S* has garnered a reputation for misogyny, the opening moments of the film alone justify why: A group of hoodlums film themselves committing acts of vandalism and sexual assault, executed with a disturbing casualness. Lured by the promise of a cash payment, they agree to rob a house to steal a videotape. Discovering the body of a dead man passed out in front of a television, they have unlimited time to locate the tape amongst the vast array of old tapes they discover. "Tape 56" plays out like a zombie narrative, but the videos selected by the criminals for viewing provide the structure for the rest of the film. The first of these is Bruckner's "Amateur Night" which recalls the male-teens-looking-for-sex trope common to 1980s slasher films. This is updated by one of the group attaching a hidden video camera to his spectacles so the group can record their sexual encounters. Their attempts at sexual exploitation is foiled at the revelation that one of the two girls they lure to their hotel room is a succubus, whose monstrous sexuality goes to fatal extremes in teaching the young men basic lessons in sexual etiquette.

West's "Second Honeymoon" is tonally more understated, and follows a young married couple on their eponymous holiday. A fortune-telling machine tells wife Stephanie (Sophia Takal) that she will be reunited with someone she loves, and after ongoing harassment by a strange masked woman, the couple's relationship begins to deteriorate (all captured, of course, on home video). At its conclusion, it is revealed that the woman is Stephanie's lover and they murder Stephanie's husband Sam (Joe Swanberg) so the two women can escape together. McQuaid's "Tuesday the 17th" also recalls 1980s slasher films, as four teens on a camping trip are told by one of their group, Wendy (Norma C. Quinones), of a series of incidents that led to the death of a number of her friends. One by one, the group is killed by a strange being whose presence is defined by technical interference on the home video camera they use to document their trip. Wendy replicates the Final Girl figure in her determination and resourceful attempts to destroy the killer, but the comparison ends when she herself is graphically murdered.

In "The Sick Thing That Happened to Emily When She Was Younger," Joe Swanberg employs a video webchat interface to tell the story of young couple Emily (Helen Rogers) and James (Daniel Kaufman) that structurally recalls the earlier films *Vlog* (Joshua Butler, 2008) and *The Collingswood Story* (Michael Costanza, 2002). Emily tells James about strange events in her past and that have recently occurred in her apartment and confesses that she believes she may be haunted by a small child. This creature knocks Emily unconscious, allowing James to enter the room from surprisingly close by, where he removes an alien fetus from Emily. Not only is there the implication that she has been used to harvest alien mutants for some time, but this story ends by revealing that James has other "girlfriends" he is apparently using in a similar way. The Radio Silence team directed the final entry "10/31/98," and like both "Tape 56" and "Amateur Night," it focuses on the dynamics of male groups. Here, four up-for-anything Halloween partygoers (one with a camera

Conclusion

From *V/H/S*'s framing story "Tape 56" (Adam Wingard, 2012) (Bloody Disgusting/The Collective/The Kobal Collection).

built into his costume) inadvertently crash an exorcism. Realizing that it is not a prank, they react to what they perceive to be the abuse of the young woman being exorcised and escape with her only to find that she is possessed and dangerous as she leads them to their violent death.

Originally developed as a television series, Wingard's wraparound narrative "Tape 56" was filmed first. According to Wingard and co-producer Brad Miska, they then approached other filmmakers to make the internal segments. Simon Barrett wrote "The Sick Thing That Happened to Emily When She Was Younger" and "Tape 56" (and starred in the latter), and has expressed a love of the earlier horror portmanteau movies from legendary British horror production house Amicus.[1] Structuring a horror anthology around a diegetic character's random viewing of stolen videotapes is not original, as demonstrated in *Screamtime* (Stanley A. Long, 1986).[2] Toetag Pictures' Fred Vogel had also sought to combine found footage into a horror anthology with his gruesome snuff-fiction *Murder Collection V.1* in 2009. Along with Damien Leone's 2013 found footage anthology *All Hallows' Eve* based on a similar discovered videotape premise, *V/H/S* undoubtedly owes a debt to these and other more famous anthology films, a category spanning back to *Uncanny Tales* (*Unheimliche Geschichten*, Richard Oswald, 1932) and Ealing Studio's *Dead of Night* (1945), across cultures from Italy's *Black Sabbath* (*I tre volti della paura*, Mario Bava, 1963) to the Japanese *Kwaidan* (Masaki Kobayashi, 1964), and including some of the most loved cult horror films of all time, such as the Karen Black vehicle *Trilogy of Terror* (Dan Curtis, 1975) and the George A. Romero–Stephen King collaboration *Creepshow* (1982).

V/H/S is much more than a retro throwback, however. In fact, its success arguably stems less from how much it adheres to the now-firmly established codes and conventions of the found footage horror category than its flagrant dismissal of them. Most overtly is how determinedly it rejects the subgenre's tendency towards occlusion, both in in relation to its Val Lewton–like coyness in revealing sources of terror and explicit gore and sexuality. In terms of the latter, Carol J. Clover argued that dismissing horror as misogynistic based solely on the latter at least may be performing a critical disservice to the more complex ideological mechanics that drive the subgenre's gender politics. Nevertheless, *V/H/S* seems almost consciously dedicated to an ambivalent position regarding its treatment of sexual difference, with varying effectiveness. "The Sick Thing That Happened to Emily When She Was Younger" is straightforward in its misogyny as it focuses on the psychological, physical and emotional abuse of women with no hope of escape. In the film's strongest segment "Amateur Night," by placing a camera inside the eyeglasses of one of its male protagonists, Laura Mulvey's delineation of cinema's dominant male gaze is rendered cleverly literal, and that this aggressive masculine gaze has its power so spectacularly removed offers tantalizing subversive potential. On one hand, that empowered female sexuality is so explicitly coded as monstrous renders the segment's more positive aspects less meaningful. But "Amateur Night" may not be so simple: As Hannah Fierman (who played the succubus Lily) poignantly pointed out, "Yes, the monster is female but she is also the strongest character as well and the most forgivable." Fierman's Lily—who the actress consciously played as "accessible and sympathetic while also terrifying"[3]—may be the literal monster, but in this instance, monstrosity itself is relative in the face of the revolting male behavior she is up against. From this perspective, "Amateur Night" satisfyingly functions as a revenge narrative against attempted sexual exploitation just as much as it adheres to the framework of an old-fashioned monster film.

In other segments, the ideological tug of war is less satisfying. The holiday home movie conceit of "Second Honeymoon" presents a symbolic power struggle between Stephanie and Sam as they shift between holding the camera and narrating events at different points on their trip. When Stephanie's girlfriend breaks into their hotel room, she significantly films both Sam and Stephanie, thus demonstrating her control of the gaze. The fact that the women film Sam's murder and then themselves kissing in the mirror after his death illustrates just how significant the camera is as a symbol of power for them. The segment's reliance in its twist ending on a construction of violent lesbianism as a supposedly "perverse" sexual spectacle renders its more interesting elements a little less impressive.

"Tuesday the 17th" suggests its subversive potential in the figure of its Final Girl figure, but then not only has her killed but viciously disemboweled by a digitized anonymous male protagonist. While not sexual as such, her death recalls famous images from the *Snuff* (1976) coda and the murder of Phyllis (Lucy Grantham) in *Last House on the Left* (Wes Craven, 1972), two films historically linked to notorious depictions of sexual violence. "10/31/98" is predicated upon a group of characters stumbling across an exorcism: This scene is normally the central spectacle in exorcism-based horror films, and by presenting it in this way, it exposes the fundamental fact that these scenes are commonly (although not always) focused on supposedly "possessed" women being tortured by men. The subversive potential of this premise is eradicated by confirming rather than challenging monstrous femininity with its conclusion: The fact that rescuing her leads to their deaths implies that they should have let the sadistic torture of the exorcism continue uninterrupted.

V/H/S is an intriguing film because its strengths *and* weaknesses all come from its ambivalence. It continually establishes subversive potential but on almost all accounts undermines its progressive promise. Regardless of its politics, *V/H/S* is historically significant for marking such a clear departure from the clichés that in large part have been felt to be responsible for the broader decline in subgenre in recent years.[4] As with the Sundance hit *The Blair Witch Project* before it, *V/H/S* is formally marked by its broader status as an independent underdog, which paradoxically granted it the credibility that made it so commercially viable.

Another significant recent independent found footage horror sensation is the YouTube series *Marble Hornets*. With regular updates posted by its protagonist Jay to the @marblehornets Twitter account and its links to broader Internet forum cultures, *Marble Hornets* is a strong example of a transmedia found footage horror success story. Unlike *Blair Witch* and *Cloverfield* that preceded it, transmedia is not a marketing gimmick for *Marble Hornets*, but rather an organic approach to contemporary storytelling. *Marble Hornets* powerfully indicates just how naturalized transmedia storytelling has become for both creators and consumers, and in doing so has blurred the boundaries between these two roles even further as fans of the broader Slender Man mythology that underscore it produce their own transmediated experiences.

The Specter of Commercialism 197

However, to pin the success of *Marble Hornets* solely upon its status as a transmedia product underplays the creative and imaginative construction of the series. Alexandra Juhasz has indicated that one of the major issues with YouTube is simply glut, as one must sift through a large volume of material to find anything of interest.[5] For every *Marble Hornets* there are countless numbers of as-yet undiscovered found footage horror videos on YouTube that have failed to attain the same cult following. Outside of word of mouth (which most often takes the form of the forum, blog or social media recommendation), it is only the roulette wheel of the related videos list that can guide us towards similarly themed material. *Marble Hornets* stands out not because of the novelty of it being a YouTube-based transmedia found footage horror series—that is no longer unique—but because it is engaging, original and creative.

As *Marble Hornets* is still an ongoing project, any synopsis will be necessarily open-ended. Its background can be found on the forums of the Something Awful website. In mid-2009, user "ce gars"—apparently writing as "Jay" (*Marble Hornets*' main character, played in the videos by director Troy Wagner)—discussed strange events that had plagued his friend Alex (Joseph DeLage), whom he knew at film school. Alex had been working on a low-budget independent feature called *Marble Hornets* (where the series gets its name) in the woods near where he lived. To the author's surprise, Alex dropped the project suddenly and began acting strangely, telling Jay to "burn" the tapes of *Marble Hornets*. Shocked at this response, Jay convinced Alex to let him look at the tapes, and Alex agreed only if Jay never returned them and did not show them to anyone else. Finding this amusing, Jay jokingly told Alex that "he must have accidentally made *The Ring* or something with the way he was talking." With tapes in hand, Alex moved interstate, leaving Jay to sort through them. Signing off on the initial Something Awful forum post, Jay writes, "If there's interest, I'll post anything that I find on here."[6]

There was interest. Jay's video documentation of his initial investigation into Alex's tapes and the complex web of paranoia and terror that followed formed the basis of arguably the Internet's most fascinating amateur found footage horror experiment to date. The markers of its amateurism are clear from the outset, some seemingly more deliberate than others. However, these simply add to the series' grassroots construction of authenticity: for example, typographical errors in some early intertitles would never slip into a big-budget commercial venture, and their presence denotes a lack of corporate contrivance. The earlier entries in the series pivot around Jay's continued investigation into Alex's tapes, but as strange events begin to unfold on the tapes—most notably the appearance of the ominous Operator (the name of the Slender Man figure in the series)—attention shifts to Jay's own bizarre experiences and those who become involved in his investigation, such as Tim (Tim Sutton) and Jessica (Jessica May).

Marble Hornets is marked by an all-encompassing paranoia that silently stops any of its characters from talking openly about The Operator. Not knowing who to trust and paralyzed by their own fears, anxieties and often the physical impact of "Slender sickness" (a respiratory-related malady that stems from exposure to The Operator and his otherworldly cohorts), Tim and Jay in particular venture to discuss him in only the most guarded of terms. (Entry #66, for instance, provides Tim's long-anticipated back-story, where he refers to The Operator only as "that person.") Both Tim and Jay's lives are devastated by The Operator and the terror he has brought to them—particularly the mysteries surrounding Alex's violent and increasingly strange behavior and Jessica's disappearance—yet they are incapable of discussing him openly. Instead, the YouTube videos and *Marble Hornets* Twitter account becomes Jay's only outlet, acting in many regards as a confessional and a place to receive support and encouragement from his followers. Crucially, because Jay is in character when on Twitter, it therefore exists in Tim's universe as well. Tim explodes angrily at Jay when he discovers the videos online, furious that Jay has been misleading him and has his own agenda. Tensions between absence and presence also play out by the YouTube "reply" videos by the mysterious user ToTheArk: These abstracted short films are considered by *Marble Hornets* fans to be drenched in clues regarding the mysteries of the series more broadly.[7] While there is speculation as to which character this figure may be, it is ToTheArk's very anonymity that makes them as such an important continuing presence in the series.

The origins of the *Marble Hornets* mythology lie deep within the countercultural underbelly of the Internet itself. The Slender Man first appeared in 2009 on the Something Awful forums, the same place that earlier spawned the notorious 4chan imageboard that has in turn been linked to hacktivist group Anonymous and the Project Chanology anti–Scientology movement. As part of a contest thread where forum members were encouraged to Photoshop paranormal-themed images, user "Victor Surge" presented two black-and-white photographs of children in otherwise innocent poses, adding in the background of each the now iconic Slender Man figure: a tall, thin man with long limbs wearing a black suit and with a featureless white face. According to Surge's origin myth, the Slender Man stalked and abducted children, and those who investigated him were also known to disappear. There are of course many antecedents to the figure, and even a cursory glance recalls a number of diverse historical predecessors. The Slender Man evokes the protagonist in George A. Romero's *Bruiser* (2000), the figure of the faceless, suited "proprietor" in Salvador Dali's dream sequence in *Spellbound* (Alfred Hitchcock, 1945), and the stick-like suited figure of Jack Skellington in the Tim Burton–produced animation *The Nightmare Before Christmas* (Henry Selik, 1993). It is also reminiscent of the cover art to the self-titled 1994 debut album by U.S. nu-metal band Korn, featuring the shadow of a bald, long-limbed figure looming over a young child on a playground swing. The ongoing *Marble Hornets* project has met with remarkable success, and at the time of writing the *Marble Hornets* YouTube channel has over 250,000 subscribers with at least 55 million views. Inspired by *Marble Hornets*, YouTube has become an obvious forum for other amateur filmmakers to experiment with the Slender Man mythology in series such as *EverymanHYBRID* and *TribeTwelve* and the feature films *Windigo* (James Hardiment, 2011) and *The Slender Man* (A.J. Meadows, 2013).

Further success appears likely for the *Marble Hornets* creators. Joseph DeLage, Tim Sutton and Troy Wagner, who have recently been involved in the production of the videogame *Slender: The Arrival*, the sequel to the popular *Slender: The Eight Pages* (2012). In early 2013, *Variety* reported that a commercial feature film based on the web series was in the works with the Mosaic Media Group (who manage stars like Judd Apatow, Jim Carrey and Will Ferrell), set to be directed by *Paranormal Activity 2, 3* and *4*'s second unit director James Moran.[8] Set in the same narrative universe as the original YouTube story but not a direct continuation of it, the film will feature legendary contortionist-turned-actor Doug Jones as The Operator, renowned for his memorable appearances in *Buffy the Vampire Slayer*, Guillermo del Toro's *Pan's Labyrinth* (2006) and the *Hellboy* franchise, and *John Dies at the End* (Don Coscarelli, 2012). In light of the seemingly inevitable rise for these young DIY filmmakers from Alabama who made the first 26 episodes on a mere $500,[9] the metaphorical presence of the Slender Man is potent. The large, looming figure of a faceless man in a suit, haunting kids with consumer-grade video cameras, is arguably nothing less than the specter of commercialism itself.

This omnipresent force has always loomed over the found footage horror subgenre. The balancing of amateur aesthetics and commercial viability is as functional a question in the subgenre as its filmic construction. After the *Blair Witch* fairy tale, the specter of commercialism rescued *Paranormal Activity* from obscurity and brought it massive financial success as it played in multiplexes around the globe, and it brought new life to the category in the shape of *V/H/S* when—like *Blair Witch* before it—it became a surprise hit at Sundance. The rapid appearance of the *V/H/S* sequel *V/H/S/2* at Sundance in 2013 highlights the commercial shrewdness of its producers, and the inclusion in this sequel of *Blair Witch*'s co-director Eduardo Sánchez and producer

Gregg Hale with their entry "A Ride in the Park" feels almost poetic, granting Sundance the status of symbolic bookends for the category's most prolific years. Responding shrewdly to criticisms of the first film and its often-problematic depictions of violence against women, *V/H/S/2* was widely viewed as a comparatively more mature project. Tweaking its gender politics to some degree certainly did not lessen its impact, however, and its highlights include Jason Eisner's "Alien Abduction Slumber Party," following the success of his film *Hobo with a Shotgun* (2011) and his breathtaking "Y Is for Youngbuck" entry in the horror anthology *The ABCs of Death* (2012). Also of note is "Safe Haven," a joint directorial effort by Gareth Evans of Indonesian *pencak silat* action film *The Raid: Redemption* (2011) fame and Timo Tjahanto (whose short "L Is for Libido" was another of *The ABCs of Death*'s most memorable entries).

So pervasive is the found footage format in horror today that it is often dismissed as a "cliché"[10] or "gimmick."[11] Found footage horror film is not yet a past-tense phenomenon, but the terrain is changing. Horror films that combine found footage with more traditional filmmaking techniques have of course been around for many years, but there has been a recent increase in these titles with movies like *Stormhouse* (Dan Turner, 2011), *Lovely Molly* (Eduardo Sánchez, 2011), *Sinister* (Scott Derrickson, 2012), *Chernobyl Diaries* (Bradley Parker, 2012), *[Rec]³ Génesis* (Paco Plaza, 2012) and *Monsters in the Woods* (Jason Horton, 2012), finding its most ingenious and sophisticated incorporation in *Resolution* (Justin Benson and Aaron Moorhead 2012). Perhaps even more significantly, some famous found footage horror franchises are now rejecting found footage altogether, such as *[Rec]⁴: Apocalipsis* (Jaume Balagueró, 2013) and *The Last Exorcism Part II* (Ed Gass-Donnelly, 2013). There has recently been a steady rise of found footage aesthetics in other genres, too, such as *Chronicle* (Josh Trank, 2012), *Project X* (Nima Nourizadeh, 2012) and *End of Watch* (David Ayer, 2012). While there is a history of non-horror titles that have done this in the past,[12] this trend appears to becoming increasingly prevalent in the mainstream as what once made found footage horror so fresh has been slowly subsumed as a readily identifiable filmmaking practice.

What all of these movies collectively suggest—and what this book has argued from the outset—is that popular film styles evolve and morph over time, rather than necessarily vanishing altogether or magically appearing overnight. Although it would be naïve to suggest that found footage horror will remain eternally in vogue, it is likely that when this current flurry of production slows (as it now appears to be), some kind of legacy will remain. This is a legacy carried on from Orson Welles' *War of the Worlds* 1938 radio broadcast through to films like *Cannibal Holocaust* (1980) and *Man Bites Dog*

The Specter of Commercialism 201

(1992), and a range of diverse screen artifacts including the safety films of the 1950s and 1960s, the controversial snuff-fictions of the 1970s and 1980s, and television experiments intersecting at the junction of form, verisimilitude and fear such as *Les Documents Interdits* (1989–1981) and *Ghostwatch* (1992). Found footage horror's watershed moments were doubtlessly the phenomenal success of *The Blair Witch Project* and *Paranormal Activity*. Along with a number of other films explored in this book—the bulk of which were sparked in its post-YouTube Renaissance such as *[Rec]* (2007), *Exhibit A* (2007), *Cloverfield* (2008), *Home Movies* (2008), *The Last Exorcism* (2010), *Trollhunter* (2010), *Shirome* (2010), *Megan Is Missing* (2011), *The Tunnel* (2011), *The Devil Inside* (2012), and *V/H/S* (2012)—this category is marked as much by its deployment of amateur filmmaking aesthetics in its construction of horror-specific verisimilitude as it is by the diversity of its cultural, ideological and production contexts.

As Internet-specific horror culture spawns the *Marble Hornets* series and other projects, found footage horror appears to be evolving and mutating again. We may at this time be too close to the popular success of found footage horror to fully identify the legacy of found footage horror, but what remains clear is that despite their myriad differences, these films collectively point to horror's broader unbending spirit of experimentation, its willingness to break the rules, its openness to new talent regardless of how cashed-up they may or may not be, and its fundamental playfulness. That the subgenre appears to be so simple but is often so complex reflects the broader challenges and charms of the horror genre itself.

Notes

Introduction

1. Sean Smith, "Curse of the Blair Witch," *Newsweek*, 143.4 (January 26, 2004): 56–8.
2. John Kenneth Muir, "Cult Movie Review: *Apollo 18* (2011)," *John Kenneth Muir's Reflections on Film/TV* (January 24, 2012) http://reflectionsonfilmandtelevision.blogspot.com.au/2012/01/cult-movie-review-apollo-18-2011.html.
3. Throughout this book I refer to found footage horror as a subgenre, according to Steve Neale's use of the term "to refer to specific traditions or groupings within ... genres." See Steve Neale, *Genre and Hollywood* (New York: Routledge, 2000), 1.
4. There is a vast range of work I can cite to support this claim, a preliminary list of which would include the following: Carol. J Clover, *Men, Women, and Chain Saws: Gender in the Modern Horror Film* (Princeton: Princeton University Press, 1992); Linda Badley, *Film, Horror, and the Body Fantastic* (Westport, CT: Greenwood Press, 1995); Rhona J. Berenstein, *Attack of the Leading Ladies: Gender, Sexuality, and Spectatorship in Classic Horror Cinema* (New York: Columbia University Press, 1996); Barry Keith Grant, ed., *The Dread of Difference: Gender and the Horror Film* (Austin: University of Texas Press, 1996); Sue Short, *Misfit Sisters: Screen Horror as Female Rites of Passage* (Basingstoke: Palgrave Macmillan, 2006); Barbara Creed, *The Monstrous-Feminine: Film, Feminism, Psychoanalysis* (London: Routledge, 1993).
5. Other additions include: *Effects* (Dusty Nelson, 1980), *Screen Kill* (Doug Ulrich, 1997), *Cradle of Fear* (Alex Chandon, 2001), *Suicide* (Raoul W. Heimrich and Yvonne Wunschel, 2001), *The Great American Snuff Film* (Sean Tretta, 2003), *My Little Eye* (Marc Evans, 2002), *Snuff-Movie* (Bernard Rose, 2005), *S&Man* (J.T. Petty, 2006), *Vacancy* (Nimród Antal, 2007), *Untraceable* (Gregory Hoblit, 2008), *Snuff Trap* (Bruno Mattei, 2003), *Hack!* (Matt Flynn, 2007), *Snuff 102* (Mariano Peralta, 2007), *Carver* (Franklin Guerrero, Jr., 2008), *The Life and Death of a Porno Gang* (Mladen Djordjevic, 2009), *Murder Collection* (Fred Vogel, 2009), *Skeleton Crew* (Tero Molin and Tommi Lepola, 2009), *Vacancy 2: The First Cut* (Eric Bross, 2009), *The Hell Experiment* (Ricardo Benz, 2010), *A Serbian Film* (Srđan Spasojević, 2010), *House with 100 Eyes* (Jay Lee & Jim Roof, 2011), *Slaughter Creek* (Brian Skiba, Liam Owen, 2011), *Cut/Print* (Nathaniel Nose, 2012) and *The Cohasset Snuff Film* (Edward Payson, 2012).
6. There are also found footage horror movies that share this interest, including *The Burningmoore Incident* (Jonathan Williams, 2010), *The Feed* (Steve Gibson, 2010), *Grave Encounters* (The Vicious Brothers, 2011), *7 Nights of Darkness* (Allen Kellogg, 2011), *The Speak* (Anthony Pierce, 2011), and *The Whispering Dead* (Hunter G. Williams, 2011). *Re-Cut* (Fritz Manger, 2010) even features ex-reality TV star Meredith Phillips from *The Bachelorette* (2004) in the lead role, and both *The Tapes* (Lee Alliston and Scott Bates, 2011) and *Penance* (Jake Kennedy, 2009) are based on the premise that they are reality TV audition tapes that go wrong.
7. There is some confusion regarding the dates of this series: as explained in Chapter Three, IMDb.com has it listed as 1993, but the official DVD release lists 1989–1991. Accordingly, I have defaulted to the latter throughout this book.
8. Jay David Bolter and Richard Grusin, *Remediation: Understanding New Media* (Cambridge: MIT Press, 2000), 42.
9. Jeffrey Sconce, *Haunted Media: Electronic Presence from Telegraphy to Television* (Durham: Duke University Press, 2000), 116–7.
10. Craig Hight, "Mockumentary: A Call to Play," in *Rethinking Documentary: New Perspectives, New Practices*, eds. Thomas Austin and Wilma de Jong (Maidenhead, England: McGraw Hill/Open University Press, 2008), 208.
11. Marjorie Garber, *Academic Instincts* (Princeton: Princeton University Press, 2000), 5.

12. Charles Leadbeater and Paul Miller, *The Pro-Am Revolution* (London: Demos. 2004).
13. Garber, 19.
14. Ibid., 20.
15. David Buckingham, Maria Pini and Rebekah Willett, "'Take Back the Tube!' The Discursive Construction of Amateur Film and Video Making," *Journal of Media Practice*, 8.2 (2007): 190.
16. "YouTube Serves Up 100 Million Videos a Day Online," *USA Today* (July 16, 2006) http://usatoday30.usatoday.com/tech/news/2006-07-16-youtube-views_x.htm.
17. Lev Grossman, "You—Yes You—Are TIME's Person of the Year," *Time Magazine* (December 25, 2006) http://www.time.com/time/magazine/article/0,9171,1570810,00.html#ixzz2OKrF1cy7.
18. Henry Jenkins, "How YouTube Became OurTube," *Confessions of an Aca-Fan: The Official Weblog of Henry Jenkins* (October 18, 2010) http://henryjenkins.org/2010/10/how_youtube_became_ourtube.html.
19. Dan Hunter, Ramon Lobato, Megan Richardson, and Julian Thomas, "Preface," in *Amateur Media: Social, Cultural and Legal Perspectives*, eds. Dan Hunter, Ramon Lobato, Megan Richardson, and Julian Thomas (Abingdon, Oxon: Routledge, 2013), vi.
20. Buckingham, Pini and Willett, 185.
21. Patricia Zimmerman, "Hollywood, Home Movies and Common Sense: Amateur Film as Aesthetic Dissemination and Social Control, 1950–1962," *Cinema Journal*, 27.4 (1988): 25.
22. Such as *Australia's Funniest Home Videos*, *You've Been Framed* in the UK and *Video Gag* in France.
23. Lucas Hilderbrand, *Inherent Vice: Bootleg Histories of Videotape and Copyright* (Durham: Duke University Press, 2009), 62.
24. Joan Hawkins, *Cutting Edge: Art-Horror and the Horrific Avant-Garde* (Minneapolis: University of Minnesota Press, 2000), 35.
25. Laura Mulvey, *Death 24x a Second: Stillness and the Moving Image* (London: Reaktion, 2005), 176.
26. Laura U. Marks, *Touch: Sensuous Theory and Multisensory Media* (Minneapolis: University of Minnesota Press, 2002), 10.
27. Ibid., 8.
28. Angela Ndalianis, *The Horror Sensorium: Media and the Senses* (Jefferson, NC: McFarland, 2012), 23.
29. Marks, 16.
30. William C. Wees, "Found Footage and Questions of Representation," in *Found Footage Film*, eds. Cecilia Hausheer and Christoph Settele (Luzern, Switzerland: Viper/Zyklop, 1992), 37.
31. Roger Luckhurst, "Found-Footage Science Fiction: Five Films by Craig Baldwin, Jonathan Weiss, Werner Herzog and Patrick Keiller," *Science Fiction Film & Television* 1.2 (2008): 193.

32. Julia Leyda, Nicholas Rombes, Steven Shaviro, Therese Grisham, "Roundtable Discussion: The Post-Cinematic in *Paranormal Activity* and *Paranormal Activity 2*," *La Furia Umana* 10 (Autumn 2011) http://www.lafuriaumana.it/index.php/locchio-che-uccide/385-roundtable-discussion-about-post-cinematic.
33. This is in the satellite YouTube entry by @totheark titled "Signal," which also contains a faux 3D anaglyph effect through the addition of red and cyan detailing. See http://marblehornets.wikidot.com/signal.
34. David Bordwell, "Return to Paranormalcy," David Bordwell's Website on Cinema (November 13, 2012) http://www.davidbordwell.net/blog/2012/11/13/return-to-paranormalcy/
35. Scott Meslow, "12 Years After 'Blair Witch,' When Will the Found-Footage Horror Fad End?" *The Atlantic* (January 6, 2012) http://www.theatlantic.com/entertainment/archive/2012/01/12-years-after-blair-witch-when-will-the-found-footage-horror-fad-end/250950/.
36. Jane Roscoe, and Craig Hight, *Faking It: Mock-Documentary and the Subversion of Factuality* (Manchester: Manchester University Press, 2001), 183.
37. Alexandra Juhasz, "Phony Definitions," in "Introduction: Phony Definitions and Troubling Taxonomies of the Fake Documentary," in *F Is for Phony: Fake Documentary and Truth's Undoing*, eds. Alexandra Juhasz and Jesse Lerner (Minneapolis: University of Minnesota Press, 2006), 7.
38. Christopher Robbins, "Crossing Conventions in Web-Based Art: Deconstruction as a Narrative Device," *Leonardo* 40.2 (2007): 162
39. Bordwell.
40. Craig Hight, *Television Mockumentary: Reflexivity, Satire and a Call to Play* (Manchester: Manchester University Press, 2010), 2.
41. Alisa Lebow, "Faking What? Making a Mockery of Documentary," in *F Is for Phony: Fake Documentary and Truth's Undoing*, eds. Alexandra Juhasz and Jesse Lerner (Minneapolis: University of Minnesota Press, 2006), 224.
42. Juhasz and Lerner, 2–3.
43. Roscoe and Hight, 184.
44. Bill Nichols, *Introduction to Documentary* (Bloomington: Indiana University Press, 2001), 33–4.
45. Ibid., 113.
46. Jane Chapman explains the difference between *cinema verité* and direct cinema as follows: "The former originated in France, and is exemplified by the work of Jean Rouch, who saw the camera as a psychological participant in the unfolding of events, so that the filming situation will sometimes draw us nearer to the truth. In contrast, Direct Cinema was a type of observational documentary practice developed in the United States and Canada from c. 1958 and throughout the 1960s. Pro-filmic events were recorded as they

happened and allowed to unfold in front of the camera without intervention by the director." See *Issues in Contemporary Documentary* (Malden, MA: Polity Press, 2009), 50.
47. Hight and Roscoe, 20.
48. Ibid., 2.
49. Ibid., 49.
50. *Hanah's Gift* (Zac Baldwin, 2008) offers a fascinating variation on the diegetic camera theme. While for all practical purposes the film formally presents as typical of found footage horror, there is in fact no diegetic camera: what we see is the actual first person perspective of an autistic child through what is otherwise relatively pedestrian slasher film terrain. Cinematic point of view experiments range from the film noir *Dark Passage* (Delmer Daves, 1947) through to the more recent remake of William Lustig's iconic 1980 slasher *Maniac* (Franck Khalfoun, 2012). More recently, the idea of the eye itself being replaced with a camera was at the heart of Adam Wingard's *V/H/S/2* segment "Phase I Clinical Trials" (2013). This recalls the premise of Bertrand Tavernier's 1980 science fiction film *Death Watch* with Romy Schneider and Harvey Keitel (itself based on the 1973 novel "The Unsleeping Eye" by D.G. Compton). A similar concept lies at the heart of the "The Entire History of You" (2011) episode of Charlie Brooker's British television anthology series *Black Mirror*, concerning a recording device implanted behind people's ears to record and allow the playback of memories.
51. James Keller, "'Nothing That Is Not There and the Nothing That Is': Language and the *Blair Witch* Phenomenon," in *Nothing That Is: Millennial Cinema and the Blair Witch Controversies*, eds. Sarah L. Higley and Jeffrey Andrew Weinstock (Detroit: Wayne State University Press, 2004), 54.
52. Craig Hight, "Mockumentary," 204.
53. Sconce, 10.
54. This is in keeping with Steven Jay Schneider's delineation of a "superhuman serial killer" category, where the spectacular and inexplicable abilities of figures like Michael Myers from the *Halloween* franchise are considered more "superhuman" than supernatural. See Steven Jay Schneider, "Introduction, PT. I: Dimensions of the Real," *Post Script* 21.3 (Summer 2002): 3–8.
55. Roscoe and Hight, 6.
56. Ibid., 8.
57. Sébastien Lefait, *Surveillance on Screen: Monitoring Contemporary Films and Television Programs* (Lanham, MD: Scarecrow Press, 2013), 80–2.
58. Christian Metz, *Psychoanalysis and Cinema: The Imaginary Signifier* (London: Macmillan, 1982).
59. Laura Mulvey, "Visual Pleasure and Narrative Cinema," *Screen* 16.3 (Autumn 1975): 6–18.
60. Brigid Cherry, *Horror* (London: Routledge, 2009), 188.
61. Roscoe and Hight, op.cit., 171.
62. "Interview: Amanda Gusack, Writer/Director 'In Memorium,'" *The Bloodsprayer* (October 27, 2010) http://www.bloodsprayer.com/interview-amanda-gusack-writerdirector-in-memorium/.
63. Michele Aaron, "Looking On: Troubling Spectacles and the Complicitous Spectator," in *The Spectacle of the Real: From Hollywood to "Reality" TV and Beyond*, ed. Geoff King (Bristol: Intellect, 2005), 214.
64. Joel Black, *The Reality Effect: Film, Culture and the Graphic Imperative* (New York: Routledge, 2002), 15.
65. Christopher Williams, *Realism and the Cinema: A Reader* (London: British Film Institute, 1980), 1.
66. Cynthia A. Freeland, "Realist Horror," in *Philosophy and Film*, eds. Cynthia A. Freeland and Thomas E. Wartenberg (New York: Routledge, 1995), 130.
67. Ndalianis, 163.
68. Gary Rhodes, "Mockumentaries and the Production of Realist Horror," *Post Script* 21.3 (Summer 2002): 46 (via Gale Cengage Learning).
69. Ibid.
70. Ibid.
71. David Ray Carter, "It's Only a Movie? Realty as Transgression in Exploitation Cinema," in *From the Arthouse to the Grindhouse: Highbrow and Lowbrow Transgression in Cinema's First Century*, eds. John Cline and Robert Weiner (Lanham, MD: Scarecrow Press, 2010), 298.

Part 1

1. Deanna Petherbridge, "Art and Anatomy: The Meeting of Text and Image," in *The Quick and the Dead: Artists and Anatomy* by Deanna Petherbridge and Ludmilla Jordanova (London: South Bank Centre, 1997), 7.
2. Marie-Hélène Huet, "The Face of Disaster," *Yale French Studies* 111 (2007): 30.
3. This is a trend that one found footage horror film at least has sought to continue: *Severed Footage* is a 2012 Canadian found footage film whose eponymous pun indicates its fictional reconstruction of the bizarre real-life Salish Sea severed human feet mystery. According to Wikipedia, "Since August 20 2007, several detached human feet have been discovered on the coasts of the Salish Sea in British Columbia (Canada) and Washington (United States). The feet belong to five men, one woman, and three other persons of unknown sex, the two left feet having been matched with two of the right feet. As of February 2012, only five feet of four people have been identified; it is not known to whom the rest of the feet belong." See http://en.wikipedia.org/wiki/Salish_Sea_human_foot_discoveries.

4. Adam Rockoff, *Going to Pieces: The Rise and Fall of the Slasher Film, 1978–1986* (Jefferson, NC: McFarland, 2002), 26.

5. Mary Shelley's *Frankenstein* is also at the core of the found footage horror film *The Frankenstein Theory* (Andrew Weiner, 2013) and *Frankenstein's Army* (Richard Raaphorst, 2013).

6. David Bordwell, "Return to Paranormalcy," *David Bordwell's Website on Cinema* (November 13, 2012) http://www.davidbordwell.net/blog/2012/11/13/return-to-paranormalcy/.

7. The Museum of Hoaxes website provides a historical overview of these and many other major media hoaxes. See http://www.museumofhoaxes.com/.

8. Joel Black, "Real(ist) Horror: From Execution Videos to Snuff Films," in *Underground USA: Filmmaking Beyond the Hollywood Canon*, eds. Xavier Mendik and Steven Jay Schneider (London: Wallflower Press, 2002), 64.

9. Harvey Fenton, "*Cannibal Holocaust*," in *Cannibal Holocaust and the Savage Cinema of Ruggero Deodato*, by Harvey Fenton, Julian Granger and Gian Luca Castoldi (Guildford, England: FAB Press, 1999), 64.

10. Mark Goodall, *Sweet and Savage: The World Through the Shockumentary Film Lens* (London: Headpress, 2006).

11. The "Video Nasties" debate concerned the introduction of the 1984 Video Recordings Bill that required the British Board of Film Censors to consider videocassette classifications on the assumption that children in private homes may see the films in question. In practice, this led to the Home Secretary and the Director of Public Prosecutions having extraordinary powers regarding what was deemed obscene, leading Martin Barker and others to compare the situation with the state censorship then active in the Communist USSR. See Martin Baker, "Introduction," in *The Video Nasties: Freedom and Censorship in the Media*, ed. Martin Baker (London: Pluto, 1984), 1–6.

12. David Kerekes and David Slater, *Killing for Culture: A History of Death Films from Mondo to Snuff* (London: Creation, 1995), 69.

13. Ibid., 68.

14. Harvey Fenton, Julian Granger and Gian Luca Castoldi, *Cannibal Holocaust and the Savage Cinema of Ruggero Deodato* (Guildford, England: FAB Press, 1999), 21.

15. Ibid., 16.

16. Fenton, 65–6.

17. Ibid., 78.

18. An alternate title for the contemporary found footage horror film *The Facility* (Ian Clark, 2012) was *Guinea Pigs*, suggesting a possible reference to this notorious Japanese predecessor.

19. Jack Hunter, *Eros in Hell: Sex, Blood and Madness in Japanese Cinema* (London: Creation, 1998), 145.

20. Ibid., 149.

21. David Ray Carter, "It's Only a Movie? Reality as Transgression in Exploitation Cinema," in *From the Arthouse to the Grindhouse: Highbrow and Lowbrow Transgression in Cinema's First Century*, eds. John Cline and Robert Weiner (Lanham, MD: Scarecrow Press, 2010), 302.

22. Jay McRoy, *Nightmare Japan: Contemporary Japanese Horror Cinema* (Amsterdam: Rodopi, 2008), 16.

23. Ibid., 17.

24. Ibid., 28.

25. Charles Masters, "World Taking Note of Belgian Film," *Hollywood Reporter* (7 December 2005), 8.

26. Martin Rubin, "The Grayness of Darkness: *The Honeymoon Killers* and Its Impact on Psychokiller Cinema," in *Mythologies of Violence in Postmodern Media*, ed. Christopher Sharrett (Detroit: Wayne State University Press, 1999), 41–64.

27. Ernest Mathijs, "*Man Bites Dog* and the Critical Reception of Belgian Horror Cinema," in *Horror International*, eds. Steven Jay Schneider and Tony Williams (Detroit: Wayne State University Press, 2005), 325.

28. Aside from work already cited, further recommended reading on *Man Bites Dog* includes Jane Roscoe, "*Man Bites Dog*: Deconstructing the Documentary Look," *Metro Magazine*, 112 (1997): 21–25; Frank Lafond, "*C'est Arrivé Près de Chez Vous, Man Bites Dog*," in *The Cinema of the Low Countries* ed. Ernest. Mathijs (London: Wallflower Press, 2004); Julian Hallam and Margaret Marshment, *Realism and Popular Cinema* (Manchester: Manchester University Press, 2000), 242–245. Further critical insight into *Cannibal Holocaust* can be found in the following: Neil Jackson, "*Cannibal Holocaust*, Realist Horror, and Reflexivity," *Post Script* 21.3 (Summer 2002): 32–45; Carolina G. Jauregui, "'Eat It Alive and Swallow It Whole!' Resavoring *Cannibal Holocaust* as a Mockumentary," *Invisible Culture* 7 (2004) http://www.rochester.edu/in_visible_culture/Issue_7/Issue_7_Jauregui.pdf; Julian Petley, "*Cannibal Holocaust* and the Pornography of Death," in *The Spectacle of the Real: From Hollywood to "Reality" TV and Beyond*, ed. Geoff King (Bristol: Intellect, 2005), 173–85; and in books including Mikita Brottman's *Meat Is Murder: An Illustrated Guide to Cannibal Culture* (London: Creation, 1998) and *EATEN ALIVE! Italian Cannibal and Zombie Movies*, ed. Jay Slater (London: Plexus, 2002).

29. Chuck Berg and Tom Erskine, *The Encyclopedia of Orson Welles* (New York: Facts on File, 2003), XV.

30. Craig Hight, *Television Mockumentary: Reflexivity, Satire and a Call to Play* (Manchester: Manchester University Press, 2010), 45.

31. This broadcast of "War of the Worlds" is in the public domain, and available to hear online

at http://archive.org/details/OrsonWelles-MercuryTheater-1938Recordings.
32. Berg and Erskine, 406–7.
33. Hadley Cantril, *The Invasion from Mars: A Study in the Psychology of Panic* (Princeton: Princeton University Press, 1940), 47.
34. Ibid., 48–9.
35. Ibid., 47.
36. Ibid., 82.
37. Ibid., 77.
38. Ibid., 83.
39. Ibid., x.
40. Jeffrey Sconce, *Haunted Media: Electronic Presence from Telegraphy to Television* (Durham: Duke University Press, 2000), 16.
41. Ibid., 117.
42. Ibid.
43. Cantril, 100.
44. Ibid., 79.
45. Marguerite H. Rippy, *Orson Welles and the Unfinished RKO Projects: A Postmodern Perspective* (Carbondale: Southern Illinois University Press, 2009), 158.
46. Ibid.
47. Rippy, 158.

Chapter One

1. Ken Smith, *Mental Hygiene: Classroom Films 1945–1970* (New York: Blast, 1999), 80.
2. Mikita Brottman "*Signal 30*," in *Car Crash Culture*, ed. Mikita Brottman (New York: Palgrave, 2001), 233.
3. Ibid., 233–4.
4. *Hell's Highway: The True Story of Highway Safety Films* (Bret Wood, 2003).
5. Ken Smith, 74–5.
6. Ibid., 81.
7. *Hell's Highway: The True Story of Highway Safety Films* (Bret Wood, 2003). Press book. Kino International www.kino.com/press/hells_pr/hells_highway_pb.pdf.
8. Martin D. Yant, *Rotten to the Core: Crime, Sex & Corruption in Johnny Appleseed's Hometown* (Columbus: Public Eye, 1994), 182–6.
9. *Hell's Highway: The True Story of Highway Safety Films*.
10. This is stated in *Hell's Highway: The True Story of Highway Safety Films*, and Wood also makes this explicit in email correspondence when discussing his conversations with Deems. He writes: "Having interviewed the guys who worked on the film (Earle Deems, John Domer), I can say with absolute certainty that there was no intent on their part to titillate or provide pleasure. They were very wary of me because they were suspicious that I was meaning to exploit the films for their entertainment value. I think if there was a little bit of a 'showman' in them, they would have taken more pleasure in being interviewed for 'Hell's Highway,' or spoken about the films with a bit more pleasure" (Bret Wood email to author, June 20, 2009).
11. Ken Smith, 81.
12. *Hell's Highway: The True Story of Highway Safety Films*.
13. Bret Wood email.
14. *Hell's Highway: The True Story of Highway Safety Films Inc.*, pressbook.
15. *Hell's Highway: The True Story of Highway Safety Films*.
16. Other non-road safety films produced by the Highway Safety Foundation include *The Shoplifter* (1964), *A Great and Honorable Duty* (1965), *Plant Pilferage* (1965), and *The Paperhangers* (1966).
17. Although Jean Hurrell and Connie Burtoch's names are not used in the film, there is enough evidence to support claims that this crime scene footage in *The Child Molester* is taken from their case. In our correspondence, Bret Wood states "it's a safe assumption. The circumstances are identical" (Bret Wood email.). Witnesses at the Hurrell-Burtoch scene recall the girls wearing "bathing suits or sun suits" ("Bodies of Two Girls Found in Creek; Suspect Murder," *Mansfield News-Journal* [24 June 1962], 1), and in the film, the outfits the girls wear (Mary in a white top and Jeannie in a pink sun suit) closely resemble these descriptions.
18. A rough outline of the events based on newspaper reports and other accounts may be found at: http://filmbunnies.wordpress.com/2011/01/30/the-child-molester-1964-the-highway-safety-foundation-beyond-the-road/.
19. John P. Butler, *The Best Suit in Town: A Generation of Cops* (Charlotte Harbor, FL: Royal Palm Press, 2001), 125.
20. William E. Jones, *Tearoom* (Los Angeles: 2nd Cannons, 2008), 42.
21. The numbers vary. As Jones explains, "estimates of the number of men convicted vary widely, and it may ultimately prove impossible to arrive at a definite total. Transfers from Lima State Hospital are noted in the register books of the Ohio Penitentiary and State Reformatory, but in the cases of men who were committed to the state mental hospital and who are not subsequently sent to prison, records are unavailable." Ibid., 34.
22. Ibid., 35.
23. Bret Wood email.
24. Carol J. Clover, *Men, Women, and Chain Saws: Gender and the Modern Horror Film* (Princeton: Princeton University Press, 1992), 56.
25. Ibid.,186.
26. Ibid.
27. Ibid., 12.
28. *Hell's Highway: The True Story of Highway Safety Films*.
29. Bret Wood email.
30. Recent statistics suggest that approximately 90 percent of child sexual abuse cases are

perpetrated by someone known to the child renders the "stranger danger" message less urgent than films like this may suggest. According to the American Psychological Association, "most children are abused by someone they know and trust." They claim approximately 30 percent of abusers are family members, while around 60 percent are other people known to the child. Only 10 percent are strangers. See http://www.apa.org/pi/families/resources/child-sexual-abuse.aspx.

31. This is ambiguous, however, as Deane Waite (the actor who plays Josh in the film) appears in an interview in the supposed news report on Megan's disappearance as the actor hired to play the role of Josh in a re-enactment.

32. Bret Wood email.

33. "Message from the Director," http://meganismissing.com/.

34. Ibid.

35. http://meganismissing.com/press/klaas.html.

36. "Message from the Director."

37. Derek Long, "The Highway Shock Film: History, Phenomenology, Ideology," *The Projector Film and Media Journal* (2012) http://www.bgsu.edu/departments/theatrefilm/projector/04-01-12/page123443.html.

38. "Classification Office Decision: *Megan Is Missing*," New Zealand Office of Literature and Film Classification (12 October 2011) http://www.censorship.govt.nz/DDA/Pages/Screens/DDA/PublicationDecisionInformationPage.aspx.

Chapter Two

1. Scott Meslow, "12 Years After *Blair Witch*, When Will the Found-Footage Horror Fad End?" *The Atlantic* (January 6, 2012) http://www.theatlantic.com/entertainment/archive/2012/01/12-years-after-blair-witch-when-will-the-found-footage-horror-fad-end/250950/.

2. Mikita Brottman, *Offensive Films: Towards an Anthropology of Cinema Vomitif* (Westport, CT: Greenwood Press, 1997), 95.

3. David Kerekes and David Slater, *Killing for Culture: A History of Death Films from Mondo to Snuff* (London: Creation, 1995), 4.

4. Ibid.

5. Eithne Johnson and Eric Schaefer, "Soft Core/Hard Gore: *Snuff* as a Crisis in Meaning," *Journal of Film and Video* 42.2–3 (1993): 40, 56.

6. See Avedon Carol, "Snuff: Believing the Worst," in *Bad Girls and Dirty Pictures: The Challenge to Reclaim Feminism*, eds. Alison Assiter and Avedon Carol (London: Pluto Press, 1993), 128; Johnson and Schaefer, Stine.

7. Julian Petley, "Cannibal Holocaust and the Pornography of Death," *The Spectacle of the Real: From Hollywood to Reality TV and Beyond* (Bristol: Intellect, 2005), 174.

8. Any doubts as to the consumption of this footage in this manner should be put to rest by its appearance on websites such as BestGore.com: http://www.bestgore.com/execution/execution-saddam-hussein-hanging-full-video/.

9. Jeffrey M. Tupas and Jeoffrey Maitem, "Bootleg DVDs of Maguindano Massacre on Sale," *Inquirer Mindanao* (December 28, 2009) http://newsinfo.inquirer.net/inquirerheadlines/metro/view/20091228-244373/Bootleg-DVDs-of-Maguindanao-massacre-on-sale. Many thanks to Ramon Lobato for bringing this to my attention in his must-read monograph *Shadow Economies of Cinema: Mapping Informal Film Distribution* (London: British Film Institute, 2012).

10. Joel Black, "Real(ist) Horror: From Execution Videos to Snuff Films," in *Underground USA: Filmmaking Beyond the Hollywood Canon*, eds. Xavier Mendik and Steven Jay Schneider (London: Wallflower Press, 2002), 69.

11. David Kerekes, "The Small World of Snuff Fetish Custom Video," in *From the Arthouse to the Grindhouse: Highbrow and Lowbrow Transgression in Cinema's First Century*, eds. John Cline and Robert Weiner (Lanham, MD: Scarecrow Press, 2010), 264–73.

12. Black, "Real(ist) Horror," 68.

13. Scott Aaron Stine, "The Snuff Film: The Making of an Urban Legend," *Skeptical Inquirer* 23:3 (1999): 29–34.

14. Julian Petley, "Cannibal Holocaust and the Pornography of Death," *The Spectacle of the Real: From Hollywood to Reality TV and Beyond* (Bristol: Intellect, 2005), 174.

15. Alan McKee, "The Aesthetics of Pornography: The Insights of Consumers," *Continuum: Journal of Media and Cultural Studies* 20.4 (December 2006): 528.

16. Deborah Cameron, "Discourses of Desire: Liberals, Feminists, and the Politics of Pornography in the 1980s," *American Literary History* 2.4 (Winter 1990): 797.

17. Avedon Carol, "Snuff: Believing the Worst," in *Bad Girls and Dirty Pictures: The Challenge to Reclaim Feminism*, eds. Alison Assiter and Avedon Carol (London: Pluto Press, 1993), 126.

18. Johnson and Schaefer, 47.

19. Catherine MacKinnon, *Only Words* (Cambridge: Harvard University Press, 1993), 15.

20. Jane Caputi, *The Age of Sex Crime* (London: Women's Press, 1987), 168.

21. Camille Paglia, *Vamps and Tramps: New Essays* (New York: Vintage, 1994), 111.

22. Carol, 130.

23. As discussed in the following: Brottman; Johnson and Schaefer; Kerekes and Slater; Stine; Black. See also Joan Hawkins, *Cutting Edge: Art-Horror and the Horrific Avant-Garde* (Minneapolis: Minnesota University Press, 2000); Neil Jackson, "The Cultural Construction of Snuff: Alejandro Amenábar's *Tesis* (*Thesis*, 1996)," *Kinoeye*

3.5 (2003) http://www.kinoeye.org/03/05/jackson05.php.
24. Joan Hawkins wrote, "In retrospect, it seems amazing that anyone mistook *Snuff*'s violence for *cinema verité*," ibid., 137. For Stine, "not only is the gore obviously fake, but the execution of the special effects is painfully inept."
25. She is called by an off-camera voice in shot 7, and is directed to "hold her down." The low quality of the sound recording here slightly blurs the sound of the name, but on careful examination, it is either June, Joan or Jude. To my ear, it sounds like the former and as such she will be referred to as this throughout this chapter.
26. Johnson and Schaefer *do* identify her presence, but only in passing. They do not mention that she is named, nor is any further significance placed upon her involvement. They noted, "After briefly embracing on an adjacent bed while fully clothed, the director pins the actress down with the help of a female crew member and beings to torture her with a knife" (49–50).
27. Johnson and Schaefer, 43.
28. Kerekes and Slater, 11.
29. Stine.
30. Johnson and Schaefer, 51.
31. Ibid.
32. Johnson and Schaefer have noted: "Continuity errors from shot to shot reveal the artifice, as does the actress's prosthetic torso, from which the director pulls the entrails" (40). For Neil Jackson, "the cutaways, multiple camera angles and unconvincing prosthetics utilized in *Snuff*'s final sequence all signal the artifice underlying the film's [...] central conceit."
33. Brottman, 104.

Chapter Three

1. Craig Hight, *Television Mockumentary: Reflexivity, Satire and a Call to Play* (Manchester: Manchester University Press, 2010), 77.
2. Cynthia Miller, "Introduction: At Play in the Fields of the Truth," *Post Script*, 28.3 (Summer 2009): 3–8. See also "On this Day: 1957: BBC Fools the Nation," http://news.bbc.co.uk/onthisday/hi/dates/stories/april/1/newsid_2819000/2819261.stm.
3. Nick Muntean, "There Is Nothing More Objectionable Than Objectivity: The Films of Peter Watkins," in *From the Arthouse to the Grindhouse: Highbrow and Lowbrow Transgression in Cinema's First Century*, eds. John Cline and Robert Weiner (Lanham, MD: Scarecrow Press, 2010), 281.
4. Keith Beattie, *Documentary Screens: Non-Fiction Film and Television* (Houndmills: Palgrave Macmillan, 2004), 152.
5. Muntean, 281.
6. Hight, Television Documentary, 93.
7. See the "Making of *Alternative 3 [qm]*" featurette on Soda Picture's *Alternative 3* DVD release from 2007.
8. See Ibid.; Hight, *Television Documentary*, 94.
9. See Paul Simpson, *That's What They Want You to Think: Conspiracies Real, Possible and Paranoid* (Minneapolis: Zenith Press, 2012), 236–45.
10. "*Alien Abduction: Incident in Lake County*," Wikipedia.org: http://en.wikipedia.org/wiki/Alien_Abduction:_Incident_in_Lake_County#Controversy.
11. Martin Harris, "The 'Witchcraft' of Media Manipulation: *Pamela* and *The Blair Witch Project*," *The Journal of Popular Culture* 34.4 (Spring 2001): 79.
12. "FAQ," *Ghostwatch: Behind the Curtains*, Official Website http://www.ghostwatchbtc.com/p/faq.html.
13. Hight, 97.
14. Jeffrey Sconce, *Haunted Media: Electronic Presence from Telegraphy to Television* (Durham: Duke University Press, 2000), 164.
15. Elizabeth Evans, "*Ghostwatch* & Interview with Stephen Volk," *Scope: An Online Journal of Film and Television Studies* 22 (February 2012) http://www.scope.nottingham.ac.uk/February_2012/ftv_reviews.pdf.
16. Stephen Volk, email to author, February 21, 2013.
17. Hight, *Television Documentary*, 96.
18. Simon Hattenstone, "Saturday Interview: Michael Parkinson," *The Guardian* (February 24, 2012) http://www.guardian.co.uk/theguardian/2012/feb/24/michael-parkinson-saturday-interview.
19. "How to Talk to Anyone in the World," *The Sun-Herald* (June 2, 2003) http://www.smh.com.au/articles/2003/06/01/1054406070303.html.
20. Hight, *Television Documentary*, 20
21. Adam Curtis, "The Ghosts in the Living Room," *BBC Blogs* (December 22, 2011) http://www.bbc.co.uk/blogs/adamcurtis/posts/the_ghosts_in_the_living_room.
22. See *Ghostwatch: Behind the Curtains* (Rich Lawden, 2012).
23. In an interview in London's *Time Out* (April 1–7, 2010), Peli openly admitted he had seen *Ghostwatch*. See "Paranormal-ier Activity," *Ghostwatch: Behind the Curtains* (June 30, 2010) http://www.ghostwatchbtc.com/2010/06/paranormal-ier-activity.html.
24. A thirteenth episode called "The Examination" was broadcast on French television network Arte on December 16, 2010.
25. The following interview describes the series as being first broadcast in France in the late 1980s. Additionally, the 2009 DVD release of *Les Documents Interdit* also dates the series as 1989–1991. "Entretien avec Jean-Teddy Filippe," *Cine-

trange (November 30, 2009) http://www.cine trange.com/support/sortie-dvd/jean-teddy-fil ippe/. Many thanks to Anna Gardner for her translation of this interview into English.
26. Ibid.

Part 2

1. Adam Lowenstein, "Spectacle Horror and Hostel: Why 'Torture Porn' Does Not Exist," *Critical Quarterly* 53.2 (2011): 42–60. While it is tempting to apply this "ambient horror" label wholesale to contemporary found footage horror, some key examples such as *V/H/S* (2012) and *Grave Encounters* (2011) have resisted this through their shocking, spectacular imagery.
2. Jane Roscoe, "*The Blair Witch Project*: Mock-documentary Goes Mainstream," *Jump Cut* 43 (July 2000) http://www.ejumpcut.org/archive/onlinessays/JC43folder/BlairWitch.html.
3. Paul Wells, *The Horror Film: From Beelzebub to Blair Witch* (London: Wallflower Press, 2000), 109.
4. James Keller, "'Nothing That Is Not There and the Nothing That Is': Language and the *Blair Witch* Phenomenon," in *Nothing That Is: Millennial Cinema and the Blair Witch Controversies*, eds. Sarah L. Higley and Jeffrey Andrew Weinstock (Detroit: Wayne State University Press, 2004), 57.
5. John Kenneth Muir, *Horror films of the 1990s* (Jefferson, NC: McFarland, 2011), 12–3.
6. Aviva Briefel and Sam J. Miller, "Introduction," in *Horror After 9/11: World of Fear, Cinema of Terror* eds. Aviva Briefel and Sam J. Miller (Austin: University of Texas Press, 2011), 1.
7. Ibid., 3.
8. Philip L. Simpson, "Whither the Serial Killer Movie?" in *American Horror Film The Genre at the Turn of the Millennium*, ed. Steffen Hantke (Jackson: University of Mississippi Press, 2010), 119–41.
9. Stephen Prince, *Firestorm: American Film in the Age of Terrorism* (New York: Columbia University Press, 2009), 284.
10. Matt Hills, "Cutting into Concepts of 'Reflectionist' Cinema? The Saw Franchise and Puzzles of Post–9/11 Horror," in *Horror After 9/11: World of Fear, Cinema of Terror*, eds. Aviva Briefel and Sam J. Miller (Austin: University of Texas Press, 2011), 108.
11. David Lyon, *Surveillance Studies: An Overview* (Cambridge, MA: Polity Press, 2007), 11.
12. Ibid., 13.
13. Adam L. Penenberg, "The Surveillance Society," *Wired*, 9.12 (December 2001) http://www.wired.com/wired/archive/9.12/surveillance.html
14. Ibid.
15. Sébastien Lefait, *Surveillance on Screen: Monitorin Contemporary Films and Television Programs* (Lanham, MD: Scarecrow Press, 2013), 82.
16. It is however crucial to remember that from a commercial perspective at least the shift from "torture porn" to the more ambient horror of the *Paranormal Activity* franchise was not considered a battle as such, but rather a shift from one commercially-viable trend to another. The two franchises almost became explicitly linked when Kevin Greutert who directed *Saw VI* (2009) and *Saw VII* (2010) and edited the first five films of that franchise. He was initially pegged to direct *Paranormal Activity 2* until he was forced instead to make *Saw VII* through the exercising of a contractual obligation. Greutert was disappointed with this decision, and released the following statement: "I just had the task of telling my 83 year old mother that no, I'm not going to be allowed to direct the movie we were all so excited about when my family last got together, and that I'm being forced to leave town before getting a chance to see her again. Yes, I'll be filming people getting tortured YET AGAIN. So we'll have to put off me making a film she can actually watch for another year. I'm not making this shit up." See Simon Brew, "Kevin Greutert Posts Statement on *Saw 7/Paranormal Activity 2* Situation," *Den of Geek* (January 27, 2010) http://www.denofgeek.com/movies/saw/15306/kevin-greutert-posts-statement-on-saw-7-paranormal-activity-2-situation.
17. David Edelstein, "Now Playing at Your Local Multiplex: Torture Porn," *New York Magazine* (January 28, 2006) http://nymag.com/movies/features/15622/.
18. Eithne Johnson, and Eric Schaefer, "Soft Core/Hard Gore: *Snuff* as a Crisis in Meaning," *Journal of Film and Video* 42.2–3 (1993): 51.
19. Lowenstein, 42.
20. Ibid.
21. Paul Schrodt, "*Paranormal Activity 4:* The Instant Trailer Review," *Esquire* (August 1, 2012) http://www.esquire.com/the-side/movie-trailers/paranormal-activity-4-11248478.
22. John Kenneth Muir, "Cult Movie Review: *Paranormal Activity* (2009)," *John Kenneth Muir's Reflections on Film/TV* (January 4, 2010) http://reflectionsonfilmandtelevision.blogspot.com.au/2010/01/cult-movie-review-paranormal-activity.html.
23. Adrian Martin, "Pity It's Phooey," *The Age* (December 2, 1999), 84.

Chapter Four

1. Sean Smith, "Curse of the Blair Witch," *Newsweek*, 143:4 (January 26, 2004): 56–8.
2. James Keller, "'Nothing That Is Not There and the Nothing That Is': Language and the *Blair Witch* Phenomenon," in *Nothing That Is: Millen-*

nial Cinema and the Blair Witch Controversies, eds. Sarah L. Higley and Jeffrey Andrew Weinstock (Detroit: Wayne State University Press, 2004): 53.

3. Keira McKenzie, "Double the Passive: The Trials of Viewer/Subject in *Cloverfield* and *The Blair Witch Project*," *Ol3Media*, 84.09 (January 2011): 37–43.

4. Martin Harris, "The 'Witchcraft' of Media Manipulation: *Pamela* and *The Blair Witch Project*," *The Journal of Popular Culture*, 34.4 (Spring 2001): 79.

5. See Higley; Higley and Weinstock; Paul Wells, *The Horror Film: From Beelzebub to Blair Witch* (London: Wallflower Press, 2000), 109; Brigid Cherry, *Horror* (London: Routledge, 2009), 189–90; Tanya Krzywinska, *A Skin for Dancing In: Possession, Witchcraft and Voodoo in Film* (Trowbridge, England: Flicks, 2000), 139; Eric S. Mallin, "*The Blair Witch Project*, *Macbeth*, and the Indeterminate End," in *The End of Cinema as We Know It: American Film in the Nineties* ed. Jon Lewis (New York: New York University Press, 2001), 105–14; Joewon Yoon, "Ghostly Imagination, History, and Femininity at Centuries' Ends: The Turn of the Screw and The Blair Witch Project," in *Nothing That Is: Millennial Cinema and the Blair Witch Controversies*, eds. Sarah L. Higley and Jeffrey Andrew Weinstock (Detroit: Wayne State University Press, 2004), 181–96; Harris, 75–107.

6. Aloi, 199.

7. Bruce Alexander, "*The Blair Witch Project*: Expulsion form Adulthood and Versions of the American Gothic," in *Nothing That Is: Millennial Cinema and the Blair Witch Controversies*, eds. Sarah L. Higley and Jeffrey Andrew Weinstock (Detroit: Wayne State University Press, 2004), 145–61.

8. As Sean Smith notes, Eduardo Sánchez and Daniel Myrick rejected offers to make studio-based horror films such as *Freddy vs. Jason* and *The Exorcist 4*, focusing their attentions on the never-realized *Heart of Love* comedy project. Myrick co-founded the direct-to-DVD label Raw Feed through Warner Home Video, and directed a number of solid genre efforts including *Solstice* (2008) and *Believers* (2007). Sánchez also directed small-scale movies such as *Altered* (2006) and *Seventh Moon* (2009), but recently has had more success with *Lovely Molly* (2011) and he co-directed one of the entries in the *V/H/S* (2012) sequel *V/H/S/2* (2013), "A Ride in the Park" with *Blair Witch* producer Gregg Hale. At the time of writing, Sánchez and Hale are working on the post-production of their found footage Bigfoot horror movie, *Exists*. There also are rumors circulating online about a possible third *Blair Witch* film. As for the actors, Michael C. Williams and Heather Donahue attained little comparative success: according to Smith, Williams returned to his original job as a furniture removalist for some time, then went on to teach acting. After a number of smaller roles in film and television, Donahue quit acting to pursue growing medical marijuana as documented in her 2012 memoir *Growgirl: How My Life After The Blair Witch Project Went to Pot*. More successful has been Joshua Leonard, who has worked consistently on a diverse range of projects post-*Blair Witch*, including in a number of horror films such as *Cubbyhouse* (Murray Fahey, 2001), *Madhouse* (William Butler 2004), and *Bitter Feast* (Joe Maggio, 2010), as well as starring in the celebrated mumblecore film *Humpday* (Lynn Shtelton, 2009). The latter won the same John Cassavetes Independent Spirit award at Sundance that year, co-incidentally the same award that *Blair Witch* received a decade earlier.

9. Jane Roscoe, "*The Blair Witch Project*: Mock-documentary Goes Mainstream," *Jump Cut* 43 (July 2000): 3–8. http://www.ejumpcut.org/archive/onlinessays/JC43folder/BlairWitch.html.

10. Sarah L. Higley and Jeffrey Andrew Weinstock, "Introduction: The Blair Witch Controversies" in *Nothing That Is: Millennial Cinema and the Blair Witch Controversies*, eds. Sarah L. Higley and Jeffrey Andrew Weinstock (Detroit: Wayne State University Press, 2004), 29.

11. Scott Dixon McDowell, "Method Filmmaking: An Interview with Daniel Myrick, Co-director of *The Blair Witch Project*," *Journal of Film and Video* 53.2:3 (Summer/Fall 2001): 140–7.

12. Sarah L. Higley, "'People Just Want to See Something': Art, Death and Document in *The Blair Witch Project*, *The Last Broadcast* and *Paradise Lost*," in *Nothing That Is: Millennial Cinema and the Blair Witch Controversies*, eds. Sarah L. Higley and Jeffrey Andrew Weinstock (Detroit: Wayne State University Press, 2004), 98.

13. Ibid., 101.

14. Alexandra Juhasz, "Phony Definitions," in "Introduction: Phony Definitions and Troubling Taxonomies of the Fake Documentary," in *F Is for Phony: Fake Documentary and Truth's Undoing*, eds. Alexandra Juhasz and Jesse Lerner (Minneapolis: University of Minnesota Press, 2006), 10.

15. McDowell.

16. Sean Smith.

17. Peg Aloi, "Beyond the *Blair Witch*: A New Horror Aesthetic?" in *The Spectacle of the Real: From Hollywood to "Reality" TV and Beyond*, ed. Geoff King (Bristol: Intellect, 2005), 197.

18. Joseph S. Walker, "Mom and the Blair Witch: Narrative, Form and the Feminine," in *Nothing That Is: Millennial Cinema and the Blair Witch Controversies*, eds. Sarah L. Higley and Jeffrey Andrew Weinstock (Detroit: Wayne State University Press, 2004), 164.

19. Laura U. Marks, *Touch: Sensuous Theory*

and *Multisensory Media* (Minneapolis: University of Minnesota Press, 2002), 52.
20. Lynden Barber, "Method in Their Fearful Madness," *The Australian* (December 10, 1999): 10.
21. According to James Castonguay, "Artisan spent $1.5 million on the early Web promotional campaign and over $25 million in total marketing costs." He continued, "Although this is less than half the promotional budget for a major studio blockbuster, at the very least it calls into question claims that the popularity of BWP simply fueled itself." See "The Political Economy of the Indie Blockbuster: Fandom, Intermediality and *The Blair Witch Project*," in *Nothing That Is: Millennial Cinema and the Blair Witch Controversies*, eds. Sarah L. Higley and Jeffrey Andrew Weinstock (Detroit: Wayne State University Press, 2004), 78.
22. Ibid., 80.
23. David Banash, "*The Blair Witch Project*: Technology, Repression, and the Evisceration of Mimesis," in *Nothing That Is: Millennial Cinema and the Blair Witch Controversies*, eds. Sarah L. Higley and Jeffrey Andrew Weinstock (Detroit: Wayne State University Press, 2004), 122.
24. J. P. Telotte. "*The Blair Witch Project*: Film and the Internet," *Film Quarterly* 54:3 (Spring 2001): 32–9. Republished in *Nothing That Is: Millennial Cinema and the Blair Witch Controversies*, eds. Sarah L. Higley and Jeffrey Andrew Weinstock (Detroit: Wayne State University Press, 2004), 37–51.
25. Chuck Tryon, "Video from the Void: Video Spectacularity, Domestic Film Cultures, and Contemporary Horror Film," *Journal of Film and Video* 61.3 (Fall 2009): 42.
26. Keller, 55.
27. Castonguay, 73.
28. Margrit Schreier, "'Please Help Me; All I Want to Know Is: Is It Real or Not?': How Recipients View the Reality Status of *The Blair Witch Project*," *Poetics Today* 25.2 (Summer 2004): 330.
29. Haxan went on to make commercial ARGs such as "The Art of the Heist" for Audi in 2005. See http://www.haxan.com/2005/06/07/interactive-storytelling/.
30. Angela Ndalianis, *The Horror Sensorium: Media and the Senses* (Jefferson, NC: McFarland, 2012), 172.
31. Jane Roscoe and Craig Hight, *Faking It: Mock-Documentary and the Subversion of Factuality* (Manchester: Manchester University Press, 2001), 16.
32. Emily Wax, "It's Enough to Make You Sick," *The Age* (August 12, 1999): B3 (reprinted from *The Washington Post*).
33. Roscoe and Hight, 17.
34. Barbara Creed, *The Monstrous-Feminine: Film, Feminism, Psychoanalysis* (London: Routledge, 1993), 2.
35. Ibid., 76.
36. Ibid., 73–83.
37. Linda C. Badley, "Spiritual Warfare: Postfeminism and the Cultural Politics of the *Blair Witch* Craze," *Intensities: The Journal of Cult Media* (Spring 2003) http://intensities.org/Essays/Badley.pdf.
38. Ibid.
39. Christina Lane, "Just Another Girl Outside the Neo-Indie," in *Contemporary American Independent Film: From the Margins to the Mainstream*, eds. Chris Holmlund and Justin Wyatt (London: Routledge, 2005), 177.

Chapter Five

1. Angela Ndalianis, *The Horror Sensorium: Media and the Senses* (Jefferson, NC: McFarland, 2012), 172.
2. Considering the notoriously disappointing commercial performance of *Book of Shadows*, it is perhaps surprising that *Grave Encounters 2* (John Poliquin, 2012) adopted a near-identical premise, where fans of the original film retrace the steps of the first film's characters. Unlike *Book of Shadows*, however, *Grave Encounters 2* was formally loyal to the original and is clearly a found footage horror movie.
3. Sarah L. Higley, "'People Just Want to See Something': Art, Death and Document in *The Blair Witch Project*, *The Last Broadcast* and *Paradise Lost*," in *Nothing That Is: Millennial Cinema and the Blair Witch Controversies*, eds. Sarah L. Higley and Jeffrey Andrew Weinstock (Detroit: Wayne State University Press, 2004), 87–110.
4. Ibid., 104.
5. Jeffrey Sconce, *Haunted Media: Electronic Presence from Telegraphy to Television* (Durham: Duke University Press, 2000), 16.
6. Guido Henkel, "The Facts About *The Last Broadcast*: An Interview with Lance Weiler," DVD Review (December 9, 1999) http://www.dvdreview.com/html/dvd_review_-_lance_weiler.shtml.
7. Higley, 88–9.
8. David Ray Carter, "It's Only a Movie? Reality as Transgression in Exploitation Cinema," in *From the Arthouse to the Grindhouse: Highbrow and Lowbrow Transgression in Cinema's First Century*, eds. John Cline and Robert Weiner (Lanham, MD: Scarecrow Press, 2010), 313.
9. *Man Bites Dog* is evoked not only through the basic premise of a diegetic camera documenting a serial killer, but in key moments such as the implied threat to Max's grandmother evoking a similar scene in the Belgian film where Ben gains access to an elderly woman's home and murders her. Aside from the serial killer link to *Henry, The Last Horror Movie* also recalls that earlier film's home invasion scene and its bathtub dismemberment sequence. *Ringu* is flagged in a scene where

Max shaves in an oval mirror: The composition of this shot is almost identical to an image of Sadako's mother brushing her hair in the "found" video in the famous J-horror.
10. Johnny Walker, "Nasty Visions: Violent Spectacle in Contemporary British Horror Cinema," *Horror Studies* 2.1 (2011): 124.
11. Susan Sontag, *On Photography* (New York: Picador, 1977), 7.
12. Walker, 126.
13. There appears to be a prequel in the works called *Before the Mask: The Return of Leslie Vernon*—alternatively referred to as *B4TM*—although details are at present limited.
14. *August Underground* (Fred Vogel, 2001), *August Underground's Mordum* (Killjoy, Fred Vogel, Cristie Whiles, Jerami Cruise, and Michael T. Schneider, 2003) and *August Underground's Penance* (Fred Vogel, 2007).

Chapter Six

1. Missy Schwartz, "A Shocking Hit," *Entertainment Weekly* 1074 (November 6, 2009): 20–3.
2. The following is a breakdown of expenses included in Peli's initial $11,000 budget: camera $3,000, Red Bull $100, miscellaneous camera equipment $1,000, editing PC and editing software $4,000, catering $500, casting costs, accommodations, trips to Los Angeles: $1,000, wood for making a cross: $20, baby powder: $3, materials and printing costs for Ouija board: $35, actors: $1,500, and police costume rental: $400. See Missy Schwartz.
3. Nicolas Rapold, "*Paranormal Activity*," *Sight & Sound* 20.1 (January 2010): 72.
4. "*Paranormal Activity 5*: Horror Franchise Sets Release For Fifth Film," *Huffington Post* (November 21, 2012) http://www.huffingtonpost.com/2012/11/21/paranormal-activity-5-horror-film-release_n_2170454.html.
5. Evan Dickson, "Finally! The Full Trailer for *Paranormal Activity 4*!!!" *Bloody Disgusting* (August 1, 2012) http://bloody-disgusting.com/news/3156933/finally-the-full-trailer-for-paranormal-activity-4/.
6. Leslie A. Hahner, Scott J. Varda and Nathan A. Wilson, "*Paranormal Activity* and the Horror of Abject Consumption," *Critical Studies in Media Communication* (2012): 2.
7. Sébastien Lefait, *Surveillance on Screen: Monitoring Contemporary Films and Television Programs* (Lanham, MD: Scarecrow Press, 2013), 89.
8. Ibid., 85.
9. Julia Leyda, Nicholas Rombes, Steven Shaviro and Therese Grisham, "Roundtable Discussion: The Post-Cinematic in *Paranormal Activity* and *Paranormal Activity 2*," *La Furia Umana* 10 (Autumn 2011) http://www.lafuriaumana.it/index.php/locchio-che-uccide/385-roundtable-discussion-about-post-cinematic.
10. Ibid.
11. David Lyon, *The Electronic Eye: The Rise of Surveillance Society* (Minneapolis: University of Minnesota Press, 1994), 4.
12. Leyda, Rombes, Shaviro and Grisham.
13. Joanna Heath, "Blame It on the Bankers," *Newsweek* (February 20, 2009). Republished on *The Daily Beast* at http://www.thedailybeast.com/newsweek/2009/02/20/blame-it-on-the-bankers.html.
14. John Kenneth Muir, "Cult Movie Review: *Paranormal Activity* (2009)," *John Kenneth Muir's Reflections on Film/TV* (January 4, 2010) http://reflectionsonfilmandtelevision.blogspot.com.au/2010/01/cult-movie-review-paranormal-activity.html.
15. Todd Ford, "*Paranormal*'s Domestic Activities," *Cinema 100 Film Society* (October 27, 2009) http://www.cinema100.com/2009/10/paranormals-domestic-activities.html.
16. There was an alternate ending to the first film that was never filmed that mirrors Michael Powell's *Peeping Tom* (1960) where the camera is literally used as a weapon: "a possessed Katie corners Micah and bludgeons him with his precious camera, while viewers watch from the camera's POV." See Missy Schwartz.
17. Barbara Creed, *The Monstrous-Feminine: Film, Feminism, Psychoanalysis* (London: Routledge, 1993), 3.
18. Leyda, Rombes, Shaviro and Grisham.
19. Muir.
20. Carol J. Clover, *Men, Women, and Chain Saws: Gender and the Modern Horror Film* (Princeton: Princeton University Press, 1992), 45.
21. Creed, 2.
22. Hahner, Varda and Wilson, 4.
23. Ibid., 6.
24. For further information, see Ewan Kirkland, "*Resident Evil*'s Typewriter: Horror Videogames and Their Media," *Games & Culture* 4.2 (April 2009): 115–26.

Chapter Seven

1. Nikolas Schreck, *The Satanic Screen: An Illustrated Guide to the Devil in Cinema, 1896–1999* (London: Creation, 2001)
2. See Mark Kermode, *The Exorcist* (London: BFI, 2003), 8; Kendall R. Phillips, *Projected Fears: Horror Films and American Culture* (Westport, CT: Praeger, 2005), 108.
3. Phillips, 109.
4. On top of its astonishing box office success, *The Exorcist* was nominated for 10 Academy Awards and won two for Best Sound and Best Adapted Screenplay in 1973. Blatty's book previously topped the bestseller list for 55 weeks straight. See: Stephen Vaughn, *Freedom and En-

tertainment: *Rating the Movies in an Age of New Media* (New York: Cambridge University Press, 2006), 97; Colleen McDannell, "Catholic Horror: *The Exorcist* (1973)," *Catholics in the Movies*, ed. Colleen McDannell (Oxford: Oxford University Press, 2008), 202.
 5. Les and Barbara Keyser, *Hollywood and the Catholic Church: The Image of Roman Catholicism in American Movies* (Chicago: Loyola University Press, 1984), 197.
 6. Bob McCabe, *The Exorcist: Out of The Shadows* (London: Omnibus Press, 1999), 20.
 7. McDannell, 201.
 8. Ibid., 202.
 9. Peter Brooks, *The Melodramatic Imagination: Balzac, Henry James and the Mode of Excess* (New Haven: Yale University Press, 1995), 4.
 10. Ibid., 16.
 11. Ibid.,17.
 12. Ibid., viii.
 13. Ibid., 20.
 14. Christine Gledhill, "Rethinking Genre," *Reinventing Film Studies*, eds. Christine Gledhill and Linda Williams (London: Arnold, 2000), 227.
 15. Ibid., 239.
 16. While not a found footage horror film, boots also play a role in *The Last Exorcism Part II* (Ed Gass-Donnelly, 2013).
 17. Roth Cornet, "*The Devil Inside* Director Defends the Movie's Ending," *Screen Rant* (2012) http://screenrant.com/the-devil-inside-ending-spoilers-discussion-rothc-147380/.
 18. Peter Travers, "*The Devil Inside*," *Rolling Stone* (January 13, 2012) http://www.rollingstone.com/movies/reviews/the-devil-inside-20120113.
 19. In an interview Bell said, "When we were shooting the film and researching and trying to interview people, we put feelers out to the Catholic Church to have discussions with them about the film. We sent them the script and things like that but they didn't really want to have anything to do with the movie and of course we relayed that to our studio and there you have it." See Tommy Cook, "Writer/Director William Brent Bell, Co-writer Matthew Peterman and Producer Morris Paulson Talk *The Devil Inside*," *Collider* (January 9, 2012) http://collider.com/the-devil-inside-william-brent-bell-matthew-peterman-morris-paulson-interview/.
 20. Ibid.
 21. Bell stated, "We knew that doing the film in a non–Hollywood, non-traditional way people would have a really harsh response to it. But it felt authentic to us" (Cornet). See also Cook; Evan Dickson, "*The Devil Inside* Filmmakers Speak on Low Budget Horror & Bold Finales!" *Bloody Disgusting* (January 6, 2012) http://bloody-disgusting.com/interviews/27810/interview-the-devil-inside-filmmakers-speak-on-low-budget-horror-bold-finales/.

 22. Isabel Cristina Pinedo, *Recreational Terror: Women and the Pleasures of Horror Film Viewing* (Albany: State University of New York Press, 1997), 29–34.
 23. Tania Modleski, "The Terror of Pleasure: The Contemporary Horror Film and Postmodern Theory," in *Studies in Entertainment: Critical Approaches to Mass Culture*, ed. Tania Modlesk (Bloomington: Indiana University Press, 1986), 155–66.
 24. W.H. Rockett, "The Door Ajar: Structure and Convention in Horror Films That Would Terrify," *Journal of Popular Film & Television* 10:3 (Fall 1982): 130–6.
 25. Mark Olsen, "*The Devil Inside* Review: Any Actual Horror Seemingly Exorcised," *Los Angeles Times* (January 7, 2012) http://articles.latimes.com/2012/jan/07/entertainment/la-et-devil-inside-20120107.
 26. Evan Dickson, "*The Devil Inside* Star Simon Quarterman Talks Exorcism Schools, Rewarding the Audience and Intelligent Horror Films!" *Bloody Disgusting* (December 26, 2011) http://bloody-disgusting.com/interviews/27684/interview-the-devil-inside-star-simon-quarterman-talks-exorcism-schools-rewarding-the-audience-and-intelligent-horror-films/.
 27. Jeffrey Sconce, *Haunted Media: Electronic Presence from Telegraphy to Television* (Durham: Duke University Press, 2000), 16.
 28. Cornet.

Chapter Eight

 1. Tony Williams, *Hearths of Darkness: The Family in the American Horror Film* (Cranbury, NJ: Associated University Presses, 1996).
 2. Vivian Sobchack, "Bringing It All Back Home: Family Economy and Generic Exchange," in *America Horrors: Essays on the Modern American Horror Film*, ed. Gregory Waller (Chicago: University of Illinois, 1987), 177.
 3. Ibid., 187.
 4. Ibid., 185.
 5. Gill Valentine, "Angels and Devils: Moral Landscapes of Childhood," *Environment and Planning D: Society and Space* 4 (1996): 581–99.
 6. William Wandless, "Spoil the Child: Unsettling Ethics and the Representation of Evil," *LIT: Literature Interpretation Theory* 22.2 (2011): 134–54.

Chapter Nine

 1. Adam Lowenstein, *Shocking Representation: Historical Trauma, National Cinema, and the Modern Horror Film* (New York: Columbia University Press, 2004), 8.
 2. Ibid., 15–6.
 3. Ibid., 2.
 4. Geoff King, "'Just Like a Movie?' 9/11 and

Hollywood Spectacle," in *The Spectacle of the Real: From Hollywood to "Reality" TV and Beyond*, ed. Geoff King (Bristol: Intellect, 2005), 47.

5. See Peter Turner, "*Zero Day* and *Cloverfield*: Shooting America's Scars," *Ol3Media* 84.09 (January 2011): 58–64; Brigid Cherry, *Horror* (London: Routledge, 2009), 192; David Ray Carter, "It's Only a Movie? Realty as Transgression in Exploitation Cinema," in *From the Arthouse to the Grindhouse: Highbrow and Lowbrow Transgression in Cinema's First Century*, eds. John Cline and Robert Weiner (Lanham, MD: Scarecrow Press, 2010), 314; Rebecca Winters Keegan, "*Cloverfield*: Godzilla Goes 9/11," *Time Magazine* (January 16, 2008) http://www.time.com/time/arts/article/0,8599,1704356,00.html; Annalee Newitz, "Nevermind the Monster—*Cloverfield* Is All About 9/11," *i09* (January 18, 2008) http://io9.com/346346/nevermind-the-monster-++-cloverfield-is-all-about-911.

6. Carter, 314.

7. Emanuelle Wessels, "'Where Were You When the Monster Hit?' Media Convergence, Branded Security Citizenship, and the Trans-Media Phenomenon of *Cloverfield*," *Convergence* 17 (2011): 77.

8. Daniel North, "Evidence of Things Not Quite Seen: *Cloverfield*'s Obstructred Spectacle," *Film & History* 40.1 (Spring 2010): 90.

9. Wessels, 74.

10. Felicity Collins and Therese Davis, *Australian Cinema After Mabo* (Cambridge: Cambridge University Press, 2004), 4.

11. The two leading parties in Australian politics are the Australian Labor Party and the Liberal Party of Australia. The capital "L" is worth emphasizing in these names: The Liberal Party is the traditionally more conservative party, while the Australian Labor Party's name stems from its roots in the labor/union movement.

12. Paul Keating, "Redfern Park Speech Transcript," *New South Wales Labor* (December 10, 1992) http://www.nswalp.com/redfern-speech.

13. Collins and Davis, 6.

14. Stuart Macintyre and Anna Clark, *The History Wars* (Melbourne: Melbourne University Press, 2004), 4.

15. Lower-case "l" liberal critic Richard Nile viewed Rudd's defeat of Howard as a step away from the discourse that had marked the past decade declaring, "the culture wars are over. The history wars are finished." But for conservative commentator Janet Albrechtsen, claims such as this were ignorant of the issues at stake: "To argue ... that the culture wars are over is fallacious. We are talking not about a war where one side declares victory, but about a continuing debate." See Richard Nile, "End of the Culture Wars," *The Australian* (November 28, 2007) http://blogs.theaustralian.news.com.au/richardnile/index.php/theaustralian/comments/end_of_the_culture_wars (Accessed October 1, 2008); Janet Albrechtsen, "Orwellian Left Quick to Unveil Totalitarian Heart," *The Australian* (December 12, 2007) http://www.theaustralian.news.com.au/story/0,25197,22908896-7583,00.html.

16. Robin Wood, "An Introduction to the American Horror Film," in *Movies and Methods Vol. 2*, ed. Bill Nichols (Berkeley: California University Press, 1985), 205.

17. Ibid., 199.

18. "AICN HORROR Talks About the Entire *[Rec]* Series with Co-Director Paco Plaza and Focuses on His New Film, *[Rec]³ Génesis!*" *Ain't It Cool News* (September 10, 2012) http://www.aintitcool.com/node/58240.

19. Roberto E. D'Onofrio, "Jaume Balagueró Talks *[Rec]4: Apocalypse*," *Fangoria* (November 15, 2011) http://www.fangoria.com/index.php?option=com_content&view=article&id=6058%3Ajaume-balaguero-talks-rec-4-apocalypse&catid=1%3Alatest-news&Itemid=167.

20. In Spain, "Roman Catholicism is the largest denomination of Christianity present in Spain by far. According to an October 2011 study by the Spanish Center of Sociological Research about 70.1 percent of Spaniards self-identify as Catholics, 2.7 percent other faith, and about 25 percent identify with no religion." See http://en.wikipedia.org/wiki/Religion_in_Spain. Additionally, "according to the American Religious Identification Survey (ARIS), which was cited by the U.S. Census Bureau in their 2012 Statistical Abstract, 76 percent identified themselves as Christians, with 25 percent identifying themselves as Catholics," see http://en.wikipedia.org/wiki/Religion_in_the_United_States.

21. Chris Eggertsen, "Interview: Andre Øvredal, Director of *TrollHunter!!*," *Bloody Disgusting* (May 6, 2011) http://bloody-disgusting.com/editorials/24457/interview-andre-ovredal-director-of-trollhunter/.

22. Damon Wise, "André Øvredal's *Troll Hunter* Makes a Mock-Doc Out of Norse Folklore," *The Guardian* (September 3, 2011) http://www.guardian.co.uk/film/2011/sep/03/andre-ovredal-troll-hunter.

23. Ethan Gilsdorf, "*Trollhunter* Director Pays Homage to Norwegian Folklore," *The Boston Globe* (June 26, 2011) http://www.boston.com/ae/movies/articles/2011/06/26/trollhunter_director_andr_ovredal_pays_homage_to_norwegian_folklore/.

24. Typified in J-horror by Sadaku in the *Ringu* series, the origins of the *onryō* have been identified as early as the 8th century. See http://en.wikipedia.org/wiki/Onryo%C5%8D.

25. Larissa Hjorth, "Cute@keitai.com," in *Japanese Cybercultures*, eds. Nanette Gottlieb and Mark McLelland (London: Routledge, 2003), 51.

Conclusion

1. Matt Barone, "Scare-A-Thon: The Stories Behind *V/H/S*, the Best, Most Unique Horror Anthology Movie in Years," *Complex Pop Culture* (October 5, 2012) http://www.complex.com/pop-culture/2012/10/vhs-horror-movie-anthology-interviews-backstory/tape-56.
2. They are not, however, home movies but rather tapes stolen from a video library.
3. Hannah Fierman, email to author, April 10, 2013.
4. See Scott Meslow, "12 Years After *Blair Witch*, When Will the Found-Footage Horror Fad End?" *The Atlantic* (January 6, 2012) http://www.theatlantic.com/entertainment/archive/2012/01/12-years-after-blair-witch-when-will-the-found-footage-horror-fad-end/250950/.
5. Alexandra Juhasz, "Documentary on YouTube: The Failure of the Direct Cinema of the Slogan," in *Rethinking Documentary: New Perspectives, New Practices* eds. Thomas Austin and Wilma de Jong (Maidenhead, England: McGraw Hill/Open University Press, 2008), 300.
6. See http://forums.somethingawful.com/showthread.php?threadid=3150591&userid=129681#post362207600.
7. See http://marblehornets.wikidot.com/theark
8. Dave McNary, "*Marble Hornets* Flying to Bigscreen," *Variety* (February 25, 2013) http://www.variety.com/article/VR1118066545/.
9. Joey Nolfi, "*Marble Hornets* Creators Talk Terrifying Audiences, Future of Digital Media," *Pop Smut* (August 25, 2011) http://popsmut.wordpress.com/2011/08/25/marble-hornets-creators-talk-terrifying-audiences-future-of-digital-media/.
10. Frank Scheck, "Apollo 18," *Film Journal International*, 114.10 (October 2011): 58.
11. Eric Kohn, "Sundance Curiosities: 5 More Observations on the 2013 Lineup, from Found Footage Horror to Transmedia," *Indiewire* (November 20, 2012) http://www.indiewire.com/article/sundance-curiosities-5-more-observations-on-the-2013-lineup-from-found-footage-horror-to-transmedia; Brian Salisbury, "Found Footage of 2012: Filmmakers Discuss the Genre's Highs and Lows," Hollywoodwww, (December 21, 2012) http://www.hollywood.com/news/movies/46603332/found-footage-of-2012-filmmakers-discuss-the-genre-s-highs-and-lows?page=all.
12. Earlier non-horror found footage films include but are not limited to war films such as *Septem8er Tapes* (2004), *Redacted* (Brian De Palma, 2007), *84C MoPic* (Patrick Sheane Duncan, 1989); crime films such as *Gang Tapes* (Adam Ripp, 2001), *Razor Eaters* (Shannon Young, 2003); and of course the blockbuster science fiction hit *District 9* (Neill Blomkamp, 2009).

Bibliography

Aaron, Michele. "Looking On: Troubling Spectacles and the Complicitous Spectator," in *The Spectacle of the Real: From Hollywood to "Reality" TV and Beyond*, ed. Geoff King. Bristol: Intellect, 2005. 213–22.
"AICN HORROR Talks About the Entire *[Rec]* Series with Co-Director Paco Plaza and Focuses on His New Film, *[Rec]³ Génesis*!" *Ain't It Cool News* (September 10, 2012) http://www.aintitcool.com/node/58240.
Albrechtsen, Janet. "Orwellian Left Quick to Unveil Totalitarian Heart." *The Australian* (December 12, 2007) http://www.theaustralian.news.com.au/story/0,25197,22908896-7583,00.html.
Alexander, Bruce. "*The Blair Witch Project*: Expulsion form Adulthood and Versions of the American Gothic," in *Nothing That Is: Millennial Cinema and the Blair Witch Controversies*, eds. Sarah L. Higley and Jeffrey Andrew Weinstock. Detroit: Wayne State University Press, 2004. 145–61.
Aloi, Peg. "Beyond the *Blair Witch*: A New Horror Aesthetic?" in *The Spectacle of the Real: From Hollywood to "Reality" TV and Beyond*, ed. Geoff King. Bristol: Intellect, 2005. 187–200.
Angier, Bradford. *How to Stay Alive in the Woods*. New York: Black Dog & Leventhal, 2001.
Badley, Linda. *Film, Horror, and the Body Fantastic*. Westport, CT: Greenwood Press, 1995.
_____. "Spiritual Warfare: Postfeminism and the Cultural Politics of the *Blair Witch* Craze." *Intensities: The Journal of Cult Media* (Spring 2003) http://intensities.org/Essays/Badley.pdf.
Baker, Martin. "Introduction," in *The Video Nasties: Freedom and Censorship in the Media*, ed. Martin Baker. London: Pluto, 1984. 1–6.
Banash, David. "*The Blair Witch Project*: Technology, Repression, and the Evisceration of Mimesis," in *Nothing That Is: Millennial Cinema and the Blair Witch Controversies*, eds. Sarah L. Higley and Jeffrey Andrew Weinstock. Detroit: Wayne State University Press, 2004. 111–24.
Barber, Lynden. "Method in Their Fearful Madness." *The Australian* (December 10, 1999): 10.
Baudrillard, Jean. *Simulacra and Simulation*. Ann Arbor: University of Michigan Press, 1994.
Beattie, Keith. *Documentary Screens: Non-Fiction Film and Television*. Houndmills: Palgrave Macmillan, 2004.
Berenstein, Rhona J. *Attack of the Leading Ladies: Gender, Sexuality, and Spectatorship in Classic Horror Cinema*. New York: Columbia University Press, 1996.
Berg, Chuck, and Tom Erskine. *The Encyclopedia of Orson Welles*. New York: Facts on File, 2003.
Black, Joel. "Real(ist) Horror: From Execution Videos to Snuff Films," in *Underground USA: Filmmaking Beyond the Hollywood Canon*, eds. Xavier Mendik and Steven Jay Schneider. London: Wallflower Press, 2002. 63–75.
_____. *The Reality Effect: Film, Culture and the Graphic Imperative*. New York: Routledge, 2002.

Bolter, Jay David, and Richard Grusin. *Remediation: Understanding New Media*. Cambridge: MIT Press, 2000.
Booth, Wayne C. *The Rhetoric of Fiction*. Chicago: University of Chicago Press, 1995.
Bordwell, David. "Return to Paranormalcy." *David Bordwell's Website on Cinema* (November 13, 2012) http://www.davidbordwell.net/blog/2012/11/13/return-to-paranormalcy/.
Brew, Simon, "Kevin Greutert Posts Statement on *Saw 7/Paranormal Activity 2* Situation." *Den of Geek* (January 27, 2010) http://www.denofgeek.com/movies/saw/15306/kevin-greutert-posts-statement-on-saw-7-paranormal-activity-2-situation.
Briefel, Aviva, and Sam J. Miller. "Introduction," in *Horror After 9/11: World of Fear, Cinema of Terror*, eds. Aviva Briefel and Sam J. Miller. Austin: University of Texas Press, 2011. 1–12.
Brooks, Peter. *The Melodramatic Imagination: Balzac, Henry James and the Mode of Excess*. New Haven: Yale University Press, 1995.
Brottman, Mikita. *Meat Is Murder: An Illustrated Guide to Cannibal Culture*. London: Creation, 1998.
_____. *Offensive Films: Towards an Anthropology of Cinema Vomitif*. Westport, CT: Greenwood Press, 1997.
_____. "Signal 30," in *Car Crash Culture*, ed. Mikita Brottman. New York: Palgrave, 2001. 233–243.
Buckingham, David, Maria Pini, and Rebekah Willett, "'Take Back the Tube!' The Discursive Construction of Amateur Film and Video Making." *Journal of Media Practice*, 8.2 (2007): 183–201.
Butler, John P. *The Best Suit in Town: A Generation of Cops*. Charlotte Harbor, FL: Royal Palm Press, 2001.
Cameron, Deborah. "Discourses of Desire: Liberals, Feminists, and the Politics of Pornography in the 1980s." *American Literary History* 2:4 (Winter 1990): 784–798.
Cantril, Hadley. *The Invasion from Mars: A Study in the Psychology of Panic*. Princeton: Princeton University Press, 1940.
Caputi, Jane. *The Age of Sex Crime*. London: Women's Press, 1987.
Carol, Avedon. "Snuff: Believing the Worst," in *Bad Girls and Dirty Pictures: The Challenge to Reclaim Feminism*, eds. Alison Assiter and Avedon Carol. London: Pluto Press, 1993. 126–30.
Carroll, Noel. *The Philosophy of Horror: Paradoxes of the Heart*. New York: Routledge, 1990.
Carter, David Ray. "It's Only a Movie? Reality as Transgression in Exploitation Cinema," in *From the Arthouse to the Grindhouse: Highbrow and Lowbrow Transgression in Cinema's First Century*, eds. John Cline and Robert Weiner. Lanham, MD: Scarecrow Press, 2010. 297–315.
Castonguay, James. "The Political Economy of the Indie Blockbuster: Fandom, Intermediality and *The Blair Witch Project*," in *Nothing That Is: Millennial Cinema and the Blair Witch Controversies*, eds. Sarah L. Higley and Jeffrey Andrew Weinstock. Detroit: Wayne State University Press, 2004. 65–85.
Chapman, Jane. *Issues in Contemporary Documentary*. Malden, MA: Polity Press, 2009.
Cherry, Brigid. *Horror*. London: Routledge, 2009.
"Classification Office Decision: *Megan Is Missing*." New Zealand Office of Literature and Film Classification (October 12, 2011) http://www.censorship.govt.nz/DDA/Pages/Screens/DDA/PublicationDecisionInformationPage.aspx.
Clover, Carol J. *Men, Women, and Chain Saws: Gender and the Modern Horror Film*. Princeton: Princeton University Press, 1992.
Collins, Felicity, and Therese Davis. *Australian Cinema After Mabo*. Cambridge: Cambridge University Press, 2004.
Cook, Tommy. "Writer/Director William Brent Bell, Co-writer Matthew Peterman and Producer Morris Paulson Talk *The Devil Inside*." *Collider* (January 9, 2012) http://collider.com/the-devil-inside-william-brent-bell-matthew-peterman-morris-paulson-interview/.
Cornet, Roth. "*The Devil Inside* Director Defends the Movie's Ending." *Screen Rant* (2012) http://screenrant.com/the-devil-inside-ending-spoilers-discussion-rothc-147380/.

Creed, Barbara. *The Monstrous-Feminine: Film, Feminism, Psychoanalysis*. London: Routledge, 1993.
Curtis, Adam. "The Ghosts in the Living Room." *BBC Blogs* (December 22, 2011) http://www.bbc.co.uk/blogs/adamcurtis/posts/the_ghosts_in_the_living_room.
Dickson, Evan. "*The Devil Inside* Filmmakers Speak on Low Budget Horror & Bold Finales!" *Bloody Disgusting* (January 6, 2012) http://bloody-disgusting.com/interviews/27810/interview-the-devil-inside-filmmakers-speak-on-low-budget-horror-bold-finales/.
_____. "*The Devil Inside* Star Simon Quarterman Talks Exorcism Schools, Rewarding the Audience and Intelligent Horror Films!" *Bloody Disgusting* (December 26, 2011) http://bloody-disgusting.com/interviews/27684/interview-the-devil-inside-star-simon-quarterman-talks-exorcism-schools-rewarding-the-audience-and-intelligent-horror-films/.
Donahue, Heather. *Growgirl: How My Life After the Blair Witch Project Went to Pot*. New York: Gotham, 2012.
D'Onofrio, Roberto E. "Jaume Balagueró Talks *[Rec]⁴: Apocalypse*." *Fangoria* (November 15, 2011) http://www.fangoria.com/index.php?option=com_content&view=article&id=6058%3Ajaume-balaguero-talks-rec-4-apocalypse&catid=1%3Alatest-news&Itemid=167.
Edelstein, David. "Now Playing at Your Local Multiplex: Torture Porn." *New York Magazine* (January 28, 2006) http://nymag.com/movies/features/15622/.
"Entretien avec Jean-Teddy Filippe." *Cinetrange* (November 30, 2009) http://www.cinetrange.com/support/sortie-dvd/jean-teddy-filippe/.
Evans, Elizabeth. "*Ghostwatch* & Interview with Stephen Volk." *Scope: An Online Journal of Film and Television Studies* 22 (February 2012) http://www.scope.nottingham.ac.uk/February_2012/ftv_reviews.pdf.
Fenton, Harvey. "*Cannibal Holocaust*," in *Cannibal Holocaust and the Savage Cinema of Ruggero Deodato*, by Harvey Fenton, Julian Granger and Gian Luca Castoldi. Guildford, England: FAB Press, 1999. 62–78.
_____, Julian Granger and Gian Luca Castoldi. *Cannibal Holocaust and the Savage Cinema of Ruggero Deodato*. Guildford, England: FAB Press, 1999.
Fisher, Bob. "Michael Goi, ASC." *OnFilm (Kodak Cinema and Television)* http://www.motion.kodak.com/motion/Publications/On_Film_Interviews/goi.htm.
Ford, Todd. "*Paranormal*'s Domestic Activities." Cinema 100 Film Society (October 27, 2009) http://www.cinema100.com/2009/10/paranormals-domestic-activities.html.
Freeland, Cynthia A. "Realist Horror," in *Philosophy and Film*, eds. Cynthia A. Freeland and Thomas E. Wartenberg. New York: Routledge, 1995. 126–142.
Garber, Marjorie. *Academic Instincts*. Princeton: Princeton University Press, 2000.
Gledhill, Christine. "Rethinking Genre," in *Reinventing Film Studies*, eds. Christine Gledhill and Linda Williams. London: Arnold, 2000.
Goodall, Mark. *Sweet and Savage: The World Through the Shockumentary Film Lens*. London: Headpress, 2006.
Grant, Barry Keith, ed. *The Dread of Difference: Gender and the Horror Film*. Austin: University of Texas Press, 1996.
Grossman, Lev. "You—Yes You—Are TIME's Person of the Year," *Time Magazine* (December 25, 2006) http://www.time.com/time/magazine/article/0,9171,1570810,00.html#ixzz2OKrF1cy7.
Hahner, Leslie A., Scott J. Varda, and Nathan A. Wilson. "*Paranormal Activity* and the Horror of Abject Consumption." *Critical Studies in Media Communication* (2012): 1–15.
Hallam, Julian, and Margaret Marshment. *Realism and Popular Cinema*. Manchester: Manchester University Press, 2000.
Harris, Martin. "The 'Witchcraft' of Media Manipulation: *Pamela* and *The Blair Witch Project*." *The Journal of Popular Culture* 34.4 (Spring 2001): 75–107.
Hattenstone, Simon. "Saturday Interview: Michael Parkinson." *The Guardian* (February 24, 2012) http://www.guardian.co.uk/theguardian/2012/feb/24/michael-parkinson-saturday-interview.

Hawkins, Joan. *Cutting Edge: Art-Horror and the Horrific Avant-Garde*. Minneapolis: University of Minnesota Press, 2000.
Hell's Highway: The True Story of Highway Safety Films (Bret Wood, 2003). Press book. Kino International www.kino.com/press/hells_pr/hells_highway_pb.pdf.
Hight, Craig. "Mockumentary: A Call to Play," in *Rethinking Documentary: New Perspectives, New Practices*, eds. Thomas Austin and Wilma de Jong. Maidenhead, England: McGraw Hill/Open University Press, 2008. 204–216.
_____. *Television Mockumentary: Reflexivity, Satire and a Call to Play*. Manchester: Manchester University Press, 2010.
Higley, Sarah L. "'People Just Want to See Something': Art, Death and Document in *The Blair Witch Project, The Last Broadcast* and *Paradise Lost*," in *Nothing That Is: Millennial Cinema and the Blair Witch Controversies*, eds. Sarah L. Higley and Jeffrey Andrew Weinstock. Detroit: Wayne State University Press, 2004. 87–110.
_____, and Jeffrey Andrew Weinstock. "Introduction: The Blair Witch Controversies," in *Nothing That Is: Millennial Cinema and the Blair Witch Controversies*, eds. Sarah L. Higley and Jeffrey Andrew Weinstock. Detroit: Wayne State University Press, 2004. 11–35.
Hilderbrand, Lucas. *Inherent Vice: Bootleg Histories of Videotape and Copyright*. Durham: Duke University Press, 2009.
Hills, Matt. "Cutting into Concepts of 'Reflectionist' Cinema? The *Saw* Franchise and Puzzles of Post-9/11 Horror," in *Horror After 9/11: World of Fear, Cinema of Terror*, eds. Aviva Briefel and Sam J. Miller. Austin: University of Texas Press, 2011. 107–123.
Hjorth, Larissa. "Cute@keitai.com," in *Japanese Cybercultures*, eds. Nanette Gottlieb and Mark McLelland. London: Routledge, 2003. 50–9.
"How to Talk to Anyone in the World." *The Sun-Herald* (June 2, 2003) http://www.smh.com.au/articles/2003/06/01/1054406070303.html.
Huet, Marie-Hélène. "The Face of Disaster." *Yale French Studies* 111 (2007): 7–31.
Hunter, Dan, Ramon Lobato, Megan Richardson, and Julian Thomas, eds. *Amateur Media: Social, Cultural and Legal Perspectives*. Abingdon, Oxon: Routledge, 2013.
Hunter, Jack. *Eros in Hell: Sex, Blood and Madness in Japanese Cinema*. London: Creation, 1998.
"Interview: Amanda Gusack, Writer/Director 'In Memorium.'" *The Bloodsprayer*, (October 27, 2010) http://www.bloodsprayer.com/interview-amanda-gusack-writerdirector-in-memorium/.
Jackson, Neil. "*Cannibal Holocaust*, Realist Horror, and Reflexivity." *Post Script* 21:3 (Summer 2002): 32–45.
_____. "The Cultural Construction of Snuff: Alejandro Amenábar's *Tesis* (Thesis, 1996)." *Kinoeye* 3:5 (2003) http://www.kinoeye.org/03/05/jackson05.php.
Jauregui, Carolina G. "'Eat It Alive and Swallow It Whole!' Resavoring *Cannibal Holocaust* as a Mockumentary." *Invisible Culture* 7 (2004) http://www.rochester.edu/in_visible_culture/Issue_7/Issue_7_Jauregui.pdf.
Jenkins, Henry. "How YouTube Became OurTube." *Confessions of an Aca-Fan: The official Weblog of Henry Jenkins,* October 18, 2010 http://henryjenkins.org/2010/10/how_youtube_became_ourtube.html.
Johnson, Eithne, and Eric Schaefer. "Soft Core/Hard Gore: *Snuff* as a Crisis in Meaning." *Journal of Film and Video* 42.2–3 (1993): 40–59.
Juhasz, Alexandra. "Documentary on YouTube: The Failure of the Direct Cinema of the Slogan," in *Rethinking Documentary: New Perspectives, New Practices* eds. Thomas Austin and Wilma de Jong. Maidenhead, England: McGraw Hill/Open University Press, 2008. 299–312.
_____. "Phony Definitions," in "Introduction: Phony Definitions and Troubling Taxonomies of the Fake Documentary," in *F Is for Phony: Fake Documentary and Truth's Undoing*, eds. Alexandra Juhasz and Jesse Lerner. Minneapolis: University of Minnesota Press, 2006. 1–35.
Keegan, Rebecca Winters. "*Cloverfield*: Godzilla Goes 9/11." *Time Magazine* (January 16, 2008) http://www.time.com/time/arts/article/0,8599,1704356,00.html.

Keller, James. "'Nothing That Is Not There and the Nothing That Is': Language and the *Blair Witch* Phenomenon," in *Nothing That Is: Millennial Cinema and the Blair Witch Controversies*, eds. Sarah L. Higley and Jeffrey Andrew Weinstock. Detroit: Wayne State University Press, 2004. 53–63.
Kerekes, David. "The Small World of Snuff Fetish Custom Video," in *From the Arthouse to the Grindhouse: Highbrow and Lowbrow Transgression in Cinema's First Century*, eds. John Cline and Robert Weiner. Lanham, MD: Scarecrow Press, 2010. 264–73.
____, and David Slater. *Killing for Culture: A History of Death Films from Mondo to Snuff*. London: Creation, 1995.
Kermode, Mark. *The Exorcist*. London: BFI, 2003.
Keyser, Les, and Barbara Keyser. *Hollywood and the Catholic Church: The Image of Roman Catholicism in American Movies*. Chicago: Loyola University Press, 1984.
King, Geoff. "'Just Like a Movie?' 9/11 and Hollywood Spectacle," in *The Spectacle of the Real: From Hollywood to "Reality" TV and Beyond*, ed. Geoff King. Bristol: Intellect, 2005. 47–57.
Kirkland, Ewan. "*Resident Evil*'s Typewriter: Horror Videogames and Their Media." *Games & Culture* 4:2 (April 2009): 115–26.
Kohn, Eric. "Sundance Curiosities: 5 More Observations on the 2013 Lineup, from Found Footage Horror to Transmedia." *Indiewire*, November 20, 2012 http://www.indiewire.com/article/sundance-curiosities-5-more-observations-on-the-2013-lineup-from-found-footage-horror-to-transmedia.
Kryzwinska, Tanya. *A Skin for Dancing In: Possession, Witchcraft and Voodoo in Film*. Trowbridge, England: Flicks, 2000.
LaBelle, Beverly. "*Snuff*—The Ultimate in Woman-Hating," in *Take Back the Night: Women on Pornography*, ed. Laura Lederer. New York: William Morrow, 1980. 272–78.
Lafond, Frank, "*C'est Arrivé Près de Chez Vous, Man Bites Dog*," in *The Cinema of the Low Countries*, ed. Ernest. Mathijs. London: Wallflower Press, 2004.
Lane, Christina. "Just Another Girl Outside the Neo-Indie," in *Contemporary American Independent Film: From the Margins to the Mainstream*, eds. Chris Holmlund and Justin Wyatt. London: Routledge, 2005. 193–210.
Leadbeater, Charles and Paul Miller. *The Pro-Am Revolution*. London: Demos, 2004.
Lebow, Alisa. "Faking What? Making a Mockery of Documentary," in *F Is for Phony: Fake Documentary and Truth's Undoing*, eds. Alexandra Juhasz and Jesse Lerner. Minneapolis: University of Minnesota Press, 2006. 223–237.
Lefait, Sébastien. *Surveillance on Screen: Monitoring Contemporary Films and Television Programs*. Lanham, MD: Scarecrow Press, 2013.
Leyda, Julia, Nicholas Rombes, Steven Shaviro, and Therese Grisham. "Roundtable Discussion: The Post-Cinematic in *Paranormal Activity* and *Paranormal Activity 2*." *La Furia Umana* 10 (Autumn 2011) http://www.lafuriaumana.it/index.php/locchio-che-uccide/385-roundtable-discussion-about-post-cinematic.
Lobato, Ramon. *Shadow Economies of Cinema: Mapping Informal Film Distribution*. London: British Film Institute, 2012.
Long, Derek. "The Highway Shock Film: History, Phenomenology, Ideology." *The Projector Film and Media Journal* (2012) http://www.bgsu.edu/departments/theatrefilm/projector/04-01-12/page123443.html.
Lowenstein, Adam. *Shocking Representation: Historical Trauma, National Cinema, and the Modern Horror Film*. New York: Columbia University Press, 2004.
____. "Spectacle Horror and Hostel: Why 'Torture Porn' Does Not Exist." *Critical Quarterly* 53.2 (2011): 42–60.
Luckhurst, Roger. "Found-Footage Science Fiction: Five Films by Craig Baldwin, Jonathan Weiss, Werner Herzog and Patrick Keiller." *Science Fiction Film & Television* 1.2 (2008): 193–214.
Lyon, David. *The Electronic Eye: The Rise of Surveillance Society*. Minneapolis: University of Minnesota Press, 1994.

_____. *Surveillance Studies: An Overview.* Cambridge, MA: Polity Press, 2007.
Macintyre, Stuart, and Anna Clark. *The History Wars.* Melbourne: Melbourne University Press, 2004.
MacKinnon, Catherine. *Only Words.* Cambridge: Harvard University Press, 1993.
Mallin, Eric S. "*The Blair Witch Project, Macbeth*, and the Indeterminate End," in *The End of Cinema as We Know It: American Film in the Nineties*, ed. Jon Lewis. New York: New York University Press, 2001. 105–14.
Marks, Laura U. *Touch: Sensuous Theory and Multisensory Media.* Minneapolis: University of Minnesota Press, 2002.
Martin, Adrian. "Pity It's Phooey." *The Age* (December 2, 1999), B3-B4.
Mathijs, Ernest. "*Man Bites Dog* and the Critical Reception of Belgian Horror Cinema," in *Horror International*, eds. Steven Jay Schneider and Tony Williams. Detroit: Wayne State University Press, 2005. 315–35.
McCabe, Bob. *The Exorcist: Out of the Shadows.* London: Omnibus Press, 1999.
McDannell, Colleen, ed. *Catholics in the Movies*, ed. Colleen McDannell. Oxford: Oxford University Press, 2008.
McDowell, Scott Dixon. "Method Filmmaking: An Interview with Daniel Myrick, Co-director of *The Blair Witch Project*." *Journal of Film and Video* 53.2:3 (Summer/Fall 2001): 140–47.
McKee, Alan. "The Aesthetics of Pornography: The Insights of Consumers." *Continuum: Journal of Media and Cultural Studies*, 20.4 (December 2006): 523–39.
McKenzie, Keira. "Double the Passive: The Trials of Viewer/Subject in *Cloverfield* and *The Blair Witch Project*." *Ol3Media*, 84.09 (January 2011): 37–43.
McNary, Dave. "*Marble Hornets* Flying to Bigscreen." *Variety* (February 25, 2013) http://www.variety.com/article/VR1118066545/.
McRoy, Jay. *Nightmare Japan: Contemporary Japanese Horror Cinema.* Amsterdam: Rodopi, 2008.
Meslow, Scott. "12 Years After 'Blair Witch,' When Will the Found-Footage Horror Fad End?" *The Atlantic* (January 6, 2012) http://www.theatlantic.com/entertainment/archive/2012/01/12-years-after-blair-witch-when-will-the-found-footage-horror-fad-end/250950/.
Metz, Christian. *Psychoanalysis and Cinema: The Imaginary Signifier.* London: Macmillan, 1982.
Miller, Cynthia. "Introduction: At Play in the Fields of the Truth." *Post Script*, 28.3 (Summer 2009): 3–8.
Modleski, Tania. "The Terror of Pleasure: The Contemporary Horror Film and Postmodern Theory," in *Studies in Entertainment: Critical Approaches to Mass Culture*, ed. Tania Modleski. Bloomington: Indiana University Press, 1986. 155–166.
Muir, John Kenneth. "Cult Movie Review: *Apollo 18* (2011)." *John Kenneth Muir's Reflections on Film/TV* (January 24, 2012) http://reflectionsonfilmandtelevision.blogspot.com.au/2012/01/cult-movie-review-apollo-18-2011.html.
_____. "Cult Movie Review: *Paranormal Activity* (2009)." *John Kenneth Muir's Reflections on Film/TV* (January 4, 2010) http://reflectionsonfilmandtelevision.blogspot.com.au/2010/01/cult-movie-review-paranormal-activity.html.
_____. *Horror Films of the 1990s.* Jefferson, NC: McFarland, 2011.
Mulvey, Laura. *Death 24x a Second: Stillness and the Moving Image.* London: Reaktion, 2005.
_____. "Visual Pleasure and Narrative Cinema." *Screen* 16.3 (Autumn 1975): 6–18.
Muntean, Nick. "There Is Nothing More Objectionable Than Objectivity: The Films of Peter Watkins," in *From the Arthouse to the Grindhouse: Highbrow and Lowbrow Transgression in Cinema's First Century*, eds. John Cline and Robert Weiner. Lanham, MD: Scarecrow Press, 2010. 274–96.
Ndalianis, Angela. *The Horror Sensorium: Media and the Senses.* Jefferson, NC: McFarland, 2012.
Neale, Steve. *Genre and Hollywood.* New York: Routledge, 2000.
Newitz, Annalee. "Nevermind the Monster—*Cloverfield* Is All About 9/11." *i09* (January 18, 2008) http://io9.com/346346/nevermind-the-monster-++-cloverfield-is-all-about-911.

Nichols, Bill. *Introduction to Documentary*. Bloomington: Indiana University Press, 2001.
Nile, Richard. "End of the Culture Wars." *The Australian* (November 28, 2007) http://blogs.theaustralian.news.com.au/richardnile/index.php/theaustralian/comments/end_of_the_culture_wars.
Nolfi, Joey. "*Marble Hornets* Creators Talk Terrifying Audiences, Future of Digital Media." *Pop Smut* (August 25, 2011) http://popsmut.wordpress.com/2011/08/25/marble-hornets-creators-talk-terrifying-audiences-future-of-digital-media/.
North, Daniel. "Evidence of Things Not Quite Seen: *Cloverfield*'s Obstructred Spectacle." *Film & History* 40.1 (Spring 2010): 75–92.
Olsen, Mark. "*The Devil Inside* Review: Any Actual Horror Seemingly Exorcised." *LA Times* (January 7, 2012) http://articles.latimes.com/2012/jan/07/entertainment/la-et-devil-inside-20120107.
Paglia, Camille. *Vamps and Tramps: New Essays*. New York: Vintage, 1994.
"Paranormal-ier Activity." *Ghostwatch: Behind the Curtains* (June 30, 2010) http://www.ghostwatchbtc.com/2010/06/paranormal-ier-activity.html.
Penenberg, Adam L. "The Surveillance Society." *Wired*, 9.12 (December 2001) http://www.wired.com/wired/archive/9.12/surveillance.html.
Petherbridge, Deanna, and Ludmilla Jordanova. *The Quick and the Dead: Artists and Anatomy*. London: South Bank Centre, 1997.
Petley, Julian. "*Cannibal Holocaust* and the Pornography of Death," in *The Spectacle of the Real: From Hollywood to "Reality" TV and Beyond*, ed. Geoff King. Bristol: Intellect, 2005. 173–85.
Phillips, Kendall R. *Projected Fears: Horror Films and American Culture*. Westport, CT: Praeger, 2005.
Pinedo, Isabel Cristina. *Recreational Terror: Women and the Pleasures of Horror Film Viewing*. Albany: State University of New York Press, 1997.
Prince, Stephen. *Firestorm: American Film in the Age of Terrorism*. New York: Columbia University Press, 2009.
Rapold, Nicolas. "*Paranormal Activity*." *Sight & Sound* 20.1 (January 2010): 72.
Rhodes, Gary. "Mockumentaries and the Production of Realist Horror." *Post Script* 21.3 (Summer 2002): 20–31 (via Gale Cengage Learning).
Rippy, Marguerite H. *Orson Welles and the Unfinished RKO Projects: A Postmodern Perspective*. Carbondale: Southern Illinois University Press, 2009.
Robbins, Christopher. "Crossing Conventions in Web-Based Art: Deconstruction as a Narrative Device." *Leonardo* 40.2 (2007): 161–6.
Rockett, W.H. "The Door Ajar: Structure and Convention in Horror Films That Would Terrify." *Journal of Popular Film & Television* 10:3 (Fall 1982): 130–6.
Rockoff, Adam. *Going to Pieces: The Rise and Fall of the Slasher Film, 1978–1986*. Jefferson, NC: McFarland, 2002.
Roscoe, Jane. "*The Blair Witch Project*: Mock-documentary goes mainstream." *Jump Cut* 43 (July 2000): 3–8. http://www.ejumpcut.org/archive/onlinessays/JC43folder/BlairWitch.html.
_____. "*Man Bites Dog*: Deconstructing the Documentary Look." *Metro Magazine*, 112 (1997): 21–25.
_____, and Craig Hight. *Faking It: Mock-Documentary and the Subversion of Factuality*. Manchester: Manchester University Press, 2001.
Rubin, Martin. "The Grayness of Darkness: *The Honeymoon Killers* and Its Impact on Psychokiller Cinema," in *Mythologies of Violence in Postmodern Media*, ed. Christopher Sharrett. Detroit: Wayne State University Press, 1999. 41–64.
Salisbury, Brian. "Found Footage of 2012: Filmmakers Discuss the Genre's Highs and Lows." Hollywoodwww (December 21, 2012) http://www.hollywood.com/news/movies/46603332/found-footage-of-2012-filmmakers-discuss-the-genre-s-highs-and-lows?page=all.
Sanders, Ed. *The Family: The Story of Charles Manson's Dune Buggy Attack Battalion*. New York: Dutton, 1971.

Scheck, Frank. "*Apollo 18.*" *Film Journal International*, 114.10 (October 2011): 58.
Schneider, Steven Jay, ed. "Introduction, PT. I: Dimensions of the Real," *Post Script*, 21.3 (Summer 2002): 3–8.
_____. *Fear Without Frontiers: Horror Cinema Across the Globe*. Godalming, England: FAB Press, 2003.
Schreck, Nikolas. *The Satanic Screen: An Illustrated Guide to the Devil in Cinema, 1896–1999*. London: Creation, 2001.
Schreier, Margrit. "'Please Help Me; All I Want to Know Is: Is It Real or Not?': How Recipients View the Reality Status of *The Blair Witch Project*." *Poetics Today* 25.2 (Summer 2004): 306–34.
Schrodt, Paul. "*Paranormal Activity 4:* The Instant Trailer Review." *Esquire* (August 1, 2012) http://www.esquire.com/the-side/movie-trailers/paranormal-activity-4-11248478.
Schwartz, Missy. "A Shocking Hit." *Entertainment Weekly* 1074 (November 6, 2009): 20–3.
Sconce, Jeffrey. *Haunted Media: Electronic Presence from Telegraphy to Television*. Durham: Duke University Press, 2000.
Short, Sue. *Misfit Sisters: Screen Horror as Female Rites of Passage*. Basingstoke: Palgrave Macmillan, 2006.
Simpson, Paul. *That's What They Want You to Think: Conspiracies Real, Possible and Paranoid*. Minneapolis: Zenith, 2012.
Simpson, Philip L. "Whither the Serial Killer Movie?" in *American Horror Film: The Genre at the Turn of the Millennium*, ed. Steffen Hantke. Jackson: University of Mississippi Press, 2010. 119–41.
Slater, Jay, ed. *EATEN ALIVE! Italian Cannibal and Zombie Movies*. London: Plexus, 2002.
Smith, Ken. *Mental Hygiene: Classroom Films 1945–1970*. New York: Blast, 1999.
Smith, Sean. "Curse of the Blair Witch." *Newsweek*, 143.4 (January 26, 2004): 56–58.
Sobchack, Vivian. "Bringing It All Back Home: Family Economy and Generic Exchange," in *America Horrors: Essays on the Modern American Horror Film*, ed. Gregory Waller. Chicago: University of Illinois, 1987. 175–94.
Sontag, Susan. *On Photography*. New York: Picador, 1977.
Stine, Scott Aaron. "The Snuff Film: The Making of an Urban Legend." *Skeptical Inquirer*, 23.3 (1999): 29–34.
Telotte, J.P. "*The Blair Witch Project*: Film and the Internet." *Film Quarterly* 54:3 (Spring 2001): 32–39. Republished in *Nothing That Is: Millennial Cinema and the Blair Witch Controversies*, eds. Sarah L. Higley and Jeffrey Andrew Weinstock. Detroit: Wayne State University Press, 2004. 37–51.
Tombs, Pete. *Mondo Macabro: Weird and Wonderful Cinema Around the World*. New York: St. Martins Press, 1998.
Travers, Peter. "The Devil Inside." *Rolling Stone* (January 13, 2012) http://www.rollingstone.com/movies/reviews/the-devil-inside-20120113.
Tryon, Chuck. "Video from the Void: Video Spectatorship, Domestic Film Cultures, and Contemporary Horror Film." *Journal of Film and Video* 61.3 (Fall 2009): 40–51.
Tupas, Jeffrey M., and Jeoffrey Maitem. "Bootleg DVDs of Maguindano Massacre on Sale," *Inquirer Mindanao* (December 28, 2009) http://newsinfo.inquirer.net/inquirerheadlines/metro/view/20091228-244373/Bootleg-DVDs-of-Maguindanao-massacre-on-sale.
Turner, Peter. "*Zero Day* and *Cloverfield*: Shooting America's Scars." *Ol3Media* 84:09 (January 2011): 58–64.
Valentine, Gill. "Angels and Devils: Moral Landscapes of Childhood." *Environment and Planning D: Society and Space* 4 (1996): 581–99.
Vaughn, Stephen. *Freedom and Entertainment: Rating the Movies in an Age of New Media*. New York: Cambridge University Press, 2006.
Walker, Johnny. "Nasty Visions: Violent Spectacle in Contemporary British Horror Cinema." *Horror Studies* 2.1 (2011): 115–130.
Walker, Joseph S. "Mom and the Blair Witch: Narrative, Form and the Feminine," in *Nothing*

That Is: Millennial Cinema and the Blair Witch Controversies, eds. Sarah L. Higley and Jeffrey Andrew Weinstock. Detroit: Wayne State University Press, 2004. 163–80.
Wandless, William. "Spoil the Child: Unsettling Ethics and the Representation of Evil." *LIT: Literature Interpretation Theory* 22.2 (2011): 134–154.
Wax, Emily. "It's Enough to Make You Sick." *The Age* (August 12, 1999): B3. Reprinted from *The Washington Post*.
Wees, William C. "Found Footage and Questions of Representation," in *Found Footage Film*, eds. Cecilia Hausheer and Christoph Settele. Luzern, Switzerland: Viper/Zyklop, 1992. 37–53.
Wells, Paul. *The Horror Film: From Beelzebub to Blair Witch*. London: Wallflower Press, 2000.
Wessels, Emanuelle. "'Where Were You When the Monster Hit?' Media Convergence, Branded Security Citizenship, and the Trans-Media Phenomenon of *Cloverfield*." *Convergence* 17 (2011): 69–83.
Williams, Christopher. *Realism and the Cinema: A Reader*. London: British Film Institute, 1980.
Williams, Tony. *Hearths of Darkness: The Family in the American Horror Film* Cranbury, NJ: Associated University Presses, 1996.
Wood, Robin. "An Introduction to the American Horror Film," in *Movies and Methods Vol. 2*, ed. Bill Nichols. Berkeley: California University Press, 1985. 195–219.
Yant, Martin D. *Rotten to the Core: Crime, Sex & Corruption in Johnny Appleseed's Hometown*. Columbus: Public Eye, 1994.
Yoon, Joewon. "Ghostly Imagination, History, and Femininity at Centuries' Ends: *The Turn of the Screw* and *The Blair Witch Project*," in *Nothing That Is: Millennial Cinema and the Blair Witch Controversies*, eds. Sarah L. Higley and Jeffrey Andrew Weinstock. Detroit: Wayne State University Press, 2004. 181–96
"YouTube Serves Up 100 Million Videos a Day Online." *USA Today* (July 16, 2006) http://usatoday30.usatoday.com/tech/news/2006-07-16-youtube-views_x.htm.
Zimmerman, Patricia. "Hollywood, Home Movies and Common Sense: Amateur Film as Aesthetic Dissemination and Social Control, 1950–1962." *Cinema Journal*, 27. 4 (1988): 23–44.

Index

À l'intérieur (2007) 92
A MOVIE (1958) 14
Aaron, Michele 24
The ABCs of Death (2012) 200
Abnormal Activity (2010) 128
Abrams, J.J. 180
Abu Ghraib 91
Albrechtsen, Janet 215n
Alexander, Bruce 96
Alien Abduction: Incident in Lake County (1998) 76, 122
All Hallows' Eve (2013) 194
Allen, Brady 133
Aloi, Peg 96, 98
Alone with Her (2006) 124
Altered (2006) 211n
Alternative Reality Games (ARGs) 101, 212n
Alternative 3 (1977) 74–75, 76, 122
amateur film and filmmaking 3, 4, 8, 9, 10, 42, 43, 45, 50, 52, 54, 57, 58, 60, 61, 65, 83, 84, 87, 89, 96, 97, 99, 112, 116, 125, 127, 180, 192, 197, 199, 201
Ambrose, David 74
American Horror Story (television series) 56
American Zombie (2007) 126, 181
America's Funniest Home Videos (television series) 10
Amuchástegui, Margarita 69
anatomical drawing 29
Andrade, Fernanda 160
Annable, Odette 179
Anneliese: The Exorcist Tapes (2011) 11, 127, 151
Anonymous 198
Aoyama, Noriko 189
Apartment 143 (2011) 5, 14, 149, 166, 174–175, 176
Apatow, Judd 199
Argentina 190
Armageddon (1988) 179
Arnold, Luke 181
Ashworth, Brittany 171, 172
The Asylum (production company) 127
The Asylum Tapes (2012) 11
Atrocious (2010) 12, 173

August Underground (film series) 125
August Underground (2001) 213n
August Underground's Mordum (2003) 213n
August Underground's Penance (2007) 213n
Australia 96, 101, 122, 176–177, 181–186, 191, 215n
Australia's Funniest Home Videos (television series) 204n
Avalos, Stefan see The Last Broadcast (2000)
avant-garde film and filmmaking 14, 16, 17, 33

The Bachelorette (television series) 203n
Bachiatari Bōryoku Ningen (2010) 189
Back from Hell (2011) 151
The Bad Seed (1956) 167
Badlands (1973) 36
Badley, Linda 105, 108
Baesel, Nathan 123
Banesh, David 100
The Banshee Chapter (2013) 123, 150
Barber, Lynden 99
The Bare Wench Project (2000) 113
Bare Wench Project 2: Scared Topless (2001) 113
Bare Wench 3: Path of the Wicked (2002) 113
The Bare Wench Project 4: Uncensored (2003) 113
Battle Royale (2000) 6
The Bay (2012) 181
BBC (television network) 7, 73, 76, 77, 78, 81
Beard, David 116
Beattie, Keith 73
Beatty, Ned 105
Behind the Mask: The Rise of Leslie Vernon (2006) 87, 112, 123
Belgium 35–36, 91, 212n
Believers (2007) 211n
Belize 190
Bell, Ashley 156, 159
Bell, William Brent 160, 164, 214n; see also The Devil Inside (2011)
Benjamin, Walter 178
Benny's Video (1992) 33
Berg, Chuck 37, 38, 41
Bevan, Gillian 78

227

Bigfoot: The Lost Coast Tapes (2012) 11
The Birds (1963) 162
Bite Back (television program) 77
Bitter Feast (2010) 211n
Bittner, Lauren 133
Black, Joel 24, 30, 60
Black, Karen 195
The Black Door (2001) 121
Black Mirror (television series) 205n
Black Sabbath (*I tre volti della paura*, 1963) 195
Black Sunday (1960) 104
The Black Witch Project (2001) 113
Blainey, Geoffrey 183
Blair, Linda 152, 175
The Blair Kitch Project (2002) 113, 191
The Blair Witch Project (1999) 1, 3, 4, 5, 6, 8, 10, 13, 18, 19, 23, 24, 26, 30, 35, 36, 46, 58, 66, 69, 71, 72, 76, 82, 84, 85, 86, 87, 88, 92, 93–111, 112–115, 116, 117, 119, 120, 121, 122, 125, 126, 128, 129, 132, 147, 158, 163, 171, 179, 187, 191, 192, 196, 199, 201, 211n
Blatty, William Peter 153, 213n; see also *The Exorcist* (1973)
Blogspot 10
Body of a Female (1965) 65
The Bogus Witch Project (2000) 113
Boland, Brian 132
Bolter, Jay David 7
Book of Shadows: Blair Witch 2 (2000) 96, 107, 113–114, 212n
Boorman, John see *Deliverance*; *Exorcist II*
bootleg videos 10, 35
Bordwell, David 14, 16, 17, 30
Borrowed Power (1951) 45
Bracken, Ashley 171
The Brave (1997) 61
Brazil 190
Brennan, Brid 76
Briefel, Aviva 89
Brinton, Tim 74, 75
Brooker, Charlie 205n
Brooks, Max see *World War Z: An Oral History of the Zombie War*
Brooks, Peter 152, 154
Brottman, Mikita 42, 59, 69
Brown, Jessica Tyler 113, 143
Bruckner, David 6, 23, 192, 193; see also *V/H/S*
Bruiser (2000) 198
Brutal Massacre (2007) 124
Bryson, Norman 99
Buckingham, David 9–10
Buffy the Vampire Slayer (television series) 89, 105
Bulger, Jamie 167
The Burningmoore Incident (2010) 85, 203
Burstyn, Ellen 152
Burtoch, Jean 46, 207n

Cam—Fürchte die Dunkelheit (2010) 190
Camera Phone (2012) 11
Camera Surveillance (1964) 46–47

Canada 45, 60, 76, 205n
Candyman (1992) 1
Cannibal Ferox (1981) 32
Cannibal Holocaust (1980) 1, 6, 8, 11, 25, 32–34, 36, 37, 61, 66, 70, 75, 86, 113, 187, 200, 206n
Cantril, Hadley 38–39
Caplan, Lizzy 179
Capturing the Friedmans (2003) 18
Caputi, Jane 63
Caravaggio 29
Carol, Avedon 63
Carrey, Jim 199
Carrie (1976) 104, 162
Carrie (Stephen King, 1974) 30
Carroll, Lewis 59
Carroll, Noel 24
Carter, David Ray 25, 26, 35, 118, 180
Cartoon Network 113
Carved: The Slit-Mouthed Woman (*Kuchisake-onna*, 2007) 189
Carver (2008) 203n
Case #342 (2012) 21
Case No. 666/2013 (2013) 21, 191
Castonguay, James 99, 100, 212n
CBS (television network) 38, 39
cellular phones see mobile phones
Celluloid Nightmares (1999) 35
Chapman, Jane 204n
Charles, Craig 78
Charmed (television series) 105
chat (online) 52, 56, 122, 193
Chen, Steve 9
Chernobyl Diaries (2012) 200
The Child Molester (1964) 31, 43, 46–57
China 190
Chō Akunin (2011) 189
Chronicle (Josh Trank, 2012) 147, 200
Chronicles of an Exorcism (2008) 127, 151
cinéma vérité 18, 204n
Citizen Kane (1940) 41
Clarke, Manning 183
Classical Hollywood 3, 22, 24
Close, Joshua 126
Closed Circuit Extreme (2012) 191
Clover, Carol J. 20, 49, 105, 140, 195
Cloverfield (2008) 1, 3, 4, 5, 13, 21, 30, 87, 102, 112, 127, 149, 170, 179–181, 186, 191, 192, 196, 201
The Cohasset Snuff Film (2012) 203n
Cohen, Larry see *It's Alive*; *Special Effects*
Cold War 73, 74, 84
Cole, Bradley 170, 172
The Collingswood Story (2002) 122, 193
Collins, Felicity 183
Colors (magazine) 33
COPS (television series) 13, 187
Cortez, Vivis 140
Costa Rica 190
Countdown to Looking Glass (1984) 176
Cradle of Fear (2001) 203n

Index 229

The Craft (1996) 105
Craven, Wes *see* *Last House on the Left*; *Nightmare on Elm Street* (film series); *Scream* (film series)
Crawley, Budge 45
Creed, Barbara 104, 108, 139, 141
Creepshow (1982) 195
Crimewatch (television series) 77
Crocodile Dundee (1986) 182
The Crow (1994) 58
Crowley, Suzan 160
Crowsnest (2012) 34
Csengery, Chloe 133, 143
CSI (television series) 7, 8
Cubbyhouse (2001) 211n
Curse of the Blair Witch (1999) 19, 72, 96, 102, 115, 121
Curtis, Adam 81

Da Hip Hop Witch (2000) 113
d'Agoty, Jacques Gautier 29
The Dark Area (2000) 190
Dark Passage (1947) 205n
Darkest Night (2012) 190
The Da Vinci Treasure (2006) 127
Davis, Therese 183
Dead of Night (1945) 194–195
Death of a Ghost Hunter (2007) 166, 173–174
Death Watch (1980) 205n
Deems, Dottie (nee Vaughn) 45
Deems, Earle 45
Deep Impact (1998) 179
Deep Throat (1972) 162
Dees, Stephanie 122
DeLage, Joseph 197
Deliá, Bel 181
Deliverance (1972) 102, 105–107
De Palma, Brian *see* *Carrie*; *Redacted*
De Quincey, Thomas 59
Desaparecidos (2011) 190
Devlin, Denise 120
Demonlover (2002) 6
The Devil Inside (2012) 5, 14, 18, 115, 149, 151, 152, 154, 155, 160–164
Devil's Experiment (*Ginī Piggu: Akuma no Jikken*, 1985) 34–35
Devils Pass (2013) 25–26
The Devil's Rejects (2005) 190
Diary of the Dead (2007) 1, 4, 14, 20, 24, 87, 112, 126–127, 171
Die Hard (1988) 179
Dimbleby, Richard 73
direct cinema 18, 204n
District 9 (2009) 216n
Dnepropetrovsk Maniacs 60
documentary film and filmmaking 16–22, 23, 25, 26, 33, 36, 73, 74, 75, 83, 96, 97, 98, 102, 103, 111, 114, 115, 117, 118, 120, 121, 123, 124, 125, 126, 151, 152, 153, 155, 156, 160, 163, 181, 186, 204n

Les Documents Interdits (television series) 7, 26, 82–85, 116, 201
Domer, John 45, 207n
domestic violence 121, 134, 137, 169, 172
Donahue, Heather 95, 211n; *see also* Blair Witch Project
Donovan, Jeffrey 114
Dowdle, John Eric *see* *The Poughkeepsie Tapes*; *Quarantine*
Dracula (Bram Stoker, 1897) 30
DreamWorks 129
driver education films 6, 31, 43, 44–45, 50
Dunham, Stephen 133
DVD 12, 102, 119
Dyatlov Pass incident 25
The Dybbuk (1937) 151

Ebert, Roger 114
Edelstein, David 90–91
Edison, Thomas *see* *Electrocuting an Elephant*; *Execution of Czolgosz with Panorama of Auburn Prison*
educational films *see* safety films
Effects (1980) 203n
8mm (1999) 6, 31, 61
84C MoPic (1989) 96, 216n
Electrocuting an Elephant (1903) 31, 91
Emanuelle in America (1977) 6
Emergo *see* *Apartment 143* (2011)
The Emperor's Naked Army Marches On (1987) 99
End of Watch (2012) 200
Ephraim, Molly 113
The Erotic Witch Project (2000) 113
Erskine, Tom 37, 38, 41
Evans, Gareth 190, 200
EverymanHYBRID (web series) 199
Evidence (2011) 21, 171
Evidence (2013) 21
Evil Dead Trap (1988) 35
Evil Things (2009) 13
Execution of Czolgosz with Panorama of Auburn Prison (1901) 30
The Execution of Mary, Queen of Scots (1895) 91
Executions (1995) 11, 60
Exhibit A (2007) 5, 21, 125, 135, 149, 166, 170–173, 201
Exhibit X (2012) 21
exorcism 5, 26, 115, 150–164, 168, 189, 194, 196
The Exorcist (1973) 151, 152–155, 157, 163, 165, 167, 175
Exorcist Chronicles (2007) 151, 160
Exorcist II: The Heretic (1977) 152
experimental film 14, 16, 17, 33, 97, 98
exploitation film 25, 31, 33, 42, 46, 54, 60, 64, 65, 160
Extreme Private Eros: Love Song 1974 (1974) 199
The Eyes of Laura Mars (1978) 24

Eyes Without a Face (*Les Yeux Sans Visage*, 1959) 25, 179
F Is for Fake (1973) 41
Fabian, Patrick 155
Facebook 10
Faces of Death (1978) 11, 32
The Facility (2012) 206n
The Fall of the City (radio broadcast) 39
The Fall of the House of Usher (Edgar Allan Poe, 1839) 170
Fatal Frame (videogame) 146
*FeardotCo*m (2002) 121
Featherstone, Katie *see Paranormal Activity*
The Feed (2010) 85, 203n
feminism 22, 32, 62–64, 65, 70, 105, 139
Fenton, Harvey 32, 34
Ferrari, Keith 77
Ferrell, Will 1999
The Fiend Without a Face (1958) 48
Fierman, Hannah 195
Fight Club (1999) 179
Filippe, Jean-Teddy 82–85
Final Girl 123, 140, 145, 193, 196; *see also* Clover, Carol J.
Findlay, Michael 6, 31; *see also Snuff*
Findlay, Roberta 6, 31; *see also Snuff*
First Person Singular (radio series) 38
Flowers of Flesh and Blood (*Za ginipiggu 2: Chiniku no hana*, Hideshi Hino, 1985) 34, 35
Foote, Hallie 132
The Forbidden Files see *Les Documents Interdits*
The Forbidden Quest (1993) 14
Forrest, Angela 172
4chan 198
Frankenstein (Mary Shelley, 1818) 30, 206n
The Frankenstein Theory (2013) 150, 206n
Frankenstein's Army (2013) 150, 206n
Fredrichs, Mark 113
Freeland, Cynthia 24–25
Friday the 13th (film series) 123, 162
Friedkin, William *see The Exorcist* (1973)
Frontière(s) (2007) 92
Frost (2012) 191
Funny Games (1997/2007) 12

Gabin, Jean 36
Gacy House (2010) 127
Gallinaro, Sergio 121
Garber, Marjorie 8–9
Garth Marenghi's Darkplace (television series) 86
gender 6, 22, 58, 59, 70, 88, 104–111, 117, 135, 137, 139, 140, 141, 145, 146, 147, 154, 157, 176, 177, 179, 200, 203n
The Gerber Syndrome (2011) 191
Gericault, Theodore 29
Germany 121, 190
Ghost Hunters (television series) 86
Ghostbusters (1984) 188

The Ghosts of Crowley Hall (2008) 14
Ghostwatch (television program) 7, 26, 76–82, 85, 122, 201
Ghostwatch: Behind the Curtains (2012) 79, 80
Gillard, Julia 184
Gilsdorf, Ethan 188
Ginsberg, Seth 134
Glascott, Fiona 174
Gledhill, Christine 154
Glee (television series) 56
Global Financial Crisis 130
Godsend (2004) 167
Godzilla 180
Godzilla (1998) 179
Goethals, Angela 123
Goi, Michael *see Megan Is Missing*
The Good Son (1993) 167
Goodall, Mark 32–33
Gore, Al 75
Grace (2009) 167
Graham, Billy 153
Grama, Ionut 161
Grand Guignol 29, 33
Grantham, Lucy 196
Grave Encounters (2011) 13, 85, 203n, 210n
Grave Encounters 2 (2012) 212n
Grayden, Sprague 132
The Great American Snuff Film (2003) 203n
A Great and Honorable Duty (1965) 207n
Greece 191
Greene, Sarah 78
Greystone Park (2012) see *The Asylum Tapes*
Grimes, Adam 155
Grisham, Therese 131
Grizzly Man (2005) 18
Grotesque (*Gurotesuku*, 2009) 189
The Grudge (*Ju-On*, film series) 188
Grusin, Richard 7
Guinea Pig (*Ginī Piggu*, film series) 6, 34–35, 37, 206n
Gulf War 82
Gunning, Tom 91

Hack! (2007) 203n
Hahner, Leslie A. 130, 146
Hale, Gregg 11, 200, 211n
Halloween (film series) 123, 162, 205n
Halloween (1978) 25, 49, 167
Halloween (2007) 167
Hanah's Gift (2008) 205n
Haneke, Michael *see Benny's Video*; *Funny Game*
Hanks, Colin 124
Hansel and Gretel (Brothers Grimm) 96
Hanzha, Alexander *see* Dnepropetrovsk Maniacs
Hara, Kazuo 98–99
A Hard Day's Night (1964) 190
Hardcore (1979) 6, 31, 61
Haunted Changi (2010) 14, 190
A Haunted House (2013) 128

Index

The Haunted House Project (2010) 190
Haunted Poland (Nawiedzona Polska, 2011) 191
Haute Tension (2003) 92
Hawkins, Joan 11, 12
Head (1968) 190
Head Case (2007) 21, 124, 125
The Hell Experiment (2010) 203*n*
Hellboy (film series) 199
Hell's Highway: The True Story of Highway Safety Films (2003) 2, 45–46, 55, 56
Helmuth, Evan 161
Henkel, Guido 116
Henry: Portrait of a Serial Killer (1986) 25, 36, 61, 118
Her Flesh (film series) 65
Herthum, Louis 156
Herzog, Werner *see Grizzly Man*; *Incident at Loch Ness*
High 8 video 110
Highway Safety Foundation 42–57
Hight, Craig 8, 16, 17, 18, 21, 23, 37, 72, 74, 75, 77, 78, 81, 102, 103
Higley, Sarah L. 96, 97, 114, 116
Hills, Matt 89
Da Hip Hop Witch (2000) 113
Hiroshima 73, 179
Hitchcock, Alfred *see The Birds*; *Psycho*; *Spellbound*
Hitler, Adolf 40
Hjorth, Larissa 190
Hobo with a Shotgun (2011) 200
Hombre y tierra (2011) 190
Home Movie (2008) 5, 6, 10, 34, 127, 149, 166, 167–170, 171, 173, 201
The Honeymoon Killers (1970) 36, 69
Hooper, Tobe *see Poltergeist*; *The Texas Chain Saw Massacre*
A Horrible Way to Die (2010) 192
Hostel (franchise) 89, 92, 112, 122
Hostel (2005) 4, 90–91
Hostel III (2011) 91
Hotel Hollywood (2010) 191
The House of the Devil (2009) 192
House with 100 Eyes (2011) 203*n*
Howard, John 183
Howarth, Kevin 118
Howell, Jerrel Ray 47
Human Centipede (2010) 91
Human Centipede 2: Full Sequence (2011) 91
Humpday (2009) 211*n*
Hunter, Dan 9
Hunter, Jack 35
Hurley, Chad 9
Hurrell, Connie 46
Hussein, Saddam 60
Hypermediacy 7
Hyperreality 26

I Sell the Dead (2008) 192
Iceland 191

Ignatow, Melvin Henry 60
In Memorium (2005) 23
In Search of... (television series) 76
Incident at Loch Ness (2004) 122
Incidente (2010) 190
An Inconvenient Truth (2006) 75
Independence Day (1996) 179
India 191
Indiana Jones (film series) 188
Indonesia 190, 200
Inferno (1980) 104
The Innkeepers (2011) 192
Interview with the Assassin (2002) 122
Italy 123, 190–191; *see also The Devil Inside*
It's Alive (1973) 165
ITV (television network) 74

J-horror 178, 188, 189, 190, 213*n*, 215*n*
J-pop 189, 190
Jackass (television series) 147
Jackson, Neil 209*n*
Japan 6, 34, 35, 98, 99, 122, 170, 180, 186, 188–190, 195, 206*n*
Jenkins, Henry 9
Jeopardy (television series) 86
Jespersen, Otto 187
Jodrell, Steve 176
John Dies at the End (2012) 199
Johnson, Eithne 59, 63, 65, 69, 90, 208*n*
Jones, Doug 199
Jones, William E. 46–47
Joshua (2007) 167
Joy, Davina 174
Juhasz, Alexandra 17, 97, 197
Jun, Lin 60
June 9 (2008) 127

K-horror *see* Korea
Karim, Jawed 9
Karloff, Boris 165
Kaufman, Daniel 193
Kawaii 190
Keating, Paul 183
Keitel, Harvey 205*n*
Keller, James 88, 93, 100
Kerekes, David 33, 59, 60, 208*n*
Killer Shrimps (2004) 126
Kinect (gaming console) 146
King, Geoff 179
King, Stephen *see Carrie*; *Creepshow*
The Kingdom (1994) 1
Klaas, Marc 56
Klaas, Polly 56
Kōhaku Uta Gassen (television program) 189–190
Korea 178, 190
Korn (band) 199
Krug, David 56
Krug, Eric 56
Kwaidan (1964) 195

LaBelle, Beverly 65
Lake, Leonard 60
Lake Mungo (2008) 5, 14, 127, 149, 166, 176–177, 191
Lane, Christina 110
Larratelli, Enrique 31
Larsen, Tomas Alf 188
The Last Broadcast (1998) 14, 40, 85, 87, 97, 115–118, 119, 123
Last Date (1950) 44
The Last Exorcism (2011) 5, 14, 17, 18, 40, 115, 149, 151, 152, 154, 155–160, 161, 162, 163, 174, 192, 200, 201
The Last Exorcism Part II (2013) 200, 214
The Last Horror Film (1982) 115, 118, 123, 126
The Last Horror Movie (2003) 40, 87, 112, 115, 118–119, 126, 212*n*
Last House on Dead End Street (1977) 6, 61
Last House on the Left (1972) 171, 196
The Last Movie (1971) 115
The Last Picture Show (1971) 115
Last Ride (2011) 191
Law & Order: SVU (television series) 43
Leadbeater, Charles 9
Leave It to Beaver (television series) 165
Lebow, Alison 17
Leder, Herbert J. 48–49; *see also The Child Molester*
Lee, Alexondra 133
Lee, Brandon 58
Lee, Oliver 171
Lefait, Sébastien 22, 90, 131
The Legend of Boggy Creek (1972) 96
Lennox, Kai 174
Leno, Jay 114
Leonard, Joshua 95, 211*n*; *see also Blair Witch Project*
Leonardo Da Vinci 29
Lessin, Barbara 125
The Levenger Tapes (2011) 11
Lewton, Val 104, 140, 163, 165, 195
Leyda, Julia 131, 140
The Life and Death of a Porno Gang (2009) 203*n*
Lobato, Ramon 9, 208*n*
Long, Derek 57
Lovekamp, Aiden 133
Lovely Molly (2011) 200, 211*n*
Long Pigs (2007) 34
The Lost Tape (2012) 11, 191
The Lost Tapes (television series) 86
Lovecraft, H.P. 30, 83, 123, 185
Lowenstein, Adam 88, 90–91, 178, 181, 186
Lucas, Jessica 179
Luckhurst Roger 14
Lugosi, Bela 25, 165
Lustig, William 205*n*
Lyon, David 89, 132

M (1931) 49
Mabo and Others vs. The State of Queensland (No. 2) (1992) 183

MacKinnon, Catherine 63
Madhouse (2004) 211*n*
The Magician (2005) 122
Magnotta, Luka 160
Maguindano Massacre (2009) 60
Malaysia 190
The Malleus Maleficarium (Dominicans Heinrich Kramer and James Sprenger, 1484) 104
Man Bites Dog (1992) 1, 6, 35–36, 37, 66, 118, 123, 125, 188, 200, 206*n*, 212*n*
Maniac (Franck Khalfoun, 2012) 205*n*
Manning, Lesley 7, 76–82, 122; *see also Ghostwatch*
Le Manoir Du Diable (1896) 151
Mansfield 1962 (2006) 46
Manson, Charles 31, 59, 65, 69, 153
Marble Hornets (web series) 6, 14, 27, 196–199, 201
Marks, Laura U. 12, 13, 98–99
Marner, Richard 74
Marsh, Mike 174
Martin, Adrian 92
Martyrs (2008) 92
Masters, Charles 35
Mathjis, Ernest 36
The Matrix (1999) 179
McCarthy, Charlie 39
McClain, Cady 167
McCloskey, Paul 165
McDowell, Scott Dixon 96
McKee, Alan 61
McKenzie, Keira 93
McQuaid, Glenn 6, 192, 193; *see also V/H/S*
McRoy, Jay 35
Megan Is Missing (2011) 3, 4, 5, 21, 43, 48, 51–57, 122, 171, 201
melodrama *see* Brooks, Peter
Mercury Theatre 37, 38
Meslow, Scott 16, 58
Metz, Christian 22
Michelangelo 29
Miles, Christopher 74
Miller, Cynthia 72
Miller, Jason 152
Miller, Paul 9
Miller, Sam J. 89
Miller, Steven 181
Miller, T.J. 179
Il mistero di Lovecraft—Road to L. (2005) 123, 150
The Mitchell Tapes (2010) 11
mobile phones 7, 52, 90
mockumentary 14, 16–21, 25, 35, 37, 72–75, 79, 81, 86, 96, 118, 122, 123, 124, 126, 175, 181, 191
Modleski, Tania 162
Monarch Releasing Corporation 65
Mondo 11, 25, 32–33, 60
Mondo Cane (1962) 33
Monster (2008) 127
Monsters in the Woods (2012) 200

Morelda, Clare 173
Morgan, Michèle 36
Morgan, Michelle 20, 127, 171
Morimo Clover 189–190
Mosaic Media Group 199
Most Haunted (television series) 86
The Mountain of the Cannibal God (1978) 32
Muir, John Kenneth 4, 88, 92, 136, 140
Muirhouse (2012) 191
Mulvey, Laura 12, 22, 108, 139, 195
Munro, Caroline 115
Muntean, Nick 73
Murder Collection V.1 (2009) 194
Murder in the Heartland: The Search for Video X (2003) 19
Mute Witness (1994) 6, 31
My Little Eye (2002) 203n
My Name Is Earl (television series) 56
Myrick, Daniel see *Blair Witch Project*

Nader, Ralph 45
Nakamura, Suzy 181
National Geographic (magazine) 33
Natural Born Killers (1994) 69
NCIS (television series) 7, 8
Ndalianis, Angela 13, 25, 101, 113
New French Extremity 91, 178
New Zealand Office of Film and Literature Classification 57
Newsweek (magazine) 3, 93, 135
Newton, Kathryn 133
Ng, Charles 60
Nichols, Bill 17–18
Night of the Living Dead (1968) 25, 103
The Nightmare Before Christmas (1993) 199
Nightmare on Elm Street (film series) 162
Nile, Richard 215n
Nine Miles to Noon (1963) 48
909 Experiment (2000) 120–121
No. 32, B District (2011) 190
Noiret, Philip 36
Noroi: The Curse (2005) 122, 189
North, Daniel 180
Norway 14, 186–188
Nuchtern, Simon 65

O'Brian, Conan 114
Occult (*Okaruto*, 2009) 189
O'Keefe, Michael 174
Olsen, Mark 162
The Omen (1976) 32, 165
100 Ghost Street: The Return of Richard Speck (2012) 127
The 100 Greatest Scary Moments (television program) 76
1 Lunatic 1 Ice Pick (2012) 60
One Missed Call (*Chakushin ari*, film series) 188
Onibaba (1964) 179
Onryō 189, 215n
Options to Live (1979) 45
The Otaku Murderer see Tsutomo, Muyazaki

Page, Lindsay 174
Paglia, Camille 63
Pamela: Or, Virtue Rewarded (Samuel Richardson, 1740) 96
Panorama (television series) 72, 74
Pan's Labyrinth (2006) 199
The Paperhangers (1966) 207n
Paradise Lost: The Child Murders at Robin Hood Hills (1996) 96
Paramount Pictures 129, 131, 132
Paranormal Activity (film series) 5, 14, 34, 86, 88, 89, 90, 92, 93, 115, 119, 127, 128, 129–147, 151, 163, 192, 201
Paranormal Activity (2007) 1, 4, 8, 15, 22, 26, 87, 88, 90, 92, 112, 120, 121, 123, 127, 128, 129–131, 133–138, 170, 199
Paranoid Activity 2 (Kevin Clark and Manzie Jones, 2011) 131, 133–134, 138–141, 171, 199
Paranormal Activity 2: Tokyo Night (*Paranōmaru Akutibiti Dai Ni Shō: Tōkyō Naito*, 2010) 140, 147, 186, 189
Paranormal Activity 3 (2011) 82, 133–134, 141–143, 147, 199
Paranormal Activity 4 (2012) 133–134, 143–147, 199
Paranormal Activity: The Marked Ones (2014) 140, 141, 147
Paranormal Effect (2010) 128
Paranormal Entity (2009) 127, 128
Paranormal Proof (2010) 128
Paranormal Whacktivity (2012) 128
Paranormal Yakutsk (2012) 191
Parent, Valérie 36
Paris Match (magazine) 74
Parkinson, Michael 78–79, 81
Parkinson (television series) 79
Pasdar, Adrian 167
Paulson, Morris 160; see also *The Devil Inside* (2011)
Peeping Tom (1960) 6, 24, 31, 61, 62, 88, 213n
Peli, Oren 22, 34, 86, 121, 127, 186, 189, 209n, 213n; see also *Paranormal Activity*; *The River*
Penance (2009) 203n
Penenberg, Adam L. 90
Penunggu istana (2011) 190
Pereiro, Chus 173
Perkins, Amber 5, 51, 53; see also *Megan Is Missing*
Peterman, Matthew 160; see also *The Devil Inside* (2011)
Petley, Julian 60, 61
The Philippines 60
Phillips, Meredith 203n
Photo (magazine) 33
Picnic at Hanging Rock (1975) 96
Pinedo, Isabel Cristina 162
Pini, Maria 9, 10
Plant Pilferage (1965) 207n
Pledger, David 176
Poe, Edgar Allan 14, 30, 170
Poelvoorde, Benoît see *Man Bites Dog*

Poltergeist (1982) 77, 85, 123
pornography 32, 45, 58–65, 90, 113
possession 126, 130, 135, 137, 146; *see also* exorcism films
Post-Mortem (2010) 125
The Poughkeepsie Tapes (2007) 11, 21, 125, 127, 187
P.O.V: A Cursed Film (*POV: Norowareta firumu*, 2012) 189
Power, Tyrone 58
Practical Magic (1998) 105
Prelinger, Rick 43–44, 45, 50
Pretty Boy Floyd (1960) 48
Pretty Dead (2012) 126
Project Chanology 198
Project X (2012) 200
Project Zero see *Fatal Frame* (videogame)
Psycho (1960) 25, 50, 165
Pulask, Michele 116

Quarantine (2008) 127–128, 187
Quarterman, Simon 161
?: A Question Mark (2012) 191
Quinn, Rachel 51; *see also Megan Is Missing*
Quinones, Norma C. 193

radio *see War of the Worlds* (1938)
Radio Silence 6, 151; *see also V/H/S*
Radio Times (magazine) 77–78
Ragini MMS (2011) 191
Raw Feed (DVD label) 211*n*
Razor Eaters (2003) 216*n*
realism 7, 17, 18, 24–25, 30, 88, 111
reality television 13, 33, 86, 90, 133, 203*n*
[Rec] (2007) 1, 4, 5, 11, 12, 20, 87, 112, 125–126, 127, 149, 151, 186–187, 191, 192, 201
[Rec]² (2009) 187
[Rec]³: Génesis (2012) 187, 200
[Rec]⁴: Apocalipsis (2013) 187, 200
Record (*Zzikhimyeon jukneunda*, 2000) 190
Redacted (2007) 216*n*
Redfern Park Speech *see* Keating, Paul
Re-Kill (2012) 126
Resident Evil (2002) 126
Resolution (2012) 200
Rhodes, Gary 25
Richardson, Megan 9
Richie, Abigail 171
Rimmer, Shane 74
Ring (*Ringu*, film series) 188, 215*n*
Ring (*Ringu*, 1998) 11, 16, 118, 212*n*
Ring 0: Birthday (*Ringu 0: Bâsudei*, 2000) 189
Rippy, Marguerite H. 40, 41
Risey, John 102
The Ritual (2009) 125
The River (television series) 34, 86
Robbins, Christopher 17
Rock n' Roll High School (1979) 190
Rockett, W.H. 162
Rockoff, Adam 29
Rodoreda, Andy 181

Rogers, Helen 193
Roman, Damian 174
Roman Catholicism 104, 151, 153–154, 160, 186, 187
Rombes, Nick 14, 131, 133
Romero, George A. *see Bruiser*; *Diary of the Dead*; *Night of the Living Dead*
Roscoe, Jane 16–19, 21, 23, 88, 96, 101, 102, 103
Rose, Bernard *see Candyman*; *Snuff-Movie*
Rose Hobart (1936) 14
Rosemary's Baby (1968) 165
Rosso, Pablo 12, 20, 126
Rouch, Jean 204*n*
Rudd, Kevin 184, 215*n*
Russia 191

S&Man (1996) 20, 203*n*
Sabrina the Teenage Witch (television series) 105
safety films 6, 26, 31, 42–57, 201
The St. Francisville Experiment (2000) 114–115
El Sanatorio (2010) 190
Sanchez, Eduardo 11, 98, 199, 200, 211*n*; *see also Altered*; *Blair Witch Project*; *Lovely Molly*; *Seventh Moon*; *V/H/S 2*
Sanders, Ed 59
Saw (film series) 89–92, 112, 122
Saw (2004) 4
Saw 3D: The Final Chapter (2010) see *Saw VII*
Saw VI (2009) 91, 210*n*
Saw VII (2010) 91, 210*n*
Sayenko, Viktor *see* Dnepropetrovsk Maniacs
Schaefer, Eric 59, 63, 65, 69, 90, 209*n*
Schneider, Romy 205*n*
Schneider, Steven Jay 178, 205*n*
Schreck, Nikolas 151
Schreier, Margrit 100
Science Report (television series) 74–75
Scientology 198
SciFi channel 72
Sconce, Jeffrey 7, 21, 39–40, 77, 115, 163
The Scooby Doo Project (1999) 113
Scream (film series) 88, 123
Screamtime (1986) 194
Screen Kill (1997) 203*n*
Secret Snow (1966) 14
September 11, 2001 88–89
Septem8er Tapes (2004) 216*n*
A Serbian Film (2010) 203*n*
Series 7: The Contenders (2001) 6
7 Nights of Darkness (2011) 85, 203*n*
Seventh Moon (2009) 211*n*
Severed Footage (2012) 205*n*
Seward, James 116
Shackleton, Allan 31, 32, 65
Shadow People (2013) 14
Sharp, Martin 176
Shaviro, Steven 131
The She Beast (1966) 104

Index

Sheen, Charlie 35
Shelley, Mary *see* Frankenstein
Shelley, Percy Bysshe 59
Shiraishi, Kôji 150; *see also* Carved: The Slit-Mouthed Woman; Grotesque; Noroi: The Curse; Shirome
Shirome (2010) 5, 149, 186, 189–190, 191, 201
Shockers (television series) 85
The Shoplifter (1964) 207n
The Signal (2007) 192
Signal 30 (1959) 42, 45
Singapore 190
*Siniste*r (2012) 200
Siren (videogame series) 147–148
16mm film 110–111
Skeleton Crew (2009) 203n
Skew (2011) 123
slasher film 13, 25, 29, 49, 50, 58, 118, 123, 140, 162, 167, 193, 205n
Slashers (2001) 6
Slater, David 33, 59
The Slaughter (1971) 31, 65, 69
Slaughter Creek (2011) 203n
Slender: The Arrival (videogame) 199
Slender: The Eight Pages (videogame) 199
Slender Man 196, 198, 199
The Slender Man (2013) 199
Sloat, Micah *see* Paranormal Activity
Smith, Chris 133
Smith, Ken 42, 44, 45
Smith, Mike 78
Smith, Wayne A. 120
Snow, Michael 14
Snuff (1976) 6, 8, 31–32, 37, 60, 63–71, 90, 196, 209n; *see also* snuff-fictions
snuff-fictions 1, 6, 26, 31, 57, 58–71, 79, 113, 194, 201
snuff films and filmmaking 60–61; *see also* snuff-fictions
Snuff-Movie (2005) 31, 203n
Snuff 102 (2007) 203n
Snuff Trap (2003) 203n
Sobchack, Vivian 165–166
Solomon and Sheba (1959) 58
Solstice (2008) 211n
Something Awful (web forum) 197–198
Soviet Union 73
The Speak (2011) 203n
Special Bulletin (1985) 75
Special Effects (1985) 61
Special Report: Journey to Mars (1996) 76
Spellbound (1945) 199
Spielberg, Steven 129, 188
Spinell, Joe 115
Stahl-David, Michael 179
Stanner, W.E.H. 183
Stine, Scott Aaron 61
Stinton, Colin 78
Stoltenberg, Jens 188
Stormhouse (2011) 200
Strange Days (1995) 6, 61

Strawberry Estates (2001) 125
Subconscious (2010) 191
Suicide (2001) 121–122
Suicide Club (2002) 121
Suicide Dolls (1999) 35
Sundance Film Festival 116, 192, 196, 199, 200, 211n
Suprunyuck, Igor *see* Dnepropetrovsk Maniacs
Suspiria (1977) 104
Sutton, Tim 198
Swanberg, Joe 122, 192; *see also* V/H/S
Sweden 35

Takal, Sophia 193
Talancón, Ana Claudia 124
Tape 407 (2012) 11, 21
The Tapes (2011) 11, 203n
Tate, Sharon 31, 66
Tearoom (1962/2007) 46–47
television 6, 7, 8, 10, 13, 16, 19, 21, 26, 32, 34, 39, 43, 52, 54, 56, 72–86, 87, 89, 90, 102, 105, 116, 117, 122, 125, 138, 155, 160, 161, 165–166, 173, 176, 180, 181, 187, 189, 193, 194, 201, 205n, 209n, 211n
Telotte, J.P. 100
TerrorVision (1987) 114
Tesis (1996) 6, 31
The Texas Chain Saw Massacre (1974) 25
Le Théâtre du Grand-Guignol *see* Grand Guignol
30 Nights of Paranormal Activity with the Devil Inside the Girl with the Dragon Tattoo (2013) 128
Thomas, Julian 9
3 Guys 1 Hammer (2008) 60
Time (magazine) 9
Tindall, Patti 173
Titticut Follies (1967) 114
Tjahanto, Timo 200
Der Todesking (1989) 121
Toetag Pictures *see* Vogel, Fred
Tombs, Pete 178
The Tony Blair Witch Project (2000) 113
torture porn 4, 90–92, 112, 120, 130, 210n; *see also* Edelstein, David
Tourneur, Jacques 140
transmedia storytelling 93, 113, 127, 196–197
Transmorphers (2007) 127
Travers, Peter 160
Traynor, Rosie 176, 177
TribeTwelve (web series) 199
Trilogy of Terror (1975) 195
Trollhunter (2010) 5, 149, 186–188, 191, 201
True Blood (television series) 8
Tryon, Chuck 100
Tsutomo, Muyazaki 35
Tumbling Doll of Flesh (1998) 35
The Tunnel (2011) 5, 149–150, 181–186, 191, 201
The Turn of the Screw (Henry James, 1898) 96, 127

Twain, Mark 30
Twin Peaks (television series) 176
Twitter 10, 196
2 Girls 1 Cup (2007) 60

UFO Abduction (1989) 76
UGC (user generated content) 9–10, 26, 89, 125
Ukraine 60
The Ultimate Degenerate (1969) 65
Uncanny Tales (*Unheimliche Geschichten*, 1932) 194
United Kingdom 26, 33, 35, 73, 74, 119, 167, 204*n*
Universal Studios 165
The Unsleeping Eye (D.G. Compton, 1973) 205*n*
Untraceable (2008) 203*n*
USSR *see* Soviet Union

Vacancy (2007) 31, 203*n*
Vacancy 2: The First Cut (2009) 203*n*
Valencia, Cristian 173
Valentine, Gill 167
Vampires (2010) 191
Varda, Scott J. 130, 146
The Vatican 126, 160, 161, 187
V/H/S (2012) 6, 11, 13, 22, 27, 122, 151, 192, 194–196, 199, 200, 210*n*, 211*n*
V/H/S/2 (2013) 11, 190, 199, 200, 205*n*, 211*n*
video 3, 8, 9, 10–13, 16, 19–20, 23, 33, 35, 52, 53, 60, 74, 75, 98, 103, 110, 111, 116, 118–119, 122, 123, 125, 127, 132, 141, 143, 159, 160, 167, 168, 169, 170, 171, 173, 176, 177, 180, 187, 191, 193, 194, 197, 198, 199
Video Gag (television series) 204*n*
Video Nasties 33, 119, 206*n*
Video X (film series) 11, 19–20, 125
Video X: The Dwayne and Darla-Jean Story (2007) 20
Video X: Evidence (2003) 20
Videodrome (1983) 6
Vietnam War 25, 96, 153, 179
viral marketing 113
Viscalo, Manuela 126
Vlog (2008) 122, 193
Vogel, Fred 20; *see also August Underground; Murder Collection*
Volk, Stephen *see Ghostwatch*
von Sydow, Max 152

Wagner, Troy *see Marble Hornets*
Walker, Johnny 119
Walker, Joseph S. 98
The Walking Dead (television series) 8
Wandless, William 167, 169
The War Game (1965) 73, 76
War of the Worlds (H.G. Wells, 1898) 30, 37–41
War of the Worlds (Orson Welles, 1938) 1, 6, 7, 25, 37–41, 42, 74, 77, 115, 122, 163, 200, 206–207*n*
Warhol, Andy 14
Warner Home Video 211*n*
Watergate scandal 153
Watkins, Peter *see The War Game*
Wayman, Richard 44–45
We Drivers (1935) 44
Web Therapy (television series) 56
webcams 7, 8, 10, 52, 132, 146
Wees, William C. 14
Weiler, Lance *see The Last Broadcast* (2000)
Weinstock, Jeffrey Andrew 96
Welcome to the Jungle (2007) 34, 125
Wells, Paul 88
Werewolves: The Dark Survivor (television series) 86
Wessels, Emanuelle 180–181
Wesson, Cherise 76; *see also Ghostwatch*
Wesson, Michelle 76; *see also Ghostwatch*
West, Ti 192; *see also V/H/S*
West Memphis Three 114
What Made Sammy Speed? (1957) 45
Wheels of Tragedy (1963) 42
The Whispering Dead (2011) 203*n*
Whitney Museum of American Art 46
The Wicksboro Incident (2003) 122
Wikipedia 9, 10, 16, 102
Wild Zero (1999) 190
Willett, Rebekah 9, 10
Williams, Amber Joy 167; *see also Home Movie*
Williams, Austin 167; *see also Home Movie*
Williams, Christopher 24
Williams, Michael C. 95, 211*n*; *see also Blair Witch Project*
Williams, Tony 165
Wilson, Jane Edith 181
Wilson, Nathan A. 130, 146
Windigo (2011) 199
Wingard, Adam 192; *see also V/H/S*
Without Warning (1994) 76, 122
Wolf Creek (2005) 90, 182
Wood, Bret 48, 54; *see also* safety films
Wood, Robin 185
World of the Dead: The Zombie Diaries 2 (2011) 126
World War Z: An Oral History of the Zombie War (Max Brooks, 2006) 30

The X-Files (television series) 89, 122, 187

Yant, Martin 45
YouTube 4, 6, 9–10, 26, 87, 89, 112, 115, 120, 122, 124, 125, 180, 196–199, 201
You've Been Framed (television series) 204*n*

Zebub, Bill 20
Zimmerman, Patricia 10
Zombie Diaries (2006) 126
Zuker, Talia 176

www.ingramcontent.com/pod-product-compliance
Ingram Content Group UK Ltd.
Pitfield, Milton Keynes, MK11 3LW, UK
UKHW041942140426
5217IPUK00014B/614